FAITH, OBEDIENCE, AND JUSTIFICATION
Current Evangelical Departures from *Sola Fide*

Samuel E. Waldron, Ph.D.

Reformed Baptist Dissertation Series # 1

Reformed Baptist Academic Press
Palmdale, CA

Copyright © 2006 Samuel E. Waldron. All rights reserved.

Requests for information should be sent to:

Reformed Baptist Academic Press
37104 Bridgeport Ct.
Palmdale, CA 93550
rbap@sbcglobal.net
www.rbap.net

No part of this publication may be reproduced, stored in a retrieval system, or transmitted in any way by any means, electronic, mechanical, photocopy, recording, or otherwise, without the prior permission of Reformed Baptist Academic Press except as provided by USA copyright law.

Printed in the United States of America.

Series: Reformed Baptist Dissertations
  #1 FAITH, OBEDIENCE, AND JUSTIFICATION:
  Current Evangelical Departures from *Sola Fide*
  Samuel E. Waldron, Ph.D.

ISBN 0-9760039-5-3

History is repeating itself once again. The gospel is under attack. *Sola fide*, as understood within Protestantism and more particularly within Reformed theology, is being reformulated. These things in themselves are not new. What is particularly alarming is that some who are doing this come from within our own theological ranks. Samuel E. Waldron has done us a tremendous service. He has culled the writings of Luther, Calvin, and Reformed symbolics on sola fide. He has identified crucial distinctions in their doctrinal formulations. He then brings his findings into our day and compares these orthodox formulations with three key contemporaries. His method is clear. His distinctions are crucial. His conclusions are cogent.

Richard C. Barcellos, pastor
Free Grace Church: A Reformed Baptist Congregation
Lancaster, CA
Managing Editor of *Reformed Baptist Theological Review*
Author of *In Defense of the Decalogue*

The undermining of classical Protestant formulations of *sola fide* (justification by faith alone) is a significant, and disheartening, feature in contemporary evangelical discussion of soteriology. This important book, after carefully reviewing *sola fide* in Luther, Calvin and the Reformed Confessions, goes on to survey and contrast the views of three influential evangelical theologians—Daniel Fuller, Norman Shepherd, and Don Garlington—and shows how they have deviated from the historic Reformation doctrine of justification *by faith alone*. As Waldron notes "there is a widespread penumbra of confusion among evangelicals regarding faith, obedience, and justification." Consequently, many who retain the slogan *sola fide* rob it of the substance of its reformational meaning and significance. This is a serious Gospel issue. Waldron understands this and provides trenchant historical and theological critique in crystal clear prose. This is a subject about which evangelical pastors and teachers need to be well-informed, and Waldron's study and conclusions are a model of theological argument and pastoral discernment.

Ligon Duncan, Ph.D.
Senior Minister, First Presbyterian Church, Jackson, Mississippi
Past Moderator, General Assembly of the Presbyterian Church in America
President, Alliance of Confessing Evangelicals
Convener, Twin Lakes Fellowship
Adjunct Professor, Reformed Theological Seminary

In various Evangelical circles today, what has come to be known as the material cause of the Reformation, the Protestant doctrine of *sola fide* (justification by grace alone through faith alone in Jesus Christ alone), is once again the subject of controversy, and with that the blurring of its historic doctrinal significance. The danger that new reformulations of *sola fide* pose goes to the very heart of the gospel itself. If the *ECT* accords, the new perspectives on Paul, together with a number of popular and prominent theologians of our day, are successful, then we must ask with John Calvin, "what will become of so many [biblical] passages in which Christ is represented as satisfied with faith alone?" With diligent and meticulous inquiries, Samuel Waldron brings us back to a review of the biblical doctrine of *sola fide* as enunciated by Luther and Calvin; and then provides us with an examination of how it was presented in the major creeds and confessions which were formulated in the crucible of the Reformation. It is not that the modern day teachers, whom Waldron goes on to critique, are devoid of impressive credentials and intellect. But as Luther himself reminded us, if the false teachers of Galatia in Paul's day "had not possessed outstanding gifts, great authority, and the appearance of holiness" and "if they had not claimed to be the ministers of Christ, pupils of the apostles, and sincere preachers of the Gospel, they could not so easily have undermined the authority of Paul and made an impression on the Galatians." Waldron's work calls us to that same vigilance today.

David T. King, pastor
Dayspring Presbyterian Church (PCA)
Forsyth, GA
Co-author of *Holy Scripture, the Ground and Pillar of Our Faith, A Biblical and Historical Defense of the Reformation Principle of Sola Scriptura*, Three Volumes.

Having delved into the labyrinth of the current justification controversy, it is with pleasure that I recommend this work by Dr. Samuel E. Waldron on the subject. I wish it had been in publication a few years ago. His clarification of the Reformers' doctrine of justification is greatly needed in the discussion simply because some misrepresent the teachings of Luther, Calvin, and the Westminster Divines, leading others astray in the process. Waldron's dealing with the errors of Daniel Fuller, Norman Shepherd, and Don Garlington is both masterful and charitable–a rare combination today. For those still studying the issues of "the obedience of faith" and its meaning in Reformation theology vs. modern "covenant nomism", this is a must read. May God bring a clearer light to the meaning of *sola fide* through this work.

Fred A. Malone, Ph.D.
Pastor, First Baptist Church, Clinton, LA
Author of *The Baptism of Disciples Alone*

TABLE OF CONTENTS

LIST OF ABBREVIATIONS … vii

LIST OF FIGURES … vii

PREFACE … ix

ABSTRACT … xi

1. PROLEGOMENA … 1
   Introduction … 1
   Background … 2
   Thesis … 3
   Methodology … 4
   Importance … 8
   Approach … 12

2. *SOLA FIDE* IN LUTHER … 13
   Introductory Considerations … 13
   The Gradual Development of *Sola Fide* in Luther … 21
   The Major Features of *Sola Fide* in Luther … 43

3. *SOLA FIDE* IN CALVIN … 47
   Thesis … 47
   The Affirmative Answer in Calvin … 48
   The Negative Answer … 50
   Conclusion … 70

4. *SOLA FIDE* IN THE REFORMATION CONFESSIONS … 73
   Thesis, Argument, and Approach … 73
   The Augsburg Confession, A. D. 1530 … 76
   The Formula of Concord, A. D. 1576 … 82
   The Second Helvetic Confession, A. D. 1566 … 88
   The Gallican Confession, A. D. 1559 … 94
   The Heidelberg Catechism, A. D. 1563 … 97
   The Belgic Confession, A. D. 1561 … 101
   The First Scottish Confession, A. D. 1560 … 104
   The Thirty-nine Articles of the Church of England, A. D. 1563 … 107
   The Irish Articles, A. D. 1615 … 108

    The Canons of the Synod of Dort, A. D. 1619 112
    The Westminster Confession of Faith, A. D. 1647
        and Related Confessions and Catechisms till A. D. 1689 115
    Conclusion 125

5. *SOLA FIDE* IN DANIEL FULLER 127
    An Introduction to Daniel Fuller 127
    Fuller and the Dichotomy between Law and Gospel 133
    The Distinction between Justifying Faith and Obedience 145
    Fuller and the Definition of Faith 150
    Fuller versus the Reformation 155

6. *SOLA FIDE* IN NORMAN SHEPHERD 157
    Introduction 157
    The Distinction between Justifying Faith and Obedience 167
    The Definition of Justifying Faith 177
    The Dichotomy of Law and Gospel 182

7. *SOLA FIDE* IN DON GARLINGTON 187
    Introduction 187
    The Definition of Justifying Faith 192
    The Distinction of Faith 195
    The Dichotomy of Faith 205
    Conclusion 223

8. CONCLUDING OBSERVATIONS 225
    Introduction 225
    Secondary Observations 225
    Principal Observations 231

BIBLIOGRAPHY 235

SCRIPTURE INDEX 255

NAME AND SUBJECT INDEX 257

LIST OF ABBREVIATIONS

CC *Creeds and Confessions of Faith in the Christian Tradition*, ed. J. Pelikan, V. Hotchkiss (New Haven: Yale University Press, 2003).

CR *Ioannis Calvini Opera quae supersunt omnia*, ed. G. Baum, E. Cunitz, and E. Reuss, Corpus Reformatorum [CR], vol. 29-87 (Halle: C.A. Schwetschke, 1864).

LW *Luther's Works: American Edition*, ed. J. Pelikan (Saint Louis: Concordia Pub. House, 1955-1986).

OS *Ioannis Calvini Opera Selecta*, ed. P. Barth, G. Niesel (Monachii: Chr. Kaiser, 1926-1959).

WA *D. Martin Luther's Werke, kritische Gesamtausgabe* (Weimarer Ausgabe), (Weimar: H. Böhlaus Nachfolger, 1883-).

WATR *D. Martin Luther's Werke, kritische Gesamtausgabe* (Weimarer Ausgabe), *Tischreden* (Weimar: H. Böhlaus Nachfolger, 1912-1921).

LIST OF FIGURES

1. Calvin's *ordo salutis*..58

PREFACE

Independence and self-sufficiency are the very opposite of the attitudes fostered by biblical Christianity. This means, of course, that the triune God alone is to be thanked and praised for all the grace, strength, and wisdom that the completion of a project like this requires. Any wisdom that this dissertation contains and any good that it may do must be ascribed absolutely to His unmerited grace and sovereign mercy.

At the same time, God has so arranged the universe that the folly of self-sufficiency should also be exposed by the kindness and help he provides through others. Thus, as I think of the completed dissertation here prefaced, a multitude of persons come to mind whose influence has been significant at different stages in its progress.

I am thankful for Dr. R. Albert Mohler, Jr. and the Trustees of the Southern Baptist Theological Seminary in Louisville, Kentucky. The wonderful reformation that God has used them to bring about at Southern created a hospitable theological environment for me to pursue a study like this. I greatly appreciate my studies at this institution.

I am also thankful for the professors who sat on my committee. Each has contributed in his own way to this dissertation. It was in Dr. Mark Seifrid's seminars that I first grasped the serious issues being raised in evangelical circles with regard to the historic doctrine of justification. I have profited much both from his friendship and interaction in my studies. It was in Dr. David Puckett's seminars that I had the opportunity to write and refine (at his direction and with his helpful comments) the research papers on Calvin and Luther that are foundational to the thesis of this dissertation. His counsel was also of significant help in clarifying its thesis and title. Finally, I need to express special appreciation to Dr. Stephen Wellum, the supervisor of my committee. A sense of his friendship and doctrinal like-mindedness has been of significant encouragement along the way.

It is not easy to leave a church where one was has ministered for almost twenty-four years and enter doctoral studies. This would not have been possible but for the kind assistance of many Reformed Baptist churches. None of that would have happened but for the vision and leadership of Pastor Ted Christman. To him I owe a debt of gratitude that I cannot express.

Heritage Baptist Church, Owensboro, Kentucky and its elders and members, have provided me and my family a wonderful, spiritual home during these studies. I thank all the brethren there for their interest and encouragement. I thank those particularly who have at some point read part or all of my dissertation and given me helpful counsel with regard to it. Eddie Goodwin and Dave Eades come to my mind especially at this point.

Finally, I must thank my God again for a better wife than I ever deserved. Almost thirty years have passed since God kindly gave me a better woman than I knew enough to seek. Thank you, Charlene, for all your love and labors for me and especially during these years of doctoral study!

Samuel E. Waldron
Louisville, Kentucky
May 2005

ABSTRACT

The thesis of this study is that influential evangelicals have adopted views regarding the relation of faith, obedience, and justification (or, in other words, justification *sola fide*) that are in conflict with the historic, Reformation doctrine of justification *sola fide*. Having departed from the historic, Reformation doctrine, their professions of holding justification *sola fide* are misleading and meaningless for the purpose of certifying their evangelical identity.

To establish the unity of the Protestant tradition with regard to the meaning of *sola fide*, the views of Martin Luther, John Calvin, and the major Protestant Creeds and Confessions are examined.

The thesis that unity existed among Protestants with regard to *sola fide* requires the examination of the development of the doctrine in Luther found in chapter two. It shows that Luther's views gradually developed in his spiritual experience and that the major features of his mature understanding of *sola fide* are consistent with Calvin's systematic development of *sola fide*.

In chapter three, the views of John Calvin are examined. Three key perspectives on the meaning of *sola fide,* through which the Reformation tradition can be examined and the views of current evangelicals tested, are isolated: the passive definition of justifying faith, the distinction between justifying faith and obedience, and the dichotomy between the law and the gospel.

Chapter four examines the Reformation tradition. An accurate assessment of the meaning of *sola fide* for that tradition may be best achieved by the examination of its major Creeds and Confessions. The three key perspectives on the meaning of justification *by faith alone* previously isolated are found consistently embedded in the 16th and 17th century Creeds and Confessions of Protestantism.

Having seen the unified meaning of justification *sola fide* in Calvin, Luther, and the Protestant tradition, chapters five, six, and seven examine the views of three influential evangelical theologians in light of this crucial tradition. The views of Daniel Fuller, Norman Shepherd, and Don Garlington are weighed in the balance of the historic Reformation doctrine of justification *by faith alone* and found to depart from the historic doctrine.

Chapter eight seeks to make clear a number of important conclusions from the study as a whole.

CHAPTER 1
PROLEGOMENA
Introduction

> In my view, a detailed defense still needs to be done on the historic Protestant view of the relationship between faith and obedience, so that the two are not conflated in the instrumentality of justification, as many in biblical-theological circles are doing these days.[1]

In this statement John Piper in his defense of the doctrine of imputed righteousness remarks that his book (*Counted Righteous in Christ*) does not address the closely related subject of *sola fide*. Piper is right. In the context of his defense of the objective side of the historic doctrine of justification, the subject of the relationship of faith and obedience in the instrumentality of justification yet requires to be addressed. There is an indissoluble connection between the objective and subjective sides of justification. Faith (the subjective) is formed or molded by imputation (the objective). Faith is only what it is, then, in relation to Christ. Yet, the meaning of "faith alone" needs distinct attention today.

The study here proposed does not claim to be the "detailed defense" for which Piper wishes. It does not take up the all-important biblical materials. It does, however, propose to address an historical issue of pointed relevance to those in the Reformation tradition[2] and the biblical defense of *sola fide* for which Piper calls. It is my conviction that those presently engaged in that conflation of faith and obedience of which Piper speaks are open to a weighty historical critique. Perhaps, and this is my hope, such a critique will prepare the way for the biblical critique so desperately needed.

---

[1] John Piper, *Counted Righteous in Christ* (Wheaton, IL: Crossway Books, 2002), 42.

[2] In chapter four I will argue that the Reformation tradition may be and is best defined in terms of the major creeds and catechisms of the Lutheran and Reformed tradition. It is not necessary for my thesis to provide a thorough definition of Protestantism. My claim in this dissertation is much simpler. It is that the Reformation tradition is basically one in its understanding of justification by faith alone, that this understanding is either its cardinal doctrine or one of its central and distinctive doctrines.

Background

It is a remarkable fact that not a few evangelicals, and especially those who identify with the Reformed tradition, manifest a tendency today to be influenced by trends that lead to a recasting of the historic, Reformation doctrine of justification. The reasons for this tendency may be obscure. Indeed, it is not the purpose of the dissertation here proposed to clarify those reasons. Yet, it is important to note that this tendency is somehow and to some degree related to important theological influences impacting evangelicalism as a whole. Those influences include "the new perspective on Paul," Daniel Fuller's polemic against the contrast between law and gospel, the reaction against the "easy-believism" prevalent among evangelicals for the last century,[3] the ecumenical movement striving to bring Evangelicals and Catholics together, and (to some extent perhaps behind each of the foregoing) the "biblical theology" movement.[4]

---

[3] For the sake of brevity, I use the phrase "easy-believism" in a number of places throughout this dissertation. I will argue, for instance, that it is a reaction against easy-believism that drives Norman Shepherd's views of *sola fide*. This phrase is, however, not immediately transparent. It is not, for example, the opposite of "hard-believism." Let me, therefore, provide at the outset my understanding of the meaning of this phrase. I argue in the following chapters that a crucial balance is held in the Reformation tradition by which it is held that justifying faith, though inseparable from evangelical obedience, is also distinguished from it. "Easy-believism," as I define it, denies this careful balance. It is the tendency among many evangelicals to separate justifying faith and evangelical obedience in such a way as to allow that justifying faith may exist without the fruit of good works or evangelical obedience. It is associated, therefore, with the view that there are "Carnal Christians" who, though saved, live no differently than unbelievers. It is also associated with a view of the eternal security of the believer that asserts that Christians will be saved regardless of their perseverance in faith, repentance, and evangelical obedience.

[4] These influences may be documented. "The New Perspective on Paul," was mediated to evangelicals especially through the writings and ministry of N.T. Wright. The impact of Wright is clear, for instance, in the position taken by John Armstrong and Reformation and Revival Ministries. See the journal of that ministry: *Reformation & Revival Journal* 11, no. 2 (Spring 2002). Its editor-in-chief is John Armstrong. Another illustration of Wright's influence is Doug Wilson, "A Pauline Take on the New Perspective," *Credenda Agenda* 15, no. 5 (Winter 2003) in which he interacts somewhat positively with Wright and the New Perspective. Another influence is that of Daniel Fuller in his *Gospel & Law: Contrast or Continuum?* (Grand Rapids: Eerdmans, 1980) and *The Unity of the Bible* (Grand Rapids: Zondervan, 1992). Fuller appears to have had a significant influence on a number of evangelicals. Among them is Scott Hafemann. See his *The God of Promise and the Life of Faith* (Wheaton, IL: Crossway Books, 2001), 222. Hafemann there remarks, "Much of what follows in this chapter and throughout this book is indebted to the work of Daniel Fuller and his student John Piper, who, as God's

Thesis

The thesis of this study is that influential theologians who are regarded as evangelicals have adopted views and made statements regarding the relation of faith, obedience, and justification (or, in other words, justification *sola fide*) that are in substantial conflict with the consistent,

---

instruments of grace, taught me how to do biblical theology and modeled how to live in light of it." See also his citations of Fuller on 228, 233, 240, 246. John Piper's endorsement is found on the back cover of my copies of both Fuller's *Gospel & Law: Contrast or Continuum?* and his *The Unity of the* Bible. This old connection may be in part responsible for Piper's writing of *Counted Righteous in Christ* in order to make clear that he holds traditional Reformed views of double imputation. A third important influence may be the ecumenical impulse visible in the attempts at rapprochement with the view of justification held by Roman Catholicism. *Declaration on the Doctrine of Justification Joint Declaration on the Doctrine of Justification*, English Language ed. (Grand Rapids: Eerdmans, 2000); *Justification by Faith: Lutherans and Catholics in Dialogue VII*, ed. H. George Anderson, T. Austin Murphy, Joseph A. Burgess (Minneapolis: Augsburg Publishing House, 1985); cf. also *Evangelicals and Catholics Together: Toward a Common Mission*, ed. Charles Colson and Richard John Neuhaus (Dallas: Word Publishing, 1995). A fourth movement that may to some degree lie behind each of the three foregoing influences is the biblical theology movement. I will argue within this dissertation, for instance, that Daniel Fuller is greatly influenced by Oscar Cullmann and his views of the Bible as salvation history. See Oscar Cullmann, *Salvation in History*, trans. Sidney G. Sowers (New York: Harper & Row, 1967). The biblical theology movement cannot be identified with the new perspective on Paul, but certainly precedes it and shares with it fundamental assumptions about Christianity. I speculate that the readiness of evangelicals and especially Reformed evangelicals to be moved by such influences may be due to an (over) reaction to the Easy-believism and Dispensationalism that have dominated so much of Evangelicalism for the last century. See for an illustration of this predominant viewpoint among evangelicals Zane Hodges, *The Gospel under Siege* (Dallas: Redencion Viva, 1981), 11-12. (I will argue within the following dissertation that this is one of Fuller's motives.) Evangelicals represented by the Grace Evangelical Society and the *Journal of the Grace Evangelical Society* separate faith and obedience and deny that perseverance is unto final salvation. One of the opening salvoes in the attack on easy-believism came from Walt Chantry in his *Today's Gospel: Authentic or Synthetic?* (London: Banner of Truth Trust, 1970). See also my *Easy Christianity* (Grand Rapids: Truth for Eternity Ministries, 1984). The public declaration of civil war among evangelicals came, however, in John MacArthur's *The Gospel According to Jesus* (Grand Rapids: Zondervan, 1994). This issued in what has been called the Lordship controversy. Note, for instance, Richard P. Belcher, *A Layman's Guide to the Lordship Controversy* (Southbridge, MA: Crowne Publications, 1990). Within the context of this debate, it is not difficult to understand a reaction especially by Reformed evangelicals into the equal and opposite extreme of identifying or (in the words of John Piper) conflating faith and obedience. I will argue that the course always steered by Reformation orthodoxy was neither to separate nor identify faith and obedience, but to *distinguish* them.

historic, Reformation doctrine of justification *sola fide*. Having departed from the historic Reformation doctrine, their claims to hold (and professions of holding) justification *sola fide* are misleading as to the true character of their views and meaningless for the purpose of certifying their "evangelical" identity.

Methodology

The thesis statement assumes that there has been a consistent, Reformation view of the meaning of justification by faith alone. It assumes, in other words, that the meaning of *sola fide* was substantially the same throughout the Reformation tradition.[5] The first business of this dissertation will be to show that such unity existed and to determine in what it consisted. In the second place, the views of certain, influential, evangelical[6] theologians today will be weighed in the balance of the

---

[5] Thomas R. Schreiner and Ardel B. Caneday, *The Race Set before Us: A Biblical Theology of Perseverance & Assurance* (Downers Grove, IL: InterVarsity Press, 2001), 88, remark, "Few disagreements, however, are as divisive and generate as much heat as the conflict that concerns the nature of faith's relationship to obedience and good works. The familiar motto *sola fide* ('by faith alone') was central to the Protestant Reformation of the church. This was the source of the famous disputation between the reformer Martin Luther and Desiderius Erasmus, the Roman Catholic. Protestants have continued to debate the meaning of 'by faith alone.' Each generation debates this Protestant motto, usually with some acrimony, because few issues concerning the gospel of Jesus Christ are as crucial as the question concerning the relationship of faith and obedience." Schreiner and Caneday are right to underscore the centrality of *sola fide*. Their statement is misleading, however, when it implies that the meaning of this phrase has been "up in the air" or debatable in the Reformation tradition. How could it be both central and debatable at the same time? I will show within this study that, in fact, substantial unity characterized the entire Reformation tradition with regard to the meaning of *sola fide*. Schreiner and Caneday seem insensitive to the fact that the debate over "easy-believism" and "lordship salvation" in the last century does not reflect a substantial disunity or lack of clarity in the Reformation tradition over faith, obedience, and justification. Easy-believism is a departure from the consensus of that tradition.

[6] My reference to "evangelical theologians" in conjunction with my reference to the Reformation tradition is not intended to make any precise claims as to the meaning or definition of *evangelical* or to provide its exact boundaries. It is a term that is notoriously difficult to delimit. I am not, for instance, saying that *Protestant* and *evangelical* are synonymous. I do think that it is undeniable that evangelicals generally emerged out of the Reformation tradition. I am assuming that Don Garlington, Daniel Fuller, and Norman Shepherd are generally regarded as evangelical. Since each of them promulgated their views of justification while teaching at seminaries that are professedly evangelical (Toronto Baptist Seminary, Fuller Theological Seminary, and Westminster Theological Seminary respectively), it seems appropriate to call them evangelical theologians. It is not

unified and historic Reformation teaching with regard to justification *sola fide*.

The first matter to be established, then, is the substantial unity of the Reformation tradition with regard to the meaning of *sola fide*. Assertions about something as massive and diverse as the Reformation traditions are certainly problematic. I believe, however, that an examination of the views of Martin Luther, John Calvin, and the major Reformation creeds and confessions will provide an adequate basis to assert the substantial unity of that tradition with regard to justification *sola fide*. This, of course, means that I will be defining the Reformation tradition and specifically what it teaches about justification by faith alone substantially in terms of Luther, Calvin, and the major Reformation confessions.[7]

---

necessary to the thesis of this dissertation, however, to defend any precise definition of *evangelical*.

[7] In chapter four I will provide a defense of the methodology of determining the views of the Reformation tradition from its public catechisms, creeds, and confessions. Perhaps it is necessary to say something about the propriety of examining Luther and Calvin as the representative progenitors of that tradition. A number of other important early Reformers seem to be ignored in such a procedure. In defense of my procedure let me say a number of things. *First*, in any case some selection is necessary. It seems to me that Luther and Calvin are generally recognized as the leading early Reformers. *Second*, the selection of these two Reformers allow us to study the leading representatives of the two major wings of the Reformation tradition—the Lutheran and the Reformed. *Third*, it is commonly acknowledged that within the Lutheran tradition no name—not even that of Melanchthon—rivals that of Luther in importance. See the discussion of Tuomo Mannermaa, *Christ Present in Faith: Luther's View of Justification* Minneapolis: Fortress Press, 2005), 4-6. *Fourth*, within the Reformed tradition other names do come closer to Calvin in importance. Ulrich Zwingli, Heinrich Bullinger, Martin Bucer, and Peter Martyr Vermigli come first to mind. Yet, I am aware of no discussion in the scholarly literature that suggests any diversity among them on the subject of justification *sola fide*. Indeed, the unity of the Reformation catechisms and confessions on this issue (which will be demonstrated in chapter four) is implicit evidence that no diversity existed among them about it. The influence of these early Reformed Reformers seems to have been taken up in that of Calvin and so passed on to the Reformed tradition. *Fifth*, the Second Helvetic Confession (as I will note in chapter four and which is surveyed there) was authored by Bullinger. Since he was the successor of Zwingli, this confession provides direct evidence for the views of Bullinger and indirect evidence of the views of Zwingli. *Sixth*, as I will show in chapter four, Melanchthon was the penman and co-author with Luther of the Augsburg Confession. Further, by common acknowledgment his views of justification are reflected in the Formula of Concord. See the statement of Mannermaa, *Christ Present in Faith*, 4, 6, that the Formula of Concord reflects the later theology of Melanchthon. For all these reasons the selection of Luther and Calvin as the representatives of the Lutheran and Reformed traditions respectively and the Reformation tradition as a whole seems eminently justified.

The thesis that a substantial unity existed among the Protestants with regard to the meaning of *sola fide* must begin with a treatment of Martin Luther. Thus, the development of the doctrine of justification by faith alone in Luther will be examined in chapter two. I will argue that because of the development inevitable in the one who pioneered the clear articulation of justification *sola fide* and other possible factors, we ought not to look to Luther for the clearest, systematic statement of this doctrine. I will demonstrate, however, that the meaning of justification *sola fide* is helpfully clarified by its development in Luther's understanding and experience. I will also show that Luther anticipated and, indeed, pioneered each of the three key perspectives on *sola fide* systematically taught by Calvin: the passive definition of justifying faith, the distinction between justifying faith and obedience, and the dichotomy between the law and the gospel (including the doctrine of forensic justification by imputed righteousness that this dichotomy implies).

In chapter three the views of John Calvin will be examined with regard to the meaning of justification *sola fide*. As "the theologian of the Reformation," his views reflect a maturity, clarity, and balance that make him a fit center-piece for this study. An examination of Calvin's treatment of justification by faith alone isolates three key perspectives on the meaning of *sola fide* through which the Reformation tradition can be examined and the views of current evangelical theologians tested. Those three perspectives on the meaning of *sola fide* are the passive definition of justifying faith,[8] the distinction between justifying faith and obedience, and the dichotomy between the law and the gospel (including the doctrine of forensic justification by imputed righteousness that this dichotomy implies). In other words, justifying faith is defined as passive,[9] a distinction (though not a separation) is maintained between

---

[8] To avoid confusion within this study I will frequently specify justifying faith as the subject of discussion. In many cases this may be unnecessary and what is said of justifying faith might be said more generally of saving faith. Nevertheless, as the *Westminster Confession of Faith* (14:2) says, there are many actings of saving faith beside that specific acting of faith which is unto justification. Thus, as I will also argue, one ought to include such actings of saving faith in sanctifying faith. The acting of faith "working through love," for instance, is not included in justifying faith, but is included in sanctifying faith. Sanctifying faith is not exclusively passive, but when the word, *passive*, is properly understood, justifying faith is exclusively passive in its actings. The distinction I am making here between justifying faith and sanctifying faith is not meant to distinguish two different kinds of faith, but to distinguish two different, but inseparable *actings*, of saving faith.

[9] The use of the adjective *passive* in the definition of justifying faith is itself controversial and in need of definition. As I will make clear in my treatment of Calvin, in

justifying faith and obedience, and a dichotomy, antithesis, or contrast is maintained between (the righteousness of) the law and (the righteousness of) the gospel.[10] These three perspectives are critical to the meaning of *sola fide* in the Reformation tradition.

The views of *sola fide* held by the theological tradition flowing from Luther and Calvin will be examined in chapter four. The examination of

---

the first place, by calling justifying faith *passive* I do not mean to adopt the thesis of R.T. Kendall, *Calvin and English Calvinism to 1649* (New York: Oxford University Press, 1979). Kendall maintains that justifying faith for Calvin and in reality is *passive* in the sense that it is simply *intellectual* assurance that Christ died for me or that I am saved. I do not mean, by using the term *passive*, to say that faith is completely non-volitional. I mean rather what Calvin means when he says that faith is a *passive work* (*Comm.*, John 6:29). Footnote citations written as *Comm.* are from *Calvin's Commentaries*, 22 vols. (Grand Rapids: Baker Book House, 1981). [*Ioannis Calvini Opera quae supersunt omnia*, ed. G. Baum, E. Cunitz, and E. Reuss, Corpus Reformatorum *CR*, [1864] 75:141]). Though faith involves a human activity (or volition), that activity, work, or volition is passive. It is the activity of resting on or receiving Christ alone for salvation.

[10] By speaking of imputed righteousness and contrasting the righteousness of the law and the righteousness of the gospel, I involve myself inevitably in the growing controversy over imputed righteousness. Questions swirl around this issue in our day. Is double imputation biblical? Is it confessional? Is it taught throughout the Reformation tradition? Is there development in regard to imputation within the Reformation tradition and confessions? See Brian Vickers, "The Imputation of Christ's Righteousness: A Study of Key Pauline Texts" (Ph.D. diss., The Southern Baptist Theological Seminary, 2003); D.A. Carson, "The Vindication of Imputation: On Fields of Discourse and Semantic Fields," in *Justification: What's at Stake in the Current Debates?*, ed. Mark Husbands and Daniel J. Treier (Downers Grove, IL: InterVarsity Press, 2004); Mark Seifrid, "Luther, Melanchthon, and Paul: Recommendations on a Current Debate," in *Justification: What's at Stake in the Current Debates?*, ed. Mark Husbands and Daniel J. Treier (Downers Grove, IL: InterVarsity Press, 2004). Seifrid desires some room for disagreement on one's precise view of imputation and opts for what he argues is Luther's as opposed to Melanchthon's view (148-151). Yet, he also argues (citing Scott Hafemann and N.T. Wright in a footnote): "Where it is argued that there is no distinction between Law and Gospel, where it is claimed that there are no unconditioned promises of God, or where justification is construed as a pronouncement upon a human quality, there is certainly cause to be concerned, for precisely the same reasons that Melanchthon once was" (149). Though I hold firmly to double imputation (the imputation of our sins to Christ and His righteousness to us) as the ground of justification, it is not in my opinion necessary to hold so clearly articulated an understanding of imputation as this in order to hold justification *sola fide* in the classical sense. It is necessary, as I will argue, to hold that justification is forensic and has for its ground the imputation of an alien righteousness. It is not necessary that this alien righteousness be understood in terms of a developed and clearly articulated doctrine of double imputation. It is true—as this study will show—that those who specifically reduce justification to the forgiveness of sins or imputed righteousness to single imputation (of our sins to Christ) tend to deviant views of *sola fide*. Nevertheless, the thesis of this study does not assume a clearly articulated doctrine of double imputation.

something as massive as the Reformation theological tradition is, of course, problematic. A fair and accurate assessment of the meaning of *sola fide* for that tradition may be achieved and, indeed, may be best achieved by the examination of its major creeds and confessions. The three key perspectives on the meaning of justification *by faith alone* will be found embedded in the sixteenth and seventeenth century creeds of Protestantism.

Having seen the meaning and, indeed, the unified meaning of justification *sola fide* in Luther, Calvin, and the Reformation tradition, chapters five through seven will examine the views of three influential evangelical theologians in light of this crucial tradition. The views of Daniel Fuller, Norman Shepherd, and Don Garlington[11] will be weighed in the balance of the historic, Reformation doctrine of justification *by faith alone*.[12] Since the order given here is generally the chronological order of the appearance of their views, I will deal in order with Fuller, Shepherd, and Garlington.

Chapter eight will seek to make clear a number of important conclusions from the study as a whole. The broader significance of the study for evangelical theology will, in particular, be considered.

Importance

If the significance of a careful examination of the Reformation doctrine of justification is to be understood and appreciated, something must be

---

[11] In the respective chapters dealing with each of these men I provide evidence that warrants my assessment that each of these men are "influential." I suppose that the most questions might be raised about the prominence of Don Garlington. Yet, because he is generally regarded as a conservative evangelical, he has peculiar significance as one who is a conduit of "new perspective" ideas into the heart of conservative evangelicalism.

[12] Lest my argument be misunderstood, let me clarify the precise claims I am making with regard to Fuller, Shepherd, and Garlington. Though it would be possible to argue that each of these theologians may be generally identified with the Reformed and evangelical tradition, this is not necessary to my argument. Nor is it necessary for my argument to prove that these men hold any particular Reformation confession. All that is required to prove my argument is to show that these men claim to believe in justification by faith alone. This claim sufficiently identifies them with the Reformation tradition within which that doctrine was classically articulated. Any claim to believe in justification by faith alone is a claim to believe it in the sense in which it was held by that tradition. To claim to believe this doctrine, and yet tacitly depart from its classical articulation, is historically and practically misleading. To claim to believe in justification by faith alone and teach contrary to its meaning in the Reformation tradition is like claiming to believe in the Trinity while teaching Arianism or some other doctrine than that articulated by Athanasius, the Cappadocian Fathers, and Augustine.

Prolegomena

said about the importance of historical theology and church history in coming to a knowledge of the truth. The idea that church history is important in coming to a knowledge of the truth would be met with confusion and even rejection by many evangelicals today. They would wonder if we really held to—another of the great *solas* of the Reformation—*sola Scriptura.*

Much might be said by way of a *biblical* response to this question. The heart of it would be the teaching of Scripture with regard to the importance of the teaching gifts that Christ promised to the church and has been giving to the church for almost 2000 years. Passages like Romans 12:3-8, Ephesians 4:11-13, 1 Peter 4:10-11, and 1 Corinthians 12:27-31 indicate that one of the great blessings of the church is the gift of pastors and teachers. This indisputable fact means that *sola Scriptura* must never be understood in such a way as to make such gifts unnecessary. Indeed, the mention of the man of God in 2 Timothy 3:15-17 (the classic statement of scriptural sufficiency) refers to the Christian minister and means that the sufficiency of Scripture is precisely its sufficiency to enable the man of God to teach the people of God. There is at least unwitting pride and lack of self-knowledge in the attitude that sees no importance in understanding the history of doctrine in the church. When we attempt to discern the meaning of the Bible, the teaching gifts of Christ faithfully given to the church for almost 2000 years cannot be ignored without folly.

Closely related to a misunderstanding of *sola Scriptura* (and also related to insensitivity to the importance of church history) are successionist views of church history. Such views (whether Roman Catholic, Baptist, or something else) assume that the once-for-all deposit of inspired truth given us in the Bible automatically means that there can be no development in the church's understanding of that deposit. Of course, this follows neither logically nor historically. In fact, the Bible itself suggests a *progressivist* view of church history. A number of the statements and parables of the Lord suggest a progressive view of the history of the church and therefore of the history of its doctrinal understanding and articulation (Matt. 16:18; Matt. 28:18-20; Mark 4:26-29; Luke 13:13-20; Eph. 4:11-15). An unbiased examination of the history of the church leads to the conclusion that its understanding of the message of the Bible has developed in a gradual and progressive way.[13]

---

[13] For helpful discussions of this issue, see James Edward McGoldrick, *Baptist Successionism: A Crucial Question of Baptist History* (Metuchen, NJ: The Scarecrow

The special relevance of this *progressivist* view of church history for this study must be specified here. Church history is, of course, not able to act as our final authority. Yet, it is able to act as a kind of quality control on our interpretation of the Bible.

Certain teaching-gifts that God has given to the church are identified with the defense of specific doctrinal issues. For instance, the presumption of orthodox Christians is that Athanasius "got it right" with regard to the deity of Christ and that the Nicene Creed and the Cappadocian fathers "got it right" with regard to the Trinity. The assumption of most theologians in the Western tradition is that Augustine "got it right" in the Pelagian controversy. Just so and for exactly the same reasons, we would be surprised to learn that Luther and the Reformation did not "get it right" on the doctrine of justification.[14] It will, therefore, serve as useful quality control for modern evangelicals to ask the meaning of *sola fide* in Luther, Calvin, and the Reformation tradition.

The reason is, of course, that Martin Luther and the Reformation are forever bound up with the doctrine of *sola fide*.[15] This is a point that might be taken for granted. It is, however, an important enough observation for the thesis of this study that it is worthy of a little comment.

Press, 1994); and also Peter Toon, *The Development of Doctrine in the Church* (Grand Rapids: Eerdmans, 1979).

[14] Of course, I am not arguing that doctrinal development ceased with the Reformation, or that nothing useful could be added to its doctrinal construction of justification. I am saying, however, that the Reformation was a pivotal point in the development of the doctrine of justification in the church.

[15] E. Gordon Rupp in his often praised work, *The Righteousness of God* (London: Hodder & Stoughton, 1943), 256, concludes that Luther was a pioneer with regard to this doctrine. Alister McGrath, *Iustitia Dei, A History of the Christian Doctrine of Justification*, 2nd ed. (Cambridge, UK: Cambridge University Press, 1998), 180-187, rejects the idea that there were in any strict sense forerunners of Luther's doctrine of justification. He notes a fundamental discontinuity in the western theological tradition at this point. Precisely at the point of the nature of justification he sees Luther's view as differing from all that precedes. Matthew C. Heckel, "Is R.C. Sproul Wrong about Martin Luther? An Analysis of Sproul's *Faith Alone: The Evangelical Doctrine of Justification* with respect to Augustine, Luther, Calvin, and Catholic Luther Scholarship," *JETS* 47, no. 1 (March 2004): 89-120, argues that Luther's *sola fide* "was not a recovery but an innovation" (93). Such views, while appropriately underscoring the newness of Luther's views, lose something of the historical progression of Luther's *sola fide*. Justification *sola fide* is not innovative in the sense of being *novel*. It is its clear articulation that is innovative—not its substance. Justification *sola fide* is a development within the church's theological tradition—not an alien addition to it.

Prolegomena

What is the cardinal doctrine of the Reformation? If this question is asked, it seems clear that the major options to be considered must be derived from the great *solas* of the Reformation. The major options must be *sola gratia*, *sola Scriptura*, and *sola fide*. I believe that the standard by which the cardinal doctrine of the Reformation should be judged is the advancement of historical theology. That is to say, it is progress with regard to the church's understanding and articulation of the deposit of truth that should serve as the measure of the cardinal doctrine of the Reformation. The evidence shows that the cardinal doctrine of the Reformation (in the sense of its unique contribution or historical development) was not *sola gratia*. This was already clarified by Augustine in the Pelagian controversy. *Sola gratia*, in the strict Augustinian understanding of it, was assumed by Luther, Zwingli, and Calvin and foundational for them. Yet, it was for that very reason not the point of historico-theological advancement in the Reformation. Nor was the cardinal doctrine *sola Scriptura*. Again this doctrine was fundamental to the Reformation. It also became a distinctive mark of the Reformation position. A sophisticated debate over this issue was, however, already going on prior to the Reformation.[16] Thus, again this doctrine does not represent actual historico-theological progress. It is rather at the point of justification *sola fide* that the real development and contribution of Luther and the Reformation consists. Two (of the many) lines of evidence for this are these. *First*, Luther, as I will argue, was conscious that in his development of the doctrine of justification he had passed beyond the formulations of Augustine.[17] Though Luther found in Augustine the platform of his understanding of the gospel, he became increasingly conscious that Augustine was not clear about justification *sola fide*. *Second*, the confusion of the Roman Catholic response in the Council of Trent to justification *sola fide* also bears eloquent witness to the advancement represented in the Reformation doctrine of justification *sola fide*.[18] This confusion is tantamount to an admission that here was a

---

[16] Heiko Oberman, *Forerunners of the Reformation* (New York: Holt, Rinehart, and Winston, 1966), 51.

[17] Heckel, "Is R.C. Sproul Wrong about Martin Luther?," 89-120.

[18] James Buchanan, *The Doctrine of Justification* (Grand Rapids: Baker Book House, 1977), 139, remarks of the Roman Catholic theologians at Trent: "They seem, indeed, to have been much perplexed in dealing with the subject. It was felt to be singularly important, as all the errors of Luther resolved themselves into his doctrine concerning it; and also singularly difficult, since Justification by faith was regarded by many as a doctrine which had never been thought of by any School-writer, and therefore never discussed or confuted before." Buchanan remarks in this same place that the

new articulation of the doctrine of justification. The conclusion must be that any proposal by evangelicals to re-define justification cannot be taken seriously unless it grapples face to face with Martin Luther and his successors on this subject.[19]

Approach

The approach of this study is somewhat unusual. It allows historical theology rather than contemporary theology to set its agenda. It asks what historical theology has to say about contemporary theological trends. It also allows systematic theology to probe the assertions of biblical theology, rather than allowing biblical theology to criticize (usually distorted characterizations of) systematic theology. In this way I hope practical concerns will set the agenda for this study and not the narrow and limited perspectives of some, popular forms of *biblical theology* or "the new perspective on Paul."[20]

---

decrees against justification are much more dogmatic, than the Council's positive exposition of it. He also shows that various Catholic theologians held different aspects of the Protestant doctrine. The Catholic confusion is symptomatic of the fact that they stood in a less advanced (as well as more errant) place in the history of dogma. James Orr, *The Progress of Dogma* (Old Tappan, NJ: Fleming H. Revell, 1901), 241-275, argues the case for this same view of the unique contribution of the Reformation to the progress of dogma.

[19] Even if one should disagree with my conviction that *sola fide* is the cardinal doctrine of the Reformation, it seems impossible to deny that it was (at least) one of its distinctive teachings. Even this claim is sufficient to ground the argument of this dissertation.

[20] D.A. Carson, "The Vindication of Imputation: On Fields of Discourse and Semantic Fields," in *Justification: What's at Stake in the Current Debates?*, ed. Mark Husbands and Daniel J. Treier (Downers Grove, IL: InterVarsity Press, 2004), 46-78, argues exegesis today is too analytic and atomistic.

CHAPTER 2

SOLA FIDE IN LUTHER

Introductory Considerations

This chapter is organized around a number of claims regarding the meaning of *sola fide* in Luther. "The Reformation was embodied in Martin Luther . . . it lived in him as in no one else."[1] In these words Thomas Lindsay summarizes the conviction that grounds this treatment of Luther. It is crucial for the thesis of this dissertation that Luther's views of justification *sola fide* be examined. This is true because an understanding of Luther's views is critical for any discussion of *sola fide*. His name and experience are identified with this doctrine in a way that is unique.

Thus, it is also appropriate that Martin Luther be treated first. His place as the widely recognized pioneer of the Reformation seems to demand such treatment. Yet this very position as pioneer, as I will argue in this chapter, brings with it problems with regard to the meaning of *sola fide* for Luther. It is not to Luther, but to Calvin, I suggest, that we must look for the most careful and systematic presentation. Nevertheless, the problems that Luther's pioneering position carries with it are not finally such, I will also argue, as to undermine the substantial unity between Luther, Calvin, and the Reformation tradition.

This chapter, then, makes two claims with regard to the meaning of *sola fide* in Luther. Each of them are closely related to the pioneering role of Luther in the Reformation. *First*, the gradual development and major features of justification *sola fide* as it was systematically presented by Calvin are to be found in Martin Luther. *Second*, and therefore, substantial unity exists between, Luther, Calvin, and the Reformation tradition with regard to justification *sola fide*. As the previous sentence has intimated, certain modern views of Luther's doctrine of justification present a challenge to the claim that substantial unity exists on this subject between Luther and his successors. In order not to perplex the subsequent treatment of Luther's understanding of justification *sola fide*, I will interact with them in this introduction.

Each of these modern views not only seek to distance Luther from Melanchthon and the later tradition, but also move in the direction of

---

[1]Thomas Lindsay, *The History of the Reformation* (New York: Scribner's, 1936), 1:193.

including the process of personal transformation or sanctification within Luther's doctrine of justification. Though I will interact with Karl Holl's views below, it is important to mention his views here.[2] Harnack remarked in his funeral oration for Holl that "he had become one of the best-known Luther scholars of all time."[3] More recently the views of Tuomo Mannermaa and the Finnish School of Luther Studies have moved in a similar direction. They have found an affinity between Luther's doctrine of justification and the doctrine of deification (or divinization) associated with Eastern Orthodoxy.[4] It is not hard to see that—finding such an affinity—they also include sanctification in justification and, thus, must distance Luther from the later tradition.[5] Mark Seifrid belongs to a school of thought that moves more moderately

---

[2] Karl Holl, *What Did Luther Understand by Religion?*, ed. James Luther Adams and Walter F. Bense, trans. Fred W. Meuser and Walter R. Wietzke (Philadelphia: Fortress Press, 1977). Bense, in his introduction, remarks, "While Ritschl (following J.C.K. von Hofmann) had sought to distinguish Luther's own thought from that of Melanchthon and Lutheran Orthodoxy, Holl was able to show that Ritschl had not gone far enough in this endeavor" (3). Later he proceeds to say, "Holl maintains that, for Luther, justification always includes the entire process of sanctification, and that it is effected by *Christ within us*" (11).

[3] Karl Holl, *What Did Luther Understand by Religion?*, 1.

[4] The recent publication of Tuomo Mannermaa's *Christ Present in Faith: Luther's View of Justification*, ed. and intro. Kirsi Stjerna (Minneapolis: Fortress Press, 2005), renews scholarly discussion of the Finnish School of Luther studies in the English-speaking world and especially their distinctive views of Luther's understanding of justification. Mannermaa is the leading light of the Finnish School. His views and those of his associates in this movement have previously been presented to the English-speaking world in the volume of essays by members of the Finnish School edited by Carl Braaten and Robert W. Jenson entitled: *Union with Christ: The New Finnish Interpretation* ed. Carl E. Braaten and Robert W. Jenson (Grand Rapids: Eerdmans, 1998). This volume was the subject of extensive comment and review in various, theological journals after its publication in 1998. Besides many brief reviews, it was the subject of numerous longer essays. Note especially: Timothy J. Wengert, "Review of *Union with Christ: The New Finnish Interpretation of Luther,*" *Theology Today* 56, no. 3 (October 1999):432-434; Ted Dorman, "The Catholic Luther," *First Things* 98 (December 1999): 49-52; James M. Kittelson, "To the Finland Station: A Review Essay," *Dialog* 38, no. 3 (Summer 1999): 235-237. The Westminster Theological Journal dedicated most of one issue to this book. This treatment comprised four essays: Paul Louis Metzger, "Mystical Union with Christ;" Mark A. Seifrid, "Paul, Luther, and Justification;" Carl R. Trueman, "Is the Finnish Line a New Beginning? A Critical Assessment of the Reading of Luther Offered by the Helsinki Circle;" Robert W. Jenson, "Response to Mark Seifrid, Paul Metzger, and Carl Trueman on Finnish Luther Research;" *Westminster Theological Journal* 65, no. 2 (Fall 2003); 201-250.

[5] Mannermaa, *Christ Present in Faith: Luther's View of Justification*, 4, 22, 41, 42, 46, 49, 54-58, 61, 87-88. See also *Union with Christ*, 27-29, 42-67.

in the same direction. This school of thought also finds some tension between Luther and Melanchthon on the subject of justification and believes that for Luther justification is both forensic and effective.[6] Seifrid says:

> As again our citation from the Galatians commentary shows, Luther thinks of "imputation" as a forensic and declaratory act. Yet it is no mere declaration, but rather an effective Word of God: "Because you believe in me . . . and your faith takes hold of Christ, therefore be righteous!"[7]

These modern views fail to undermine the substantial unity predicated between Luther and the Reformation tradition for three reasons. *First*, they fail to present sufficient evidence to overturn the *prima facie* and presumptive evidence for the substantial unity on justification *sola fide* between Luther, Calvin, and the Reformation tradition. *Second*, they fail to take into serious account factors which may explain away any supposed disagreement between Luther and his successors. *Third*, they fail to prove such significant disagreement as to disrupt the substantial unity on *sola fide* between Luther and his successors. It will be helpful to enlarge briefly on each of these points.

There is, *first, prima facie* and presumptive evidence for the substantial unity of Luther with Calvin and the Reformation tradition. The broad, doctrinal dependence of Calvin on Luther and agreement between them is widely acknowledged. The earliest edition of the *Institutes* provides striking evidence of the influence of Luther on Calvin's view of the law, justification, and many other matters. A glance

---

[6]Mark Seifrid, "Luther, Melanchthon, and Paul on the Question of Justification," in *Justification: What's at Stake in the Current Debates*, ed. Mark Husbands and Daniel J. Treier (Downers Grove, IL: InterVarsity Press, 2004); 137-152; Timothy J. Wengert, *Law and Gospel: Philip Melanchthon's debate with John Agricola of Eisleben over Poenitentia* (Grand Rapids: Baker Book House, 1997), 177-210; Oswald Bayer, "The Being of Christ in Faith," *The Lutheran Quarterly* 10 (1996), 135-150; Robert Kolb, "Luther on the Two Kinds of Righteousness; Reflections on His Two-dimensional Definition of Humanity at the Heart of His Theology," *Lutheran Quarterly* 13 (1999): 449-466. See Stephen Westerholm, *Perspectives Old and New on Paul: The "Lutheran" Paul and His Critics*, (Grand Rapids: Eerdmans, 2004), 219-225, for an interesting overview of Seifrid's work.

[7]Mark Seifrid, "Luther, Melanchthon, and Paul on the Question of Justification," 145. See also idem, "Paul, Luther, and Justification," 229-230. I see no need to take such language in an effective sense. Luther, *Luther's Works: American Edition* (ed. J. Pelikan) *LW* [1955-1986], 26:277, also said that the Father told Christ, "Be Peter the denier." Are we to take this effectively?

at the extensive references to Luther in the indices and annotations provided by Battles to the 1536 edition illustrates the extensive dependence of Calvin on Luther.[8]

Also striking is the fact that with regard to the doctrinal rock that ruptured the doctrinal unity of the Reformation movement, the Lord's Supper, Calvin felt himself closer to Luther than Zwingli. At the outset of his ministry, in fact, he was considerably prejudiced against the Zwinglian view. T.H.L. Parker says with regard to the Lord's Supper controversy, "In this particular situation, Calvin early took Luther's side and even conceived such a dislike for Luther's sake against the writings of Zwingli and Oecolampadius that he would not read them."[9]

Striking testimonies to Calvin's *reverence* for Luther exist. They may be found in his single, extant letter to Luther and in his comments about Luther in a letter to Bullinger.[10] These testimonies receive clear confirmation in Calvin's *The Necessity of Reforming the Church*. Again and again in this writing dated in 1544 (at least seven times by my count), Calvin respectfully refers to the reformatory example of Luther by name, while never mentioning by name any other contemporary reformer.[11] The first such reference is characteristic.

> We maintain, then, that at the commencement, when God raised up Luther and others, who held forth a torch to light us into the way of salvation, and who, by their ministry, founded and reared our churches, those heads of doctrine in which the truth of our religion, those in which the pure and legitimate worship of God, and those in which the salvation of men are comprehended, were in great measure obsolete.[12]

---

[8] John Calvin, *The Institutes of the Christian Religion: 1536 Edition*, trans. and annot. Ford Lewis Battles (Grand Rapids: The H.H. Meeter for Calvin Studies with William B. Eerdmans Publishing Company, 1975), 394.

[9] T.H.L. Parker, *John Calvin* (Tring, Herts, England: Lion Publishing, 1988), 162. The discussion of Francois Wendel, *Calvin: Origins and Development of His Religious Thought*, trans. by Philip Mairet (Grand Rapids: Baker Book House, 2002), 329-334, makes the same point.

[10] *Selected Works of John Calvin: Tracts and Letters*, ed. Henry Beveridge and Jules Bonnet, trans. David Constable (Grand Rapids: Baker Book House, 1983), 4:429-441. [*Ioannis Calvini Opera quae supersunt omnia*, ed. G. Baum, E. Cunitz, and E. Reuss, Corpus Reformatorum CR, [1864] CR 39:772-775; 40:6-8].

[11] *Selected Works of John Calvin: Tracts and Letters*, 1:125, 134, 145, 183, 220 [CR 34:459, 465, 473, 499, 524-525].

[12] *Selected Works of John Calvin: Tracts and Letters*, 1:125 [CR 34:459].

Calvin's dependence on Luther and consequent, close agreement with Luther is, therefore, indisputable. One of the purposes of this chapter is to show that this same dependence and agreement existed in regard to justification *sola fide*.

The modern views we are discussing posit a rather stark contrast between Luther's view, on the one hand, and, on the other hand, that of Melanchthon and *The Formula of Concord*.[13] If these views are to make their case, they must squarely and realistically face the improbability of this claim. Even more improbable, however, is the fact that these views posit a contrast between Luther and the view of justification assumed in the *Augsburg Confession*. Though they recognize and accept the contrast with *The Formula of Concord*, they do not recognize or believe that their views are in conflict with the *Augsburg Confession*. If their views are in such conflict, then in a couple of respects this presents a greater problem for them. While the *Formula of Concord* was written after Luther's death, the *Augsburg Confession* was written during Luther's life. Though Melanchthon penned it, he did so with Luther—so to speak—looking constantly over his shoulder.[14] Not only so, as I will show in the chapter four, the Formula of Concord was anything but a *formula of concord*. It never enjoyed anything like the universal submission among Lutherans that the *Augsburg Confession* enjoyed. Thus, if it can be shown that the *Augsburg Confession* expresses a view of justification at variance with these views, this creates the strongest presumption that their view of Luther is mistaken.

But does the *Augsburg Confession* differ from the view of justification that the modern views under discussion argue Luther held? It seems clear that it does. Though the *Augsburg Confession* does not, of course, contain the overt and specific denial (provoked by Osiander) that the indwelling of God is part of justification that is contained in the *Formula of Concord*, it still clearly asserts a justification that is exclusively forensic in nature. Here is its statement:

> Also they teach that men can not be justified [obtain forgiveness of sins and righteousness] before God by their own powers, merits, or works, but are justified freely [of grace] for Christ's sake through faith, when

---

[13] Mannermaa, *Christ Present in Faith*, 4, 87.

[14] *The Creeds of Christendom with a History and Critical Notes*, ed. Philip Schaff, rev. David S. Schaff (Grand Rapids: Baker Book House, 1983), 1:229, discusses the relation of Melanchthon and Luther in the framing of the Augsburg Confession. See the discussion in chapter four.

they believe that they are received into favor, and their sins forgiven for Christ's sake, who by his death hath satisfied for our sins. This faith doth God impute for righteousness before him. Rom. iii and iv.[15]

It seems evident to me that here we have an exclusively forensic understanding of justification. To be justified is defined as to *obtain forgiveness of sins and righteousness*. Forgiveness is, of course, forensic in character, but equally so is the reference to righteousness in this context. This is clear, in the first place, from the later reference to righteousness in this paragraph where we are told that the righteousness in view in justification is a righteousness that *God doth impute*. This is clear, in the second place, from the way in which justifying faith is described in the paragraph. Justifying faith is believing "that they are received into favor, and their sins forgiven for Christ's sake, who by his death hath satisfied for our sins." Favor, forgiveness, and satisfaction for sins are the categories by means of which justification is described. These categories are exclusively forensic.

The agreement between Luther, Melanchthon, and Calvin on *sola fide* was continued, reflected, and confirmed in the agreement on this issue of the churches that descended from them. The summary of Jaroslav Pelikan may be cited as representative of scholarly opinion on the matter.

> Although Luther's "discovery" of justification by faith took place in the struggle of his own conscience as it sought an answer to the question, "How do I obtain a God who is gracious to me?", the doctrine of justification by faith was to become one that "all churches reformed, with a sweet consent, applaud, and confess," including those churches that opposed Luther on many other points. Thus the seventeenth-century Reformed followers of John Calvin knew that they disagreed with the followers of Luther on many questions, but they recognized that all of them agreed on this doctrine of the entire Reformation, in fact, the chief doctrine of Christianity and the chief point of difference separating Protestantism from Roman Catholicism.
>
> Repeatedly, the various efforts in the sixteenth and seventeenth centuries to unite Lutheran and Reformed teachings were able to affirm this doctrine as one that they shared, diverge though they did on other doctrines. It was a Swiss Reformed theologian, Heinrich Bullinger, who, in the title of a book published in 1554 and dedicated to the Lutheran king of Denmark, managed to include all the constituents of

---

[15]*The Creeds of Christendom*, 3:10. Augsburg Confession, Part First, Article IV.

this common confession more trenchantly than any one title had: *The Grace of God that Justifies Us for the Sake of Christ through Faith Alone, without Good Works, while Faith Meanwhile Abounds in Good Works.*[16]

Second, modern views positing disagreement between Luther and his successors with regard to *sola fide* fail to take into serious account factors which may explain away any supposed disagreement between Luther and his successors. Two such factors are Luther's role as pioneer of the Reformation and his passionate temperament.

Luther, as we have noted, was the doctrinal pioneer of the Reformation.[17] In his unfolding experience and theological development the Reformation emerged and sprang up as nowhere else.[18] For this very reason difficult questions arise over the timing of the emergence of his distinctive view of *sola fide*. Also for this reason, questions arise with regard to a certain lack of clarity in some of Luther's early utterances. Such questions will perforce be discussed below in this chapter. In this regard Calvin is quite different. He seems to have been converted immediately into a circle (around 1530) where Luther's distinctive and more mature views were understood and accepted.[19] Thus, he began his spiritual life, and certainly his writing life, with a view of justification by faith alone clearly and consciously distinguished from that of Medieval Catholicism.[20]

---

[16]Jaroslav Pelikan, *The Reformation of Church and Dogma*, vol. 4 of *The Christian Tradition: A History of the Development of Doctrine* (Chicago: The University of Chicago Press, 2000), 138-139.

[17]I am aware that it is arguable that Zwingli's views developed independently (and at about the same time as those) of Luther. My point is that, even acknowledging this and giving Zwingli his due, Luther was preeminently useful in spreading the doctrine of justification *sola fide* and is identified with the Reformation *breakthrough* as no one else.

[18]Thomas Lindsay, *The History of the Reformation* 1:193.

[19]Parker, *John Calvin*, 26-27, 186-196, has a detailed discussion of the various views of the chronology of Calvin's life and the timing of his conversion. He shows that Lutheran influences were clearly instrumental in Calvin's conversion.

[20]Calvin, *The Institutes of the Christian Religion: 1536 Edition*, 16-17, 29-35, [*OS* 1:38-40, 54-61.] emphasizes the distinction between law and gospel, the first use of the law to condemn our sins and lead us to Christ, and the purely forensic view of justification by imputed righteousness. With regard to justification by imputed righteousness, he remarks in this first edition of the *Institutes*: "But Christ's righteousness, which alone can bear the sight of God because it alone is perfect, must appear in court on our behalf, and stand surety for us in judgment . . . . Received from God, this righteousness is brought to us and imputed to us, just as if it were ours. Thus in faith we continually and constantly obtain forgiveness of sins; none of the filth or

It is widely acknowledged that in his temperament and subsequently in his flaming utterances Luther lacked something important to the careful articulation of the doctrinal viewpoints of the Reformation he instigated. The very temperament and boldness that fitted Luther to be the fiery reformer, pamphleteer, and leader crusading against Rome to some degree unfitted him for the task of precisely systematizing Reformation doctrine. This is sometimes affirmed by saying that Luther needed his Melanchthon. It was Melanchthon who again and again for Luther did the careful theological work necessary.[21] The fact is, however, that a strong case might be made that it was Calvin rather than Melanchthon who most faithfully articulated Luther's insights.[22] Just because he was the firebrand of reform, Luther's preaching and teaching lacks the thorough and steady balance of Calvin.[23]

Third, modern views positing disagreement between Luther and his successors on *sola fide* fail to prove such significant disagreement as to disrupt the substantial unity on *sola fide* between Luther and his successors. Mark Seifrid, for instance, though inclined toward the view that Melanchthon and the Reformation tradition moved away from the view of justification held by Luther, does not wish to deduce from this disagreement a fundamental division in the Reformation tradition. He remarks:

> Be that as it may, my point at the moment is that, as was the case with Luther and Melanchthon, both sides have reason to harbor suspicions about the Reformational status of the other's views. Surely the outcome of their debate is instructive for us. Although they maintained their

---

uncleanness of our imperfection is imputed to us, but is covered over by that purity and perfection of Christ" (Ibid., 35).

[21] Perhaps the classic illustration of this is Melanchthon's work for Luther on the Augsburg Confession. Cf. the comments of James M. Kittelson, *Luther the Reformer: The Story of the Man and His Career* (Minneapolis: Augsburg Publishing House, 1986), 184-186, 230-239.

[22] If it is true that Calvin remained closer to the views of Luther in *The Bondage of the Will* and was ultimately no farther away from Luther's view of the Lord's Supper than Melanchthon, then (given the dependence of Calvin on Luther) it is hard to see how this thesis might be refuted.

[23] The fiery and even volatile character of Luther is well known. It is illustrated from the fact that Melanchthon was afraid even to pass on to Luther the letter that Calvin had sent to him for Luther because of the reaction it might provoke. See *Selected Works of John Calvin: Tracts and Letters*, 4:440.

differences, Luther and Melanchthon accepted one another's teaching on justification[24]

In this chapter, therefore, the claims identified above regarding the meaning of *sola fide* for Luther will be carefully examined from three vantage points. The meaning of *sola fide* in Luther will be clarified by an examination of its gradual development through his life, experience, and ministry. The meaning of *sola fide* for Luther will then be identified through a presentation of its major features in order to show that the views of Luther and Calvin on this matter with regard to justification *sola fide* were substantially identical.

The Gradual Development of *Sola Fide* in Luther

The instructive development of Luther's *sola fide* will be traced by examining the major factors in its emergence. We will look in turn at its experiential milieu, scholastic context, biblical foundation, Augustinian insight, and Reformation advance.

- **The Experiential Milieu: *Anfechtung***

Sola fide was the discovery that brought peace to a troubled Martin Luther. This is not to say that having made this discovery Luther was once and for all freed from his *Anfechtungen*, but it is to say that Luther's doctrine can never be understood in a barrenly doctrinal way. It must always be understood within the context of "an unnerving and enervating fear that God had turned his back on him once and for all, had repudiated his repentance and prayers, and had abandoned him to suffer the pains of hell."[25] Pelikan says:

---

[24]Mark Seifrid, "Luther, Melanchthon, and Paul on the Question of Justification," 150.

[25]David C. Steinmetz, "Luther against Luther," in *Luther in Context* (Bloomington: Indiana University Press, 1986), 1. Steinmetz concludes this account of Luther's *Anfechtungen* and its relation to his understanding of the sacrament of penance with these sentences: "Luther sees that contrition cannot be the proper disposition for grace, since only the already justified can experience sorrow for their sins. Moreover, justifying grace which is the proper disposition for the experience of contrition can only be given to sinners who have nothing to offer to God but their sins. The good news of the gospel (at least as Luther understands it) is that that is all that God asks sinners to offer" (Ibid., 12).

Luther's discovery of justification by faith took place in the struggle of his own conscience as it sought an answer to the question, "How do I obtain a God who is gracious to me?"[26]

If we are to understand *sola fide,* we must, therefore, attempt to understand Luther's trouble. His spiritual troubles began in a horrifying confrontation with sudden death. James Atkinson gives this version of the story of how Luther decided to join a monastery:

> It would appear, though there is some uncertainty about details, that he and his companion were overtaken by a violent storm, when Martin had the horrifying experience of seeing his friend struck dead by lightning. Certainly there was some extraordinary experience. In this Luther believed he saw the hand of God in His wrath; and in great fear, and gratitude for his preservation, he immediately offered himself to God and His service. In those days that meant only one thing, entering a monastery.[27]

Luther later left no doubt about the mission that brought him to the monastery by saying that he wanted to escape hell by being a monk.[28] At first the remedy seemed to work. Years later he commented that he knew from his own experience that one's first years as a monk could be peaceful.[29] Nevertheless, as the years passed Luther failed to enjoy the peace he thought he had found. *Anfechtung,* the distress of soul that combined all the troubles of his life with the worries of one uncertain of escaping the wrath of God, began to plague Luther. All Luther could see was hell and the wrath of the eternal God that can never have an end.[30]

---

[26]Pelikan, *The Reformation of Church and Dogma,* 138.

[27]James Atkinson, *The Great Light: Luther and the Reformation* (Grand Rapids: Eerdmans, 1968), 12-13.

[28]*D. Martin Luther's Werke, Kritische Gesamtausgabe* (Weimarer Ausgabe) *WA* [1883-], 47:90 (line 35). The statement is from 1538. I will also cite below from *Luther's Works: American Edition* (ed. J. Pelikan) *LW* [1955-1986]. Cf. also Gerhard Ebeling, *Luther: An Introduction to His Thought,* trans. R.A. Wilson (Philadelphia: Fortress Press, 1964), 35.

[29]*WA,* 8:660 (line 31); E. Gordon Rupp, *The Righteousness of God* (London: Hodder & Stoughton, 1943), 103.

[30]*WA,* 5:210 (line 13); Rupp, *The Righteousness of God,* 107.

Staupitz, his confessor and friend, was of some help. He pointed Luther to the "wounds of Jesus."[31] Luther always remained grateful and expressed this with typical emphasis.[32] Luther's woes, however, went beyond Staupitz's consolations. Timothy George records:

> He would confess to Staupitz for hours, walk away, then come rushing back with some little foible he had forgotten to mention. At one point Staupitz, quite exasperated, said: Look here, Brother Martin. If you're going to confess so much, why don't you go do something worth confessing?[33]

Luther's spiritual needs exceeded Staupitz's ability to meet them.[34]

- **The Scholastic Context**

Luther eventually found the source of his spiritual struggles in the spiritual structure and theological system in which he had been schooled.[35] It is not easy to summarize the shape of the doctrine of

---

[31] Rupp, *The Righteousness of God*, 119.

[32] Rupp records this statement that sounds characteristic of Luther: "If I didn't praise Staupitz I should be a damned, ungrateful, papistical ass, for he was my very first father in this teaching, and he bore me in Christ" (Ibid., 117-118).

[33] Timothy George, *Theology of the Reformers* (Nashville: Broadman Press, 1988), 64-65.

[34] Bernard Lohse, *Martin Luther: An Introduction to His Life and Work* (Philadelphia: Fortress Press, 1986), 28. Lohse remarks, "Staupitz was a very wise pastor who was personally formed by the *devotio moderna* and on this basis he was able to be of some help to Luther in his spiritual temptations. Neither through his interpretation of biblical passages nor through his theological reflections, however, was he able to overcome Luther's terrors in the face of God the divine judge. Scholars still have not yet entirely clarified Staupitz's theological position. In particular, we still are not clear about the extent to which Staupitz's theology was genuinely oriented to Augustine."

[35] Starting at Luther's testimonies to the emotional trauma with which these years were filled for him, some modern Luther scholars have argued that the source of these struggles was that he was emotionally or mentally disturbed. This analysis probably provides more insight about its purveyors than Luther! Lohse provides a summary of what has been said on this issue (Lohse, *Martin Luther*, 25-27). Ebeling seems reasonable when he notes the workload carried by Luther during these years and says, "This was a programme of work of which someone who was mentally disturbed would have been incapable. Thus, a superficial explanation should not be sought for his temptations" (Ebeling, *Luther: An Introduction to His Thought*, 37). Lohse concludes his summary: "Any psychiatric study of a person who lived several hundred years ago confronts extraordinary difficulties. It is extremely difficult for us to determine the significance that ideas then universally accepted could have had for the personal development of the

justification in late Medieval Scholasticism. This is perhaps the very problem for Luther. The doctrine of justification was obscured by a myriad of distinctions. The righteousness of Christ was distinguished from the righteousness of God and was constantly understood in terms of an infused *habitus* of grace.[36] Different kinds of merit (*de condigno* and *de congruo*) were involved. The discussion was over whether men could on their own supply to God one of these two kinds of merit. The sacraments, especially baptism and penance, played a part.[37] All of this was understood predominantly through the lens of a professedly Augustinian view of grace that was actually largely Pelagian.[38] This mixture was mediated to Luther (as I will argue below) as the *via moderna* by such an Augustinian, Gabriel Biel:

> Finally, it is clear that Biel has a remarkable doctrine of justification: seen from different vantage points, justification is at once *sola gratia* and *solis operibus*!
>
> *By grace alone*—because if God had not decided to adorn man's good works with created and uncreated grace, man would never be saved. *By works alone*—because not only does man have to produce the framework of substance for this adornment, but God by two laws of grace is committed, even obliged to add to this framework infused

---

individual. Certainly it is not particularly helpful in understanding a person like Luther to deny the uniqueness of the religious factors. We thus continue to need a description of Luther from a medical viewpoint that does justice to Luther in both historical and theological terms. If such a description should ever be written, it would be necessary for theologians to be very open to the psychoanalytic and psychiatric dimensions. It would, however, be equally necessary for the psychoanalysts and psychiatrists to be ready basically to admit the unique character of religious ideas and experiences" (Lohse, *Martin Luther: An Introduction to His Life and Work*, 27).

[36]Heiko Oberman, *The Dawn of the Reformation* (Edinburgh: T & T Clark, 1986), 104-125.

[37]Heiko Oberman, *Forerunners of the Reformation* (Chicago: Holt, Rinehart, and Winston, 1966), 131-133.

[38]Ibid., 126-127, says, "If one applies the standards of the Council of Trent (1545-1563), one can well argue that no medieval theologian, Pelagius himself included, was ever a 'Pelagian,' that is, no one taught that man can really earn his salvation without the aid of divine grace. With equal validity one can defend the thesis that all medieval theologians attempted to be as faithful as possible to St. Ausgustine's teaching with regard to man's justification and final salvation, and, in this sense, all were Augustinians. St. Augustine's thesis that the merits of men were the gifts of God, the rewards for His own work in and through them, has been subject to interpretation but never to elimination."

grace and final acceptance. Once man has done his very best, the other two parts follow automatically.[39]

If others found peace within this theological system, he came to believe that it was because they allowed their spiritual maladies to be treated superficially and lacked real earnestness of soul. Rupp notes: ". . . he believed that a false security of conscience was one of the great evils of the age."[40]

Roman Catholic apologists have found this assessment of the state of Medieval theology to be based on great ignorance of its best representatives. It is likely that such apologists held Luther accountable for knowing Scholastic theologians he had never read and to whom he was not referring. Rupp says:

> But it is no proof of Luther's bad faith or ignorance to cite against him scholastic writings he could never have read, or even to contrast St. Thomas Aquinas with Luther's account of scholastic teaching, when we consider the overwhelming bias of his teachers towards the systems of Ockham and Scotus and the new theological problems raised (e.g. by Peter of Auriol and Gregory of Rimini) in the fourteenth and fifteenth centuries.[41]

What was the lens through which Luther viewed and rejected Scholastic theology? The evidence suggests that within the general context of Occamist and Nominalist thought, Luther was influenced by a view of justification taught by Gabriel Biel.[42] This view was (in Luther's opinion) Pelagian and incapable of offering the concerned sinner any assurance. Alister McGrath in his monumental *Iustitia Dei* supports this view:

> There is every indication that Luther is referring to the specific concept of *iustitia Dei* associated with the *via moderna*: God is *iustus*, in the sense that he rewards the man who does *quod in se est* with grace, and punishes the man who does not. In view of Gabriel Biel's unequivocal assertion that man cannot know for certain whether he has, in fact, done *quod in se est*, there is clearly every reason to state that Luther's early

---

[39]Heiko Oberman, *The Harvest of Medieval Theology* (Grand Rapids: Baker Book House, 1983), 176.
[40] Rupp, *The Righteousness of God*, 115.
[41]Ibid., 91-92.
[42]Pelikan, *Reformation of Church and Dogma*, 130, provides a summary of Gabriel Biel's doctrine on this point that seems to confirm this assessment.

concept of *iustitia Dei* was that of the righteousness of an utterly scrupulous and impartial judge, who rewarded or punished man on the basis of an ultimately unknown quality. . . .

Luther's early understanding of justification (1513-1514) may be summarised as follows: man must recognise his spiritual weakness and inadequacy, and turn in humility from his attempts at self-justification to ask God for grace. God treats this humility of faith (*humilitas fidei*) as the precondition necessary for justification under the terms of the *pactum* (that is, as man's *quod in se est*), and thus fulfils his obligations under the *pactum*, by bestowing grace upon him.[43]

Further exacerbating of the tendency of the theology in which he was schooled to cast the sinner on his own resources was the doctrine that Luther called *synteresis*. *Synteresis* was classically defined by Jerome "as that spark of conscience . . . which is not extinguished in Adam even as a sinner, after he was ejected from Paradise . . . and by which we know we are sinning."[44] This definition would not have troubled Luther greatly. Indeed, even in the lectures on Romans (when discussing Romans 1:20) in which his new theology first becomes clearly manifest, he "discusses the pagan knowledge of God which he ascribes to a 'syntheresis theologica,' and which, he says, is 'inobscurable in all.'"[45] The problem, however, with *synteresis* is that in the Scholastic theology with which Luther was familiar it came to mean a tiny or weak inclination to good in the sinner. This tiny motion to good "they dream to be an act of loving God above all things," says Luther.[46] Luther with his deep experience of his own sinfulness and with growing Augustinian views of the deep sinfulness of man no longer could accept this concept. It clearly was for Luther part and parcel of a Pelagianizing system of salvation. In *Lectures on Romans* in his comments on Romans 4:7-8 he heaps scorn on the whole idea.[47]

Here, then, is something of the spiritual dilemma in which Martin Luther, the serious-minded monk, found himself. He was tormented by terrible worries about his soul and confronted with a God of wrath. He was trained in a system that told him of a covenant in the sense of a pact

---

[43]Alister McGrath, *Iustitia Dei: A History of the Christian Doctrine of Justification*, 2nd ed. (Cambridge: Cambridge University Press, 1998), 192.

[44]Rupp, *The Righteousness of God*, 150.

[45]Ibid., 152.

[46]Ibid.

[47]Ibid. See also Martin Luther, *Luther: Lectures on Romans*, ed. and trans. Wilhelm Pauck (London: S. C.M. Press., 1961), 128-131[WA 56:273-77; *LW* 25:261-264]; George, *Theology of the Reformers*, 67.

that God had made with man to bless him with grace if he did "what was in him." This covenant, however, offered him no assurance or way of knowing that he, the sinner, had actually done *quod in se est*. This covenant addressed itself to a tiny inclination of good that it assumed to be in men even after the fall. Both experientially and theologically Luther came to doubt that such an inclination to good could be found in the sinner.

Luther came finally to see how this was a recipe for spiritual disaster. Bitter experience had taught him the improbability of finding even a tiny inclination of good in himself. Sometimes he was more inclined to hate God than love Him. He could not even be sure that he had confessed all his sins in the sacrament of penance. How in the world could he be sure that he had done *quod in se est*? How, finally, could he live without assurance that his soul was saved from eternal fire? Everything about this theological system served to focus Luther's attention on himself and his own deeds with the result of utter despair.

Staupitz—moved perhaps by a profound pastoral instinct—half persuaded and half ordered Luther into the study of theology and especially biblical studies.[48] These studies God used to lead Luther out of the spiritual and scholastic morass outlined above.

- **The Biblical Foundation: *Sola Scriptura***

The significance of Luther's biblical insights can only be understood and appreciated against the backdrop of the scholastic system of thought just discussed. This system cast him on his own resources spiritually and, thus, robbed him of spiritual hope. It was an escape from this hopeless system of self-help that his biblical insights gave to him.

It is generally agreed that the *Reformation breakthrough* came sometime in Luther's early lectures on various books of Scripture. The first matter to be understood, then, is the course of the early, biblical lectures in which Luther's saving insights developed. These lectures began shortly after Luther received his doctorate in theology. "On October 18, 1512, the degree was solemnly conferred."[49] Timothy George succinctly provides the scholarly consensus with regard to this matter.

---

[48] Rupp, *The Righteousness of God*, 117. See also Henry Chadwick, *The Reformation* (Harmondsworth, England: Penguin Books Ltd., 1978), 45.

[49] George, *Theology of the Reformers*, 55.

In the winter of 1512, the Reverend Doctor Martin Luther began preparation for his lectures on the Psalms (1513-1515), which were followed in turn by Romans (1515-1516), Galatians (1516-1517), Hebrews (1517), and again Psalms (1518-1519). He later remarked: "In the course of this teaching, the papacy slipped away from me."[50]

But where in the course of these lectures did these insights come to Luther? This is a famous crux of Luther studies. It is not necessary to the thesis of this chapter or this dissertation to provide an extensive discussion of the debate or a firm answer to the question.[51] Indeed, the claims of this chapter rather assume some ambiguity in Luther on this very point. Nevertheless, clarity will be assisted by a modest discussion.

Modesty is appropriate because, though the *Reformation breakthrough* may be spoken of in the singular, it is necessary to speak of the biblical insights—*plural*—leading to justification *sola fide*. While justification *sola fide* is an essentially unified and coherent doctrine, this is not to say that it became clear all at once to Luther, or that several different biblical insights over a period of time did not contribute to clarifying his vision of this doctrine. It may not, therefore, be possible to specify one final date for *the breakthrough*. As Steinmetz states:

> New ideas about sin, faith, justification, preaching, and prayer came tumbling from his pen in 1513-1518. It was not a single insight but a score of insights which gave Luther the courage to face what he feared and to grasp the promises of the gospel by faith.[52]

This being said, it still seems unlikely that a late date is demanded by one of the major pieces of evidence for the dating of *the breakthrough*. A reading of the important and autobiographical 1545 quotation suggests to some a later date, the year 1519.

> In that year (1519), I had meanwhile turned once more to the interpretation of The Psalms, relying on the fact that I was better schooled after I had dealt in the classroom with the letter of Saint Paul to the Romans and the Galatians and that to the Hebrews. I had been seized with a really extraordinary ardor to understand Paul in the letter

---

[50]Ibid.

[51]Martin Brecht, *Martin Luther: His Road to Reformation, 1483-1521*, trans. James L. Schaaf (Fortress Press: Philadelphia, 1985) provides a magisterial account of Luther's early life and what he calls the Reformatory discovery. Cf. especially 221-238.

[52]Steinmetz, "Luther against Luther," 10.

to the Romans, but until then there stood in my way not coldness of blood, but this one word, i. e. Rom. 1:17: "The justice of God is revealed in it." For I hated this word 'the justice of God' which by the use and usage of all the doctors I was taught to understand philosophically in terms of that so-called formal or active justice with which God is just and punishes the sinners and the unrighteous.

For however irreproachably I lived as a monk, I felt myself before God to be a sinner with a most unquiet conscience, nor could I be confident that I had pleased with my satisfaction. I did not love, nay, rather I hated, this righteous God who punished sinners, and if not with tacit blasphemy, certainly with huge murmurings I was angry with God, saying: 'As though it really were not enough that miserable sinners should be eternally damned with original sin and have all kinds of calamities laid upon them by the law of the Ten Commandments, God must go and add sorrow upon sorrow and even through the gospel itself bring his justice and wrath to bear!'

I raged in this way with a wildly aroused and disturbed conscience, and yet I knocked importunately at Paul in this passage, thirsting more ardently to know what Paul meant.[53]

A closer look at these words suggests that we need not (against much other evidence) date the breakthrough in 1519 or shortly before. Luther had clearly developed his new theology in its substance by the time of the lectures on Romans and even more clearly by the time of his famous lectures on Galatians. A more careful reading of this citation leads to the conclusion that Luther is referring to a period of time during his first lectures on the Psalms when he refers to his murmuring against God's justice.[54]

The following points seem sufficiently clear. *First*, Luther does not say in the quotation that the change came at or shortly before 1519. He only says that before he returned to the Psalms he felt better prepared to expound them because of his previous studies of Romans, Galatians, and Hebrews. *Second*, the reference to the *iustitia Dei* that troubled Luther so much likely does not refer only or even mainly to Romans 1:17, but to

---

[53] *WA* 54:185-186; *LW* 34:336-337. The translation is Wilhelm Pauck's in his general introduction to *Luther: Lectures on Romans*, xxxvi-xxxvii.

[54] Rupp, *The Righteousness of God*, 122-127; McGrath, *Iustitia Dei*, 192-194. McGrath agrees with Rupp that the 1545 quotation does not imply a 1519 date for the great change and that the decisive change took place before the lectures on Romans and therefore sometime during Luther's first lectures on the Psalms in the years 1513-1514. McGrath discusses the dating of Luther's new insights extensively in *Luther's Theology of the Cross* (Oxford: Blackwell Publishers Inc., 1990), 92-147.

that phrase as it frequently occurred throughout the Psalms. Luther's lectures on Romans 1:17 in 1515 show that by then he had unraveled the puzzle of that passage. In the 1545 quotation Luther says that he read Augustine *On the Spirit and the Letter* after coming to his new insight. *On the Spirit and the Letter* is cited in his exposition of that verse in his *Lectures on Romans*.[55] Third, McGrath shows that Luther's exposition of the early Psalms reflects an understanding of justification that is immature and primitive compared even to the lectures on Romans. All this means that we must date the inception of important, new, biblical insights in Luther's thinking sometime after he began to lecture for the first time on the Psalms, but sometime before he began his lectures on Romans or, in other words, between 1513 and 1515.[56]

Oswald Bayer has, however, argued that the Reformation *breakthrough* (what he calls a *turn*) occurred in 1518. He connects this with Luther's new understanding of faith in terms of divine promise. It is possible that Bayer is correct. If a number of new biblical insights combined to clarify Luther's vision of *sola fide*, then Bayer's dating of the *breakthrough* need not completely contradict the suggestion that important new insights were also gained between 1513 and 1515.[57]

The possibility that a number of biblical insights combined to clarify Luther's understanding of justification *sola fide* is also consistent with

---

[55]*Luther: Lectures on Romans*, 18-19. [*WA* 56:171-173; *LW* 25:151-153]. Luther also clearly says there that "the righteousness of God is the cause of salvation" and refers to "faith alone."

[56]It must be remembered, however, that we are talking in terms of substantial insights and not prejudging the question of a remaining lack of clarity at certain points. I will discuss below the possibility that Luther's doctrine of imputed righteousness is not consistently clear even in his *Lectures on Romans*.

[57]Oswald Bayer, *Promissio: Geschichte der reformatorischen Wende in Luthers Theologie* (Göttingen: Vandenhoeck&Ruprecht, 1971) connects Luther's insight with his interpreting faith in terms of divine promise. Bayer believes that a *promissio* hermeneutic is key to the Reformation turn in Luther's theology and sees such an understanding of faith in Luther coming in 1518. Bayer, "Rupture of Times: Luther's Relevance for Today," *Lutheran Quarterly* 13 (1999): 49, remarks, "The presuming of the divine promise is shown paradigmatically by the Reformation breakthrough in Luther's theology as he interprets Heb. 4:16 . . . in March, 1518: 'This faith alone makes them pure and worthy. This faith does not prop itself up on those works, but on the most pure, reliable and firm word of Christ who speaks: 'Come here to me all of you who labor and are heavy-laden, and I will give you rest.' In short: in the presumption of these words . . . one should come near, and those who approach in this manner will not be confounded.'" If we have to do with multiple insights over the years 1513-1518, then I need not contradict Bayer's idea that Luther's insight came (in one respect) in 1518 in order to maintain a somewhat earlier date for other key insights.

the view that the emergence of *sola fide* involved a complex doctrinal event. The 1545 quotation, in other words, enables us to say that two major doctrinal perspectives combined in the Reformation *breakthrough*. That quotation identifies the two major insights that combined to make Luther feel that he had been born anew. The new circle of theology that Luther drew had, we might say, both a circumference and a center. What may be called the Augustinian understanding of sin and grace (emphasizing *sola gratia*) is the circumference of this new theology. What may be called the Reformation advance (focusing on *sola fide*) is the center.

- **The Augustinian Insight: *Sola Gratia***

By the "Augustinian insight" I refer specifically to an insight provided by the Augustine of the anti-Pelagian writings. Though in the Medieval Church everyone thought of themselves as Augustinian and anti-Pelagian, this, of course, was quite different from actually understanding and really holding the views of Augustine himself on sin and grace.[58] Yet more, the corpus of Augustine's writings was so massive and filled with its own cross-currents that it was not difficult plausibly to compromise Augustine's mature views of sin and grace from his own writings.[59] It is with these qualifications that it may (and must!) be said that the Reformation was founded on a revival of strict Augustinianism.

---

[58] For a nuanced discussion of Luther's Augustinianism in the late Medieval context, see Heiko Oberman, *The Forerunners of the Reformation: the Shape of Late Medieval Thought*, trans. Paul L. Nyhus (New York: Holt, Rinehart, and Winston, 1966), 123-141. Oberman remarks, "Indeed it is not our concern to deny the uniqueness of Luther in his constructive thought, but rather to see it as—initially—a particular articulation of the preceding anti-Pelagian medieval tradition in which he was to be supported by Ulrich Zwingli . . . and John Calvin" (125). He goes on, however, to note, "With equal validity one can defend the thesis that all medieval theologians attempted to be as faithful as possible to St. Augustine's teaching with regard to man's justification and final salvation, and in this sense, all were Augustinians" (127). Pelikan, *Reformation of Church and Dogma*, 139, remarks, "The presupposition for the doctrine of justification was a vigorous reassertion of Augustinian anthropology." Following this statement Pelikan spends several pages explaining in what precise sense Luther was Augustinian and anti-Pelagian.
[59] B.B. Warfield, *The Works of Benjamin B. Warfield*, vol. 4, *Tertullian and Augustine* (Grand Rapids: Baker Book House, 1981), 114, comments as follows on the cross-currents in Augustine's writings, "If we cannot quite allow that there were in very truth many Augustines, we must at least recognize that within the one Augustine there were very various and not always consistent currents flowing, each of which had its part to play in the future."

The practical upshot of the *via moderna* in which Luther had been educated was to his way of thinking Pelagian. It focused attention on what man had to do first in order to move God to give him grace and meet the condition of the covenant. This was the meaning or practical purport of the *synteresis* and the *quod in se est*. The really pivotal movement and action in salvation depended on the sinner. Somewhere in 1513 or 1514 Luther came to the understanding that in reality the really pivotal thing was the grace of a sovereign God.

> Then and there, I began to understand the justice of God as that by which a righteous man lives by the gift of God, namely, by faith, and this sentence 'The justice of God is revealed in the gospel' to be that passive justice with which the merciful God justifies us by faith, as it is written: 'The just shall live by faith.' This straightway made me feel as though reborn and as though I had entered through open gates into Paradise itself.
>
> From then on, the whole face of Scripture appeared different. I ran through the Scriptures then as memory served, and found that other words had the same meaning, for example: the work of God with which he makes us strong, the wisdom of God with which he makes us wise, the fortitude of God, the salvation of God, the glory of God.[60]

This statement makes clear that faith is now viewed as a gift of God and that the righteousness of God is that righteousness with regard to which we are passive and by which God justifies us.[61] It is clear that from this time on Martin Luther rejected both the idea of the *synteresis* and that salvation depended on doing *quod in se est*. He was convinced that there was nothing good in him spiritually by which he could do anything pleasing to God. Some of Luther's most violent denunciations are launched against the Pelagianizing of late Medieval theology. In his first lectures on Romans at chapter 4 and verses 7 and 8, vituperation against scholastic Pelgianizing abounds:

> For this reason it is sheer madness to say that man can love God above everything by his own powers and live up to the commandment in terms of the substance of the deed but not in terms of the intention of

---

[60]*WA* 54:179-87; *LW* 34:337. The translation is Wilhelm Pauck's in his general introduction to Luther, *Lectures on Romans*, xxxvi-xxxvii. Pelikan, *Reformation of Church and Dogma*, 139, remarks, "The presupposition for the doctrine of justification was a vigorous reassertion of Augustinian anthropology."

[61]McGrath, *Iustitia Dei*, 202, 205. McGrath thinks that Luther went even beyond Augustine in the matter of sin, grace, and predestination.

Him who gave it, because he does not do so in the state of grace. O you fools, you pig-theologians! So then grace was not necessary except in connection with a new exaction over and above the law! For if we can fulfill the law by our own powers, as they say, grace is not necessary for the fulfillment of the law but only of a divinely imposed exaction that goes beyond the law. Who can tolerate such sacrilegious opinions![62]

Later in his famous response to Erasmus entitled *De Servo Arbitrio* Luther made clear his complete rejection of free will and his embrace of a thoroughly predestinarian view of grace.[63] In the way Luther puts it in the 1545 quotation it seems clear that the "blessed Augustine" (as he often called him) had provided him with the foundational insight that changed his view of salvation and justification. It was God who justified and not man who justified himself!

And now, much as I hated the word 'justice of God' before, so much the more sweetly I extolled this word to myself now, so that this passage in Paul was made a real gate to Paradise. Afterward, I read Augustine *On the Spirit and the Letter*, where unexpectedly I came upon the fact that he, too, interpreted the justice of God in a similar way: namely, as that with which God endues us when he justifies us. And although this was said still imperfectly, and he does not clearly explain about 'imputation,' it was gratifying to me that he should teach a justice of God by which we are justified.[64]

Here is Luther's comment on Augustine. He interpreted the righteousness of God in a similar way to Luther. He simply spoke imperfectly. *Sola fide* for Luther must be understood in this Augustinian framework. The faith alone that saves is a faith that is the gift of God—a faith in which He takes the initiative and not man.

---

[62]Luther, *Lectures on Romans*, 129. [*WA* 56:274-275; *LW* 25:261-262].

[63]In *De Servo Arbitrio*, written in 1525, Luther indicates how crucial and even central the Augustinian insight is for him. Roland H. Bainton, *Here I Stand: A Life of Martin Luther* (New York: Abingdon Press, 1950), 196, remarks, "Luther thanked him for centering the discussion at this point. 'You alone have gone to the heart of the problem instead of debating the papacy, indulgences, purgatory, and similar trifles. You alone have gone to the core, and I thank you for it.' Luther's fundamental break with the Catholic church was over the nature and destiny of man, and much more over the destiny than the nature."

[64] *WA* 54:179-187; *LW* 34:337. The translation is Wilhelm Pauck's in his general introduction to Luther, *Lectures on Romans*, xxxvi-xxxvii.

- **The Reformation Advance:** *Sola Fide*

Two issues come up for discussion here. The first is the question whether Luther's insight is not simply a new appreciation of strict Augustinianism. The second is the possibility that there was a remaining lack of clarity in Luther's views.

The section of the 1545 quotation just cited makes clear that Luther's breakthrough cannot be characterized as simply a return to a thoroughgoing Augustinian anti-Pelagianism.[65] Luther is, of course, speaking from the vantage point of 30 years in the future, but he leaves no doubt that there remained something imperfect and unclear in Augustine's explanation of grace. As Luther says, he did not clearly explain *imputation*. This also is crucial for the meaning of *sola fide* in Luther.

The preceding quotation of Luther makes clear that he did not find Augustine's views of justification satisfactory: "And although this was said still *imperfectly, and he does not clearly explain about 'imputation,'* it was gratifying to me that he should teach a justice of God by which we are justified."[66]

Luther makes this point repeatedly. Heckel in an important article in *JETS* provides two further such quotations. The first comes from the year 1531 and the second from about a year later.[67]

> It was Augustine's view that the law, fulfilled by the powers of reason, does not justify, even as works of the moral law do not justify the heathen, but that if the Holy Spirit assists, the works of the law do justify. The question is not whether the law or the works of reason

---

[65] Matthew C. Heckel, "Is R.C. Sproul Wrong about Martin Luther? An Analysis of R.C. Sproul's *Faith Alone: The Evangelical Doctrine of Justification* with respect to Augustine, Luther, Calvin, and Catholic Luther Scholarship," *JETS* 47, no. 1 (March 2004): 89-120, presents additional and irrefutable (in my opinion) evidence that Augustine did not have clear views of justification *sola fide* (actually held a different view which based justification on infused righteousness) and that Luther was quite aware of this. In this sense I agree that Luther's *sola fide* "was not a recovery but an innovation" (93). The term *innovation*, however, loses the historical progression, development, or advance that is taking place with Luther's *sola fide*. Justification *sola fide* is not innovative in the sense of being *novel*. It is its clear articulation that is innovative—not its substance.

[66] *WA* 54:186; *LW* 34:337. The translation is Wilhelm Pauck's in his general introduction to *Luther: Lectures on Romans*, xxxvi-xxxvii. The emphasis is mine.

[67] Heckel, "Is R.C. Sproul Wrong about Martin Luther?," 99.

justify, but whether the law, kept with the Spirit's help, justifies. I reply by saying No. . . . Works never give a peaceful heart.[68]

Ever since I came to an understanding of Paul, I have not been able to think well of any doctor [of the church]. They have become of little value to me. At first I devoured, not merely read, Augustine. But when the door was opened for me in Paul, so that I understood what justification by faith is, it was all over with Augustine.[69]

McGrath is correct, then, in rejecting the thesis that *sola fide* is simply an implication of Luther's Augustinianism.

It must be emphasized that it is totally unacceptable to characterise the doctrines of justification associated with the Reformation solely with reference to their anti-Pelagian character, or their associated doctrines of predestination. Although an earlier generation of scholars argued that the Reformation resulted from the sudden discovery of the radical anti-Pelagianism of Augustine's soteriology, it is clear that this judgement cannot be sustained.[70]

The difference here has everything to do with the nature and function of faith in justification. For Augustine and Medieval Catholicism the righteousness in view in justification and on the basis of which (at least partly) men are justified is the faith working by love that fulfills the righteousness of God as required in the law of God. For Luther (in contrast) faith was a grasping (*fides apprehensiva*) of a righteousness extrinsic to ourselves.

It is clear that an extrinsic (synthetic) rather than an intrinsic (analytic) view of justification is contained already in Luther's lectures on Romans:

The saints are intrinsically always sinners, therefore they are always extrinsically justified; but the hypocrites are intrinsically always righteous, therefore they are extrinsically always sinners. . . . Hence, we are extrinsically righteous in so far as we are righteous not in and from ourselves and not in virtue of our works but only by God's regarding us so. For inasmuch as the saints are always aware of their sin and implore God for the merciful gift of his righteousness, they are for this very

---

[68] *D. Martin Luther's Werke, kritische Gesamtausgabe* (Weimarer Ausgabe), *Tischreden* (Weimar: H. Böhlaus Nachfolger, 1912-1921), 1:32; *LW* 54:10.
[69] *WATR* 1:140; *LW* 54:49.
[70] McGrath, *Iustitia Dei*, 183.

reason also always reckoned righteous by God. Therefore they are before themselves and in truth unrighteous, but before God they are righteous because he reckons them so on account of this confession of their sin; they are sinners in fact, but by virtue of the reckoning of the merciful God they are righteous . . . .[71]

It is clear that faith functions very differently in the Augustinian and Lutheran views of justification. In the Augustinian system faith formed and working by love creates the righteousness that is in view in justification. In such a view it makes no sense to speak of faith alone justifying. In the Lutheran view, however, faith neither creates nor constitutes the righteousness in view in justification. *In this sense* it is not active, but passive. It is simply the *fides apprehensiva*.[72] It personally grasps, receives, and entrusts itself to the righteousness of another, Jesus Christ. In this way, it is faith alone that justifies. Faith is only what it is, then, in relation to Christ. It is Christ alone come into the heart of the sinner.

In the foregoing it was assumed that the doctrine of Martin Luther and that of his orthodox Lutheran and Reformed successors were one and the same. Questions have, however, been raised about this very issue. In the *Lectures on Romans*, for instance, Luther is fond of illustrating justification from the parable of the Good Samaritan with the said Samaritan interpreted as Christ.

> In the same way, our Samaritan Christ took the man who was half dead in order to cure him by promising him the most perfect well-being in the life to come. Therefore, also, this man was righteous and sinful at the same time, a sinner in fact but a righteous man by virtue of his faith in the promise and of his hope that it would be kept. It is as with a sick man who believes his physicians as he assures him that he will most certainly get well. In the meantime, he obeys his orders in the hope of recovery and abstains from whatever is forbidden to him, lest he slow up the promised cure and get worse again until finally the physician accomplishes what he has so confidently predicted. Can one say that this sick man is healthy? No; but he is at the same time both sick and healthy. He is actually sick, but he is healthy by virtue of the sure prediction of the physician whom he believes. For he reckons him already healthy because he is certain that he can cure him and does not reckon him his sickness as death.

---

[71] *Luther: Lectures on Romans*, 124-125. [*WA* 56:268-270; *LW* 25:257-258].
[72] McGrath, *Iustitia Dei*, 201.

In the same way, Christ, our good Samaritan, brought the man who was half dead, his patient, to an inn and took care of him . . . and commenced to heal him, having first promised to him that he would give him that he would give him absolutely perfect health unto eternal life. He does not reckon him his sin, i. e. his sinful desires, for death, but in the meantime, i. e. holding up to him the hope that he will get well, he forbids him to do or not to do anything that might impede his recovery and make his sin . . . worse. Now can we say that he is perfectly righteous? No; but he is at the same time both a sinner and righteous, a sinner in fact but righteous by virtue of the reckoning and certain promise of God that he will redeem him from sin in order, in the end, to make him perfectly whole and sound.[73]

This illustration seems to ground justification at least partly in the future or prospective "perfect health" of the patient. Karl Holl presses this aspect of Luther's early statements so far as to raise questions about Luther's understanding of imputed righteousness.[74] Whatever may be said by way of explaining and placing into context Luther's illustration of justification in the above quotation, it seems to imply something other than an extrinsic or forensic justification by an alien righteousness. Thus, it suggests a remaining lack of clarity, if not in Luther's thinking, at least in his teaching about justification.[75]

Of course, this implication must not be exaggerated. Even the strictest view of forensic justification does not and need not deny that its purpose includes the eventual "perfect health" of the sinner. It is, of course, one thing to say that this is the purpose of justification and quite another to make this the ground or basis of God's justifying verdict. This is the point at which Luther's statement quoted above seems nebulous.

In another remark found in *Two Kinds of Righteousness* written in 1519 Luther seems to exhibit a lack of clarity with regard to a forensic justification based on an imputed righteousness. Surprisingly, it is made

---

[73] *Luther: Lectures on Romans*, 126-127. [*WA* 272-273; *LW* 25:260].

[74] Karl Holl, *Gesammelte Aufsatze zur Kirchengeschichte* (Tubingen, 1928), 1:11-154.

[75] Rudolf Hermann, "Beobachtungen zu Luthers Rechtfertigungslehre," in *Gesammelte Studien zur Theologie Luthers under der Reformation* (Gottingen: Vandenhoeck & Ruprecht, 1960), 77-89, provides a contemporary analysis of the debate Holl generated. In personal correspondence Mark Seifrid suggests that its analysis is helpful in that it argues that "Luther understood our present health to lie not in us, but in our relationship to Christ (the Physician), i. e., in his word of promise and our faith. Holl misses the Word and focuses on the future completion of salvation. But his counterparts also miss an important element in Luther's thought."

in connection with one of those phrases that is thought to strikingly state his doctrine of justification by imputed righteousness.

> Therefore this alien righteousness, instilled in us without our works by grace alone—while the Father, to be sure, inwardly draws us to Christ—is set opposite original sin, likewise alien, which we acquire without our works by birth alone. Christ daily drives out the old Adam more and more in accordance with the extent to which faith and knowledge of Christ grow. For alien righteousness is not instilled all at once, but it begins, makes progress, and is finally perfected at the end through death. The second kind of righteousness is our proper righteousness, not because we alone work it, but because we work with that first and alien righteousness. This is that manner of life spent profitably in good works . . .[76]

Luther's statements here certainly raise all sorts of questions with regard to the doctrine of imputed "alien" righteousness. How can an alien righteousness be "instilled in us?" In what sense is it similar to "alien" original sin? In what sense can "alien righteousness be said to "grow" and not be "instilled all at once?" Each of these questions seem to require an answer that implies that even our "alien righteousness" is somehow "infused."

In response it may be argued that there is a great deal that Luther says in the context of these remarks that do not seem to fit with the idea of an "infused" alien righteousness. There is, first, the contrast that ends the quotation above. Luther seems clearly to contrast alien righteousness with "our proper righteousness . . . that manner of life spent profitably in good works." There is, second, the earlier description of alien righteousness in this treatise. A few paragraphs previously Luther has said:

> The first is alien righteousness, that is the righteousness of another, instilled from without. This is the righteousness of Christ by which he justifies through faith. . . . Therefore a man can with confidence boast in Christ and say: "Mine are Christ's living, doing, and speaking, his suffering and dying, mine as much as if I had lived, done, spoken, suffered, and died as he did."[77]

---

[76]*Martin Luther's Basic Theological Writings*, ed. Timothy F. Lull (Minneapolis: Fortress Press, 1989), 157. [*WA* 2:146-147; *LW* 31:298-299].

[77]*Martin Luther's Basic Theological Writings*, 155. [*WA* 2:145; *LW* 31:297].

It is difficult to understand such language on any other assumption than that alien righteousness is imputed righteousness.

There is a third difficulty in the way of understanding alien righteousness as infused. It is the illustration of alien righteousness from marriage that he provides. This is also found in the paragraphs immediately preceding the problematic quotation cited above.

> Just as a bridegroom possess all that is his bride's and she all that is his—for the two have all things in common because they are one flesh [Gen. 2:24]—so Christ and the church are one spirit [Eph. 5:29-32]. . . .
>
> Through faith in Christ, therefore, Christ's righteousness becomes our righteousness and all that he has becomes ours; rather, he himself becomes ours . . . .
>
> This is an infinite righteousness, and one that swallows up all sins in a moment, for it is impossible that sin should exist in Christ. On the contrary, he who trusts in Christ exists in Christ; he is one with Christ, having the same righteousness as he. It is therefore impossible that sin should remain in him. This righteousness is primary; it is the basis, the cause, the source of all our own actual righteousness. For this is the righteousness given in place of the original righteousness lost in Adam. It accomplishes the same as that original righteousness would have accomplished; rather, it accomplishes more.[78]

Sometimes in contemporary writings the typical courtroom illustration of imputed righteousness has been contrasted with this marital illustration. It is not necessary to set up such a contrast. Both illustrations clearly make the point that in justification we come into possession of an "alien righteousness." At any rate, Luther's marital illustration of justification by an alien righteousness is again difficult to make coherent with the idea of an "infused" alien righteousness.

What, then, shall we make of the problematic quotation? It seems clear that Luther does not mean to imply by "instilled" the Medieval idea of infused righteousness. Rather, when Luther says that "alien righteousness is not instilled all at once, but it begins, makes progress, and is finally perfected at the end through death," he may mean by alien righteousness the subjective power for holiness and assurance of grace that such alien righteousness alone can give. This subjective effect of alien righteousness only gradually takes over the soul until our faith is perfected at death. In this regard, we must not overlook this sentence from the problematic quotation; "Christ daily drives out the old Adam

---

[78]Ibid., 155-157. [*WA* 2:146; *LW* 31:298].

more and more in accordance with the extent to which faith and knowledge of Christ grow." It is faith and knowledge of Christ which drive out the old Adam. This seems to be a reference to our ability to understand and trust the doctrine of alien righteousness. Such faith in and knowledge of alien righteousness drive out the guilt and fear of the old Adam and the sin that results from it. This would be consistent with Luther's very practical and pastoral approach to such issues. It would also be consistent with the immediately preceding paragraph in which Luther has said that alien righteousness "is the basis, the cause, the source of all our own actual righteousness."

This tentative explanation does not imply that there is no lack of clarity in this problematic quotation from *Two Kinds of Righteousness*. Perhaps Luther indulged modes of statement here that he himself would later have found confusing and even unacceptable.

It seems that this lack of clarity in Luther was later cleared up. McGrath, for instance, responds to Holl by showing that Luther's anthropology of the "whole man (*totus homo*)" makes necessary and clear his commitment to imputed righteousness, even in spite of the lack of clarity in such statements.[79] It was by his *totus homo* anthropology that Luther was able to make his famous statements that the believer is *iustus et peccator simul* and *semper peccator, semper penitens, semper iustus*. Elsewhere Luther strikingly says, "In myself outside of Christ, I am a sinner; in Christ outside of myself, I am not a sinner."[80] Again he remarks:

> You know that we are certainly righteous, pure, and holy even though we are sinners, unrighteous, and damned. We are, however, righteous in terms of the imputation or mercy of God promised in Christ, that is, on account of Christ in whom we believe.[81]

Thus, Luther can describe the righteousness by which we are justified as a righteousness that is both outside of us and alien to us. "Christ or Christ's righteousness is outside of us and alien . . . to us."[82]

---

[79] *Totus homo* or "whole man" anthropology refers to the way in which Luther could speak of the believer as simultaneously completely righteous and yet completely sinful.

[80] *WA* 38, 205; *LW* 38:149-150 as translated in Paul Althaus, *The Theology of Martin Luther*, trans. Robert C. Schultz (Philadelphia: Fortress Press, 1966), 243. Althaus at the same place also provides a number of other cogent confirmations of Luther's firm hold on imputed, extrinsic, and alien righteousness as the basis for justification.

[81] *WA* 39:492 as translated in Althaus *The Theology of Martin Luther*, 243.

[82] *WA* 39:83; *LW* 34:153. See Althaus *The Theology of Martin Luther*, 228.

McGrath, therefore, properly remarks, "The justified sinner is, and will remain, *semper peccator, semper penitens, semper iustus*. This point is important, on account of the evident divergence from Augustine." McGrath concludes, "It will therefore be clear that Luther was obliged to develop a radically different understanding of the nature of justifying righteousness if he was to avoid contradicting the basic presuppositions implicit in the *totus homo* anthropology."[83] Inconsistencies and some lack of clarity there may have been especially in Luther's early statements of this issue, but his fundamental and increasing commitment to an alien and imputed righteousness is clear.[84] At least by the time of the Augsburg Confession in 1530 which, though penned by Melanchthon, had the complete support of Luther,[85] justification was defined in an exclusively forensic fashion as being received into God's favor and obtaining the forgiveness of sins.[86]

The "lack of clarity" noted above does witness to an important practical point that is essential to Luther's *sola fide* and always continues in his teaching. Faith was always for Luther a deeply religious matter.[87] In the first place, for Luther it is born in an acceptance of the judgment of God against our sins.

> For inasmuch as the saints are always aware of their sin and implore God for the merciful gift of his righteousness, they are for this very reason also always reckoned righteous by God. Therefore they are before themselves and in truth unrighteous, but before God they are righteous because he reckons them so on account of this confession of

---

[83] McGrath, *Iustitia Dei*, 199: "Luther's concept of faith represents a significant departure from Augustine's rather intellectualist counterpart:" Althaus, *The Theology of Martin Luther*, 241-242, also ably criticizes Karl Holl's understanding of Luther's doctrine of justification.

[84] Althaus, *The Theology of Martin Luther*, 227-233.

[85] *The Creeds of Christendom with a History and Critical Notes*, ed. Philip Schaff, rev. David S. Schaff (Grand Rapids: Baker Book House, 1983), 1:229. Cf. also *Creeds and Confessions of Faith in the Christian Tradition* (ed. J. Pelikan, V. Hotchkiss) *CC* [2003], 2:49-50; Roland H. Bainton, *Here I Stand*, 253; and Kittelson, *Luther the Reformer*, 233-234.

[86] *The Creeds of Christendom*, 3:10. Augsburg Confession, Part First, Article IV reads: "Also they teach that men can not be justified [obtain forgiveness of sins and righteousness] before God by their own powers, merits, or works, but are justified freely [of grace] for Christ's sake through faith, when they believe that they are received into favor, and their sins forgiven for Christ's sake, who by his death hath satisfied for our sins. This faith doth God impute for righteousness before him. Rom. iii and iv." [*CC* 2:60-61].

[87] McGrath, *Iustitia Dei*, 200.

their sin; they are sinners in fact, but by virtue of the reckoning of the merciful God they are righteous . . .[88]

Faith grasps (*fides apprehensiva*) Christ and brings him near.[89] This means in the words of McGrath "the real and redeeming presence of Christ."[90] Thus, faith always bears the fruit of good works. Luther can even speak of two dimensions of justification.[91] Faith justifies before God, but good works demonstrate the believer's justification by God and reveal the falseness of hypocrites.[92] Luther says, "We must therefore most certainly maintain that where there is no faith there also can be no good works; and conversely, that there is no faith where there are no good works."[93]

Justifying faith is born out of a deep and feeling acceptance of the judgment of God against our sins. It is *semper penitens*. Says Luther:

> You will therefore judge yourselves one way in accordance with the severity of God's judgment and another in accordance with the kindness of his mercy. Do not separate these two perspectives in this life.[94]

---

[88]Luther, *Lectures on Romans*, 125. [*WA* 56:270; *LW* 25:258]

[89]Althaus, *The Theology of Martin Luther*, 230, remarks: "Luther sees the essence of justifying faith in the fact that it grasps Christ. It is a 'grasping' and appropriating faith (*fides apprehensiva*)." Among other statements of Luther he cites this one from *WA* 39:319: "Our faith is the power which takes hold [*virtus apprehensiva*]."

[90]McGrath, *Iustitia Dei*, 201.

[91]Ibid., 204.

[92]Althaus, *The Theology of Martin Luther*, 250.

[93] *WA* 12:282; *LW* 30:25-26. The translation is that found in Althaus, *The Theology of Martin Luther*, 246.

[94]*WA* 8:96; *LW* 32:213. Mark Seifrid, "Luther, Melanchthon, and Paul," 151, comments, "Luther's dynamic conception of justification much more effectively conveys the way in which God's mercy is granted only in judgment. The justification of the sinner takes place only in and through the justification of God in the event of the cross and resurrection of Jesus Christ. 'Justification' is no mere transaction to be applied to my account. God's 'yes' is given only in and with his 'no,' a 'no' and 'yes' which are mine only in so far as faith echoes them in my heart. . . . All growth in the Christian life, both individually and corporately, is found not in the triumph of progress and ascent (as one might suppose from the usual scheme of 'sanctification'), but in that daily repentance and self-judgment by which God 'makes out of unhappy and proud gods, true human beings, that is, wretches and sinners.'" Whatever we might think of Seifrid's distinction between Luther and Melanchthon and his understanding of sanctification, there is no doubt that here Seifrid has given us a penetrating and critical insight into the religious and penitential character of Luther's understanding of *sola fide*.

Justifying faith has in view the eventual perfection of the believer.[95] It brings Christ and the Spirit into the heart and life. It produces good works inevitably and these good works demonstrate our justification by God to others and to ourselves. For all these reasons, we must conclude that for Luther the true and saving faith that justifies by resting on Christ also works by love. It is not merely an intellectual acceptance of the facts of the gospel or a momentary decision to accept Christ as Savior.

The Major Features of *Sola Fide* in Luther

This survey of the major factors involved in the development of Luther's *sola fide* helpfully clarifies its meaning for Luther. In particular it enables us to assert that Luther anticipates the three perspectives on the meaning of *sola fide* that we will find in Calvin.

For Luther *faith alone justifying* assumed a distinctively passive *definition of faith*. Justifying faith involved for Luther the humble and yet joyful realization that the whole origin of salvation and justification was in God and not in oneself. This insight meant that the soul must look outside itself to another for salvation. Testimonies too numerous to cite could be brought forward to illustrate Luther's passive definition of faith. One of the most striking may be found, however, in Luther's preface to his commentary on Galatians in which he describes the righteousness of faith as a passive righteousness:

> There is yet another righteousness which is above all these: to wit the righteousness of faith, or Christian righteousness, the which we must diligently discern from the other afore-rehearsed: for they are quite contrary to this righteousness . . . .But this most excellent righteousness, of faith I mean (which God through Christ, without works, imputeth unto us), is neither political nor ceremonial, nor the righteousness of God's law, nor consisteth in our works, but is clean contrary: that is to say, a mere passive righteousness, as the other above are active. For in this we work nothing, we render nothing unto God, but only we receive and suffer another to work in us, that is to say, God. Therefore it seemeth good unto me to call this righteousness of faith or Christian righteousness, the passive righteousness. . . .

---

[95]*LW* 30:245-246 [WA 20:655]: "The remission of sins has not been instituted in order that we may have permission to sin or that we may sin; it has been instituted in order that we may recognize sin and know that we are in sin, that we may fight against sin. A physician reveals an illness, not because he takes delight in the illness, but rather that the person who is sick may sigh and ask to be delivered from the illness."

Wherefore the afflicted and troubled conscience hath no remedy against desperation and eternal death, unless it take hold of the promise of God freely offered in Christ, that is to say, this passive righteousness of faith, or Christian righteousness. Which if it can apprehend, then may it be quiet and boldly say: I seek not the active or working righteousness, although I know that I ought to have it, and also to fulfil it. But be it so that I had it, and did fulfil it indeed, yet notwithstanding I cannot trust unto it neither dare I set it against the judgment of God.

Thus I abandon myself from all active righteousness, both of mine own and of God's law, and embrace only that passive righteousness, which is the righteousness of grace, mercy, and forgiveness of sins. Briefly [I rest upon] the righteousness of Christ and of the Holy Ghost, *which we do not, but suffer, and have not, but receive; God the Father freely giving it unto us through Jesus Christ.*[96]

Justification *sola fide* also meant, however, an advance on the Augustinian insight. In other words, an inconsistency in Augustine's views was overcome. After pointing the sinner to God, Augustine pointed the sinner back to himself—of course, with the Spirit's aid—to perform those works of love by which he could be justified. To Luther this was both an imperfect and inconsistent view of justification. The sinner is not justified by faith working through love, but by faith resting on Christ. Luther, thus, taught a *distinction between justifying faith and evangelical obedience*. It is well-known that Luther regarded faith as the fulfillment of the first commandment. It seems clear, however, that Luther did not regard faith's fulfillment of the first commandment as the quality or power by or for which it justified. Though faith was the beginning of new obedience, this was not the way in which it justified. It justified rather as apprehending Christ and having righteousness imputed through him. Thus, we find Luther distinguishing faith and obedience again and again.

In him we are by faith, and he in us. The bridegroom must be alone with the bride in his secret chamber, all the servants and family being put apart. But afterwards, when he openeth the door and cometh forth, then let the servants and handmaidens return, to fulfill their ministry. There let charity do her office, and let good works be done.[97]

---

[96] Martin Luther, *A Commentary on St. Paul's Epistle to the Galatians*, A revised and completed translation based on the 'Middleton' edition of the English version of 1575 (London: James Clarke & Co. Ltd., 1953), 22-23. [*WA* 40:41-43; *LW* 26:4-6].

[97] Luther, *Galatians*, 142. *Comm. Gal* 2:16. [*WA* 40:241; *LW* 26:137-138].

> We conclude therefore with Paul, that we are justified by faith only in Christ, without law and works. Now after that a man is once justified, and possesseth Christ by faith, and knoweth that he is his righteousness and life, doubtless he will not be idle, but as a good tree will bring forth good fruits. For the believing man hath the Holy Ghost, and where the Holy Ghost dwelleth, he will not suffer a man to be idle, but stirreth him up to all exercises of piety and godliness . . .[98]
>
> These four things therefore must be perfectly distinguished. For as the law hath his proper office, so hath the promise. To the law pertaineth doing, and to the promise believing. Wherefore, as far as the law and the promise are separate asunder, so far also are doing and believing, that he may separate charity from faith and shew that faith alone justifieth, because the law, whether it be done morally or spiritually, or be not done, helpeth nothing at all unto justification. For the law pertaineth unto doing; and faith is not a thing of this kind, but a thing altogether diverse, which is required before the law is done, that it may be pre-existent and so there may come to pass a lovely incarnation.
>
> Wherefore, faith always justifieth and quickeneth: yet it abideth not alone, that is to say, it is not idle. Indeed it abideth alone in its degree and office, for it justifieth always alone; but it becometh incarnate and is made, that is to say, it is never idle or without charity.[99]

Luther, therefore, also taught a clear *dichotomy between the law and the gospel* and their respective righteousnesses. Faith was directed outside of itself to an alien, but perfect, righteousness of Christ it could possess while the believer was still a sinner in himself. This distinction has already become clear in the quotations above, but is confirmed in the following quotation:

> Here is to be noted, that these three things, faith, Christ, acceptation, or imputation, must be joined together. Faith taketh hold of Christ, and hath him present, and holdeth him inclosed, as the ring doth the precious stone. And whosoever shall be found having this confidence in Christ apprehended in the heart, him will God account for righteous.
>
> This is the mean, and this is the merit whereby we attain the remission of sins and righteousness. Because thou believest in me, saith the Lord, and thy faith layeth hold upon Christ, whom I have freely given unto thee that he might be thy mediator and high priest, therefore be thou justified and righteous. Wherefore God doth accept or account us as righteous, only for our faith in Christ.

---

[98]Ibid., 157. *Comm.* Gal 2:18. [*WA* 40:265; *LW* 26:154-155].
[99]Ibid., 265. *Comm.* Gal 3:13. [*WA* 40:247; *LW* 26:272].

And this acceptation, or imputation, is very necessary: first, because we are not yet perfectly righteous . . . .

We therefore do make this definition of a Christian, that a Christian is not he which hath no sin, or feeleth no sin, but he to whom God imputeth not his sin because of his faith in Christ.[100]

All this emerges from the study of the development of Luther's views of *sola fide*. In each of these three respects (the definition of justifying faith as passive, the distinction between justifying faith and evangelical obedience, and the dichotomy between law and gospel), Luther is one with Calvin. As we will see in the next chapter Calvin provides a balanced, consistent, and systematic articulation of Luther's views of justification by faith alone.

---

[100]Ibid., 137-138. *Comm.* Gal 2:16. [*WA* 40:233, 235; *LW* 26:132-133].

CHAPTER 3
SOLA FIDE IN CALVIN
Thesis

John Calvin frequently and explicitly affirmed justification *sola fide*.[1] In this chapter the views of Calvin regarding *sola fide* will be examined with reference to the contemporary tendency to identify faith and obedience. We will ask, *Does justifying faith include evangelical obedience in the theology of John Calvin?* To put this same question in other words, we will ask, *For Calvin, is evangelical obedience included in justifying faith?*

Calvin could not avoid this issue in articulating the doctrine of *sola fide*.[2] It becomes clear at a number of points in his writings that his Roman Catholic adversaries specifically argued that it was simply impossible to separate justifying faith and the obedience flowing from love and born of the gospel of Christ. Thus, for the Roman Catholics of his day to speak of being justified by faith alone is meaningless because such faith always includes love for God and the obedience to God that flows from it.[3]

It is the thesis of this chapter that Calvin responded to his Roman Catholic opponents both affirmatively and negatively. His answer depended on a careful analysis of the meaning of the question. If he took the question to mean, Does justifying faith have the character of

---

[1] W. Stanford Reid, "Justification by Faith according to John Calvin," *Westminster Theological Journal* 42, no. 2 (Spring 1980): 290-307. Reid concludes this article with the assertion, "In this teaching Calvin saw eye to eye with Martin Luther, and those who would make a distinction between them, would seem to be misrepresenting one or both of the reformers" (307). Within this article Reid notes how frequently Calvin affirmed *sola fide* (296) and cites especially 3:17:7, 8, 10 of the *Institutes* [*Joannis Calvini Opera Selecta* (ed. P. Barth, G. Niesel) *OS* [1926-1959] 4:259-264]. Calvin also frequently affirms *sola fide* in his commentaries. Cf. *Comm.* Rom. 1:16, 17 [*Ioannis Calvini Opera quae supersunt omnia*, ed. G. Baum, E. Cunitz, and E. Reuss, Corpus Reformatorum *CR*, [1864] 77:39-41]; 3:21 [*CR* 77:57-60], 28 [*CR* 77:65-66]; 4:6-8 [*CR* 77:71-73]; Gal 2:16 [*CR* 78:196]; 5:6 [*CR* 78:246-247]. Note: Footnote citations written as *Inst.* in this chapter are from John Calvin, *Institutes of the Christian Religion*, trans. Ford Lewis Battles, ed. John T. McNeill (London: S.C.M. Press, 1961). Footnote citations written as *Comm.* are from *Calvin's Commentaries*, 22 vols. (Grand Rapids: Baker Book House, 1981).

[2] By evangelical obedience, I refer to obedience to the gospel leading to the moral renewal of the sinner.

[3] *Inst.* 3:11:20 [*OS* 4:203-04]; *Comm.* Rom. 3:27-28 [*CR* 77:65-66].

evangelical obedience? or, Does it produce evangelical obedience? then Calvin answered the question affirmatively. If, however, Calvin took the question to mean, Why does faith justify? or, Does faith justify as evangelical obedience? or, Does faith justify in its character as evangelical obedience? then Calvin answered the question with an emphatic negative.

Calvin's answer is of considerable contemporary significance. For when his answer is understood, it exposes the weakness of both parties specified in Chapter One. In other words, those who separate faith and obedience and those who fail to distinguish them both have deviated from the theological balance of Calvin (and, as we shall see, the entire Reformation tradition). Justifying faith and evangelical obedience must, according to Calvin, be neither separated nor identified. In other words, justifying faith both is (in one sense) and is not (in another sense) evangelical obedience. *Sola fide* for Calvin involves a crucial distinction between justifying faith and evangelical obedience, but not a separation of them. Though the burden of this chapter is to show that Calvin distinguished justifying faith and evangelical obedience, we will begin by briefly arguing that he also saw them as inseparable.

The Affirmative Answer in Calvin

Faith and evangelical obedience in Calvin are inseparable not in one but two senses. Faith is evangelical obedience. It is also inseparable from evangelical obedience in that it produces it. We need proceed no further than Calvin's understanding of Romans 1:5 to see that for Calvin faith is obedience.

In recent years the phrase, "the obedience of faith," occurring in both Romans 1:5 and 16:26 and so bracketing Paul's crucial letter to the Romans, has become an exegetical crux as debates about the meaning of faith and its relation to justification have heated up among evangelicals. Is it the obedience that springs from or results from faith or is it the obedience that consists in faith? Or is it one of several other alternatives?[4] Much theologically, perhaps too much, has been made to

---

[4] C.E.B. Cranfield, *The Epistle to the Romans*, The International Critical Commentary (Edinburgh: T. & T. Clark Limited), 1:66-67, illustrates how the interpretation of this text has become a crux of Pauline studies. Cranfield actually adopts, as we shall see, the same interpretation of this phrase as Calvin: "the obedience which consists in faith."

Sola Fide in Calvin

ride on the exegesis of this difficult phrase.[5]

Calvin does not appear to be in any doubt about the meaning of this phrase. He straightforwardly affirms that the obedience of faith is the obedience to the gospel that consists in faith. Commenting on the verse in question he says:

> That is, we have received a command to preach the gospel among all nations, and this gospel they obey in faith. . . . We must also notice here what faith is; the name of obedience is given to it, and for this reason—because the Lord calls us by his gospel; we respond to his call by faith; as on the other hand, the chief act of disobedience is unbelief. . . . Faith is properly that by which we obey the gospel.[6]

Faith is inseparable from obedience. Here Calvin's understanding of Galatians 5:6 is sufficient to clarify his view. In his comments on this text he makes clear that faith is not to be separated from obedience in the sense of good works. Good works always accompany and follow it. In the *Institutes*, as we shall see, he makes clear that faith unites us to Christ and thus inevitably and inseparably bestows the moral renewal that he variously describes as repentance, sanctification, and regeneration.[7]

Galatians 5:6 is a key text for Calvin. He not only comments on it in his commentary, but alludes to it in the discussion just mentioned in the *Institutes*.[8] In his commentary on this text (in words that anticipate later Reformed confessional statements) he affirms that saving faith is never alone, but is always accompanied by good works. Commenting on the phrase, "but faith working through love," in Galatians 5:6, he remarks:

> When they attempt to refute our doctrine, that we are justified by faith alone, they take this line of argument. If the faith which justifies us be that "which worketh by love," then faith alone does not justify. I answer, they do not comprehend their own silly talk; still less do they comprehend our statements. It is not our doctrine that the faith which justifies is alone; we maintain that it is invariably accompanied by good works; only we contend that faith alone is sufficient for justification . . . We, again, refuse to admit that, in any case, faith can be separated from

---

[5]Don B. Garlington, *The Obedience of Faith* (Tubingen: J. C. b. Mohr, 1991), 1-6, 233-254; idem, *Faith, Obedience, and Perseverance* (Tubingen: J. C. B. Mohr, 1994), 10-30, provides extensive treatments of this phrase that illustrate how important this phrase has become in Pauline studies.
[6]*Comm.* Rom. 1:5 [*CR* 77:11-12].
[7]*Inst.* 3:3:1-11 [*OS* 4:55-67].
[8]*Inst.* 3:11:20 [*OS* 4:77-78].

the Spirit of regeneration; but when the question comes to be in what manner we are justified, we then set aside all works.[9]

In these passages, Calvin makes clear that faith is not the opposite or contrary of obedience. If it were the primary point of this chapter, many other passages might be cited to show that faith is not the opposite of obedience. From one point of view, faith for Calvin is in itself obedience. From an alternate point of view, faith is the source of obedience and inseparable from it. The consequences of this alternate point of view will become significant as we proceed.

When it is asked, then, if saving faith includes evangelical obedience for Calvin, the answer from one perspective is surely that *it does*! Saving faith is obedience to the gospel. Thus, in the strictest sense it includes evangelical obedience. It also includes evangelical obedience in the sense of always bestowing it and always being accompanied by it.

The Negative Answer

If the affirmative answer were all there was to the matter for Calvin, this would be a very short chapter (and dissertation) indeed. Calvin, however, affirms, as just noted, the point that saving faith is never alone but is always accompanied by good works and the other graces of the Christian life. This affirmation implicitly contains a distinction between faith and obedience. Faith is not simply and without further ado to be equated with obedience. Calvin must also say that it is the source of the moral renewal that results in obedience and is accompanied by good works. These statements imply, as I shall attempt to prove in the rest of this discussion, that there is also for Calvin an important—even critical—distinction to be maintained between faith and evangelical obedience.

There is, in fact, another side to the matter for Calvin that is critically important to his theology. If the question is put this way: *Does faith justify as obedience for Calvin?* Or in this way, *Is it because faith is obedience and the beginning of new obedience that justification is by*

---

[9]*Comm.* Gal. 5:6 [*CR* 78:246-247]. Note how similar this statement is to the later affirmations of the British Calvinists in their confessions. *The Westminster Confession*, *The Savoy Declaration*, and *The 1689 Baptist Confession* all affirm in identical language (at chapter 11, paragraph 2) that "faith thus receiving and resting on Christ and his righteousness, is the alone instrument of justification; yet it is not alone in the person justified, but is ever accompanied with all other saving graces, and is no dead faith, but worketh by love." This says something about the multifaceted debate about the relation of Calvin and the Calvinists.

faith alone for Calvin? the burden of Calvin's thought on this issue begins to press in upon us and show that much more must be said.

In the rest of this chapter, then, I will argue that, though faith is obedience for Calvin, faith does not justify as obedience. This may seem a fine distinction. In the context of Calvin's debate with Rome over *sola fide*, it was, however, anything but a fine or minor distinction. On the vindication of this distinction the whole defense of *sola fide* rested.

An illustration may clarify the issue, make this distinction seem less technical, and bring out its immense, practical importance. Faith is like an oval mirror of the fancy kind that one may find in the hall or lounge of a nice restaurant. Such a mirror has more than one quality, property, or characteristic. It is oval. It is also reflective. The mirror possesses both qualities. The peculiar quality, however, that makes this oval mirror a mirror is not that it is oval, but that it reflects. It is called a mirror—not an oval! It is just such an analysis that I believe (and will now attempt to prove) is crucial to Calvin's view of *sola fide*. Faith is obedience, but it is not this quality, property, or characteristic that makes it faith. It is rather the fact that it rests and reposes on Christ that makes it faith—that is, in other words, its distinctive characteristic in the matter of justification. Faith is justifying (is a mirror) not because it is obedience (is oval), but because it rests on Christ (reflects Christ to the Father as He looks at us).[10]

Does saving faith justify as obedience for Calvin? Phrased in this way, an unqualifiedly negative answer is required to this question. This negative answer will be argued in the rest of this chapter from three facets of Calvin's theology: the definition of justifying faith, the relationship of justifying faith and repentance (or evangelical obedience), and the contrast between law and grace.

- **The Definition of Justifying Faith in Calvin**

Calvin begins Book Three of the *Institutes* by stressing that it is the agency of the Holy Spirit that produces faith. Calvin asks why it is that

---

[10] No illustration is perfect. In a conversation with the author, Peter Leithart inquired whether faith was only "accidentally" obedience. One of the imperfections of this illustration is that it might imply that faith is only "accidentally" obedience, just as the mirror is only "accidentally" oval (Mirrors come in many shapes and sizes.). Suffice to say, I do not mean to imply this at all. The mirror of faith must be oval-shaped and can only have in the context of the gospel and the Creator-creature relationship the character of obedience.

all do not embrace the grace of the gospel and insists that this requires that "we climb higher and examine into the secret energy of the Spirit."[11] He then stresses that the Holy Spirit is first given to Christ before He is given to us and discusses the titles (and thus the works) of the Spirit.[12] Paragraph Four of this chapter then begins, "But faith is the principal work of the Holy Spirit."

This discussion of the Holy Spirit as the spring of faith in Christ must not be quickly passed over in order to come immediately to Calvin's attempt to define faith. It serves to set the stage and create the context for his definition by emphasizing the fact that faith itself is the gift of the Father's grace, through the Son's work, in the Spirit's power. It is in some sense true that it is by our faith that we unite ourselves to Christ. Yet, for Calvin, it is also true and even more important that it is Christ who unites us to Himself by the bond of the Spirit who creates the faith in us which unites us to Christ.

Calvin comes to his attempt to define faith in the first seven paragraphs of the third chapter in Book Three of the *Institutes*. He then states his carefully crafted definition in Paragraph Seven. Calvin's classic definition runs as follows:

> Now we shall possess a right definition of faith if we call it a firm and certain knowledge of God's benevolence toward us, founded upon the truth of the freely given promise in Christ, both revealed to our minds and sealed upon our hearts through the Holy Spirit.[13]

Calvin follows this statement by discussing various questions and difficulties related to his definition of faith in Paragraphs 8 through 43. This careful and extended treatment of the subject manifests how critical and central the subject of faith is for Calvin.

This detailed treatment has, however, not prevented the subject of saving faith from becoming one of the cruxes of Calvin studies.[14] It has given rise to discussions of whether Calvin's doctrine of faith is intellectualist or voluntarist.[15] It has also given rise to the related

---

[11]*Inst.* 3:1:1 [*OS* 4:1-2].

[12]*Inst.* 3:1:2-3 [*OS* 4:2-5].

[13]*Inst.* 3:2:7 [*OS* 4:15-16].

[14]George Gordh, "Calvin's Conception of Faith," *Review & Expositor* 50 (April 1953): 207-215; Brian A. Gerrish, "The Doctrine of Faith," *Princeton Seminary Bulletin* 16, no. 2 (1995): 202-215.

[15]See the discussion of R.T. Kendall's notorious thesis in Richard A. Muller, *The Unaccommodated Calvin* (Oxford: New York, 2000), 159-173. Note also George W.

discussion of the relation of faith and assurance in Calvin's doctrine.[16] It has given rise, furthermore, to the inter-twined discussions of unbelief in the elect and of belief in the non-elect.[17] Finally, the place of knowledge in Calvin's view of faith became a subject of discussion as Neo-orthodoxy attempted to lay claim to Calvin.[18]

The meaning of faith for the purpose of the question raised in this chapter is, however, clear. The simple point I want to make with regard to Calvin's definition of faith seems relatively unaffected by the discussions mentioned above.

Harper, "Calvin and English Calvinism to 1649: A Review Article," *Calvin Theological Journal* 20 (1985): 255-262; Stephen Thorson, "Tensions in Calvin's View of Faith: Unexamined Assumptions in R.T. Kendall's *Calvin and English Calvinism to 1649*," *JETS* 37, no. 3 (September 1994): 413-426.

[16]Besides the books and articles cited in the previous note, see my discussion of the *Westminster Confession of Faith* in chap. 4. See also Joel R. Beeke, "Does Assurance Belong to the Essence of Faith? Calvin and the Calvinists," *The Master's Seminary Journal* 5, no. 1 (Spring 1994): 43-71; idem, *Assurance of Faith: Calvin, English Puritanism, and the Dutch Second Reformation* (New York: P. Lang, 1991); Paul Helm, *Calvin and the Calvinists* (Edinburgh: Banner of Truth Trust, 1982); Michael Eaton, *No Condemnation: A New Theology of Assurance* (Downers Grove, IL: InterVarsity Press, 1997). Beeke and Helm argue against Kendall that assurance of salvation is not of the essence of justifying faith for Calvin. It seems clear to me from the evidence I will cite in this chapter that at this point Beeke and Helm are incorrect. Nevertheless, they are right in saying that Calvin clearly did not follow the logic of this definition of faith to the conclusions of Kendall. For instance, it is not clear that Calvin rejected the practical syllogism, believed that true Christians always had (full) assurance of salvation, or defined faith exclusively as an intellectual conviction. As I indicate in this chapter, Calvin did teach that justifying faith was more than a passive assurance of salvation. He also taught that it was a passive human activity and could speak of faith as a *passive work* and as a *receiving* of Christ. Calvin, *Comm*. John 6:29 [*CR* 75:141], can say, "It is, therefore, if we may be allowed the expression, a passive work, to which no reward can be paid, and it bestows on man no other righteousness than that which he receives from Christ." It is, furthermore, commonly acknowledged that Luther understood faith to be *fides apprehensiva*, a faith that lays hold of Christ. See chapter two. For the purposes of the thesis of this dissertation, all this is important for the following reasons. Even if differences exist between the early Reformers, Calvin and Luther, and the later tradition over the definition of faith, there is no disagreement as to the fact that justifying faith must be understood as passive. In fact, however, Luther and Calvin do not always or simply define justifying faith as assurance of salvation, but—in perfect accord with the later tradition and the Westminster Confession—agree in seeing the passive quality of justifying faith as receiving and resting on Christ.

[17]John Clark Smith, "Calvin: Unbelief in the Elect," *Evangelical Quarterly* 54 (1982): 14-24.

[18]James M. Bulman, "The Place of Knowledge in Calvin's View of Faith," *Review and Expositor* 50 (July 1953): 323-329.

Clearly, Calvin says nothing about obedience in this definition of faith. The central word in this definition is "knowledge." Faith is not doing anything. It is knowing something. If faith is knowledge, this surely makes it something that in an important respect is passive. Fundamentally, for Calvin faith is knowing something—not doing something.

Furthermore, this knowledge is not pictured as the result of striving, acquisitiveness, or discovery by the active mind of the believer. It is portrayed as the result of a divine activity in which man is passive. Calvin's definition emphasizes this in several ways. It is the effect of "the freely given promise in Christ, both revealed to our minds and sealed upon our hearts through the Holy Spirit." Faith is knowing the freely given and divinely revealed promise in Christ—not the Word of God in general.[19] I will enlarge later on the fact that it is the promise in Christ and not the law of God that is the object of faith. It is the result of the work of the Holy Spirit sealing the promise upon our minds and hearts.[20]

Finally, the object of this knowledge—what is known by faith—also serves to underscore this same point. It is knowledge of "God's benevolence toward us." It seems clear that in saying this Calvin has defined faith as assurance of salvation. It is not knowledge of anything we have done or anything to which we have contributed. It is simply the blessed realization that God freely and gratuitously loves us specially and with personal mercy for us in particular. Faith is, then, for Calvin, *the blessed assurance that Jesus is mine.*

Now defining faith in this way surely creates problems for Calvin and for us. If faith is assurance of God's benevolence toward us in particular, what of those who (claim to) experience such assurance, but live an ungodly life? What about the experience of believers who struggle with doubts and fears about this very point? What about Calvin's relation to the Puritans and the practical syllogism? These are all difficult questions stemming from the way in which Calvin defines faith in his classic definition. They may suggest that there is something in his definition that needs tweaking. The fact is, however, that Calvin's definition of faith at least includes assurance in faith. More probably it makes faith consist in a kind of assurance of God's benevolence (His saving grace) toward us in particular. If, however, faith includes or actually is assurance, and I cannot see how Calvin's words can be

---

[19]*Inst.* 3:2:6-7 [*OS* 4:13-16].
[20]*Inst.* 3:1:1-4 [*OS* 4:1-6].

otherwise interpreted, then clearly faith is very different from obedience.[21]

Calvin's definition of faith is often taken as proof of an intellectualist conception of faith.[22] If faith is knowledge, this seems to imply that Calvin is to be identified with the intellectualist tradition as over against voluntarism.

R.T. Kendall concludes from this that for Calvin faith is merely a matter of the mind and not of the will and is, therefore, wholly passive. Against Kendall, Richard Muller argues that Calvin affirms from the very beginning of his career a fiducial aspect of faith in which it is seen as *placing*[23] all hope and trust in God.[24]

It may well be true—I think it is true—that in other places Calvin makes clear that there is a voluntarist aspect to his view of faith.[25] There is a voluntarist element in Calvin's view of faith that does not find clear articulation in his classic definition of faith in the *Institutes*. Calvin's mention in his definition of the promise being sealed to our *heart* implies, however, this voluntarist element. This element emerges more clearly in the surrounding paragraphs when Calvin says that we will be saved "if, indeed, with firm faith we *embrace* this mercy and *rest* in it with steadfast hope."[26] It also emerges when he remarks, "This, then, is true knowledge of Christ, if we *receive* him as he is offered by the Father: namely, clothed with the gospel."[27]

Does, however, this voluntarist aspect or activist element introduce the idea of obedience or works as the peculiar, distinguishing, and

---

[21]It should not be overlooked that defining faith in terms of a personal assurance of God's benevolence toward us safeguards the important and essential idea that saving faith is a *personal and trustful appropriation* of God's promise in Christ by the sinner. Calvin's definition, while perhaps somewhat problematic in other respects, is in my opinion very biblical and crucial in this respect.

[22]R.T. Kendall, *Calvin and English Calvinism to 1649* (New York: Oxford University Press, 1979).

[23]John Calvin, *The Institutes of the Christian Religion: The 1536 Edition*, trans. and annotated by Ford Lewis Battles (Grand Rapids: Eerdmans, 1975), 42-43. Battles translates here, ". . . faith . . . is not only to adjudge true all that has been written or is said of God and Christ, but to put all hope and trust in one God and Christ . . ."

[24]Muller, *The Unaccommodated Calvin*, 159.

[25]George W. Harper points out in "Calvin and English Calvinism to 1649: A Review Article," 259, that there is an alternative to the voluntarist and intellectualist medieval, philosophical traditions. He calls this "the Augustinian voluntarist perspective" and argues that this is the tradition to which Luther and Calvin returned.

[26]*Inst.* 3:2:1 [*OS* 4:6-9].

[27]*Inst.* 3:2:6 [*OS* 4:13-15]. The emphasis is mine.

justifying feature of faith? The answer to this question is clearly no. This active element of faith—if it can be so called—is embracing and resting in mercy. It is receiving Christ as He is offered in the gospel. The movement of the will in faith is, therefore, consistent with its peculiarly, passive character. In fact, we may even say that the very movement of the will in justifying faith is essentially passive in nature.

Calvin makes this abundantly clear at other points. Faith is no work or obedience meriting salvation or grace for him. It is the opposite of such a work. His *Commentary* on Galatians 5:6 has been cited above. Calvin also refers to the words of Galatians 5:6 in his discussion of faith and justification in the *Institutes*. His words there are of pointed relevance for the subject at hand:

> Also, they pointedly strive after the foolish subtlety that we are justified by faith alone, which acts through love, so that righteousness depends upon love. Indeed, we confess with Paul that no other faith justifies "but faith working through love" [Gal. 5:6]. But it does not take its power to justify from that working of love. Indeed, it justifies in no other way but in that it leads us into fellowship with the righteousness of Christ.[28]

Walter E. Stuermann raises a question that leads him to discuss this very point: "Can an objection be sustained to the effect that, since faith is sometimes called a work, therefore it is proper to speak of justification by works?" He then remarks that Calvin shuts the door on such reasoning.[29] Indeed he does! Commenting on John 6:29's reference to *faith as the work of God*, Calvin has this to say:

> It is idle sophistry, under the pretext of this passage, to maintain that we are justified by works, if faith justifies, because it is likewise called *a work*. First, it is plain enough that Christ does not speak with strict accuracy, when he calls faith *a work*, just as Paul makes a comparison between *the law of faith* and *the law of works*, (Rom. iii. 27). Secondly, when we affirm that men are not justified by *works*, we mean *works* by the merit of which men may obtain favour with God. Now *faith* brings nothing to God, but, on the contrary, places man before God as empty and poor, that he may be filled with Christ and with his grace. It is, therefore, if we may be allowed the expression, a passive work, to

---

[28]*Inst.* 3:11:20 [*OS* 4:203-204].
[29]Walter E. Stuermann, *A Critical Study of Calvin's Concept of Faith* (Ann Arbor, MI: Edwards Brothers, 1952), 170.

which no reward can be paid, and it bestows on man no other righteousness than that which he receives from Christ.[30]

The phrase, *passive work*, epitomizes Calvin's view of faith. There is a voluntarist element. It is a work—a human activity, but it is a *passive* work. It is such a work as simply presents "man before God as empty and poor, that he may be filled with Christ."

The main point here is that Calvin's classic definition of faith makes no mention of obedience, but rather defines it in ways that contrast justifying faith with obedience. This is all the more striking because, as we have seen, he could describe faith as obedience and as the beginning of new obedience. Yet when setting himself to define faith, faith as obedience—faith as response to commandment—plays no part in his definition. Faith is defined as *knowledge*, as *gift*, as *assurance*.

The fact surely is striking, but the reason for it is not hard to find. Calvin says nothing about faith as obedience in his classic definition because to him the fact that faith is obedience is not the important, peculiar, or justifying power of faith. It justifies only "in that it leads us into fellowship with the righteousness of Christ." Already we may say, then, that for Calvin saving faith does not justify as obedience. In this sense of the question addressed in this chapter (i.e., Does saving faith itself include evangelical obedience in the theology of John Calvin?), the answer is no. There is, however, much more to be said in defense of this answer to the question posed above.

- **Faith and Repentance in Calvin**

The relationship between (justifying) faith and repentance (evangelical obedience) in Calvin's writings also points to a negative answer to the question raised previously.

One may reconstruct from the early chapters of Book Three of the *Institutes* a kind of structure in terms of which Calvin presents his view of the application of salvation. One might almost say that Calvin provides us here with his *ordo salutis*! It is in terms of this structure that Calvin responds to a number of important, theological issues in his day and ours—including the one addressed in above.

Calvin teaches in these chapters that the way of salvation is as follows. The Holy Spirit creates faith in Christ. This is His *principal*

---

[30]*Comm.* John 6:29 [*CR* 75:141].

58   *Faith, Obedience, and Justification*

work.[31] In this way the Spirit and faith unite the believer to Christ and to all the benefits of redemption to be found in Him.[32] The two great benefits of salvation to be found in Christ are forgiveness of sins and moral renewal (justification and sanctification).[33] Moral renewal is variously termed *repentance, regeneration,* and *sanctification* by Calvin.[34] Calvin divides sanctification or moral renewal into mortification and vivification.[35] Forgiveness of sins or justification is the other great blessing possessed in union with Christ.[36]

```
                    ┌──────────────────┐
                    │   Holy Spirit    │
                    │  Creates Faith in│
                    │     Christ       │
                    └────────┬─────────┘
                             ▼
            Union with Christ and All His
            Redemptive Benefits, Especially
            Repentance and Forgiveness
                    of Sins

  Including:        Forgiveness of    Repentance:      Including:
  Forgiveness       Sins or           (Regeneration    Mortification
  and               Justification     or               and Vivification
  Acceptance                          Sanctification)
                    (Forensic         (Moral
                    Status)           Renewal)
```

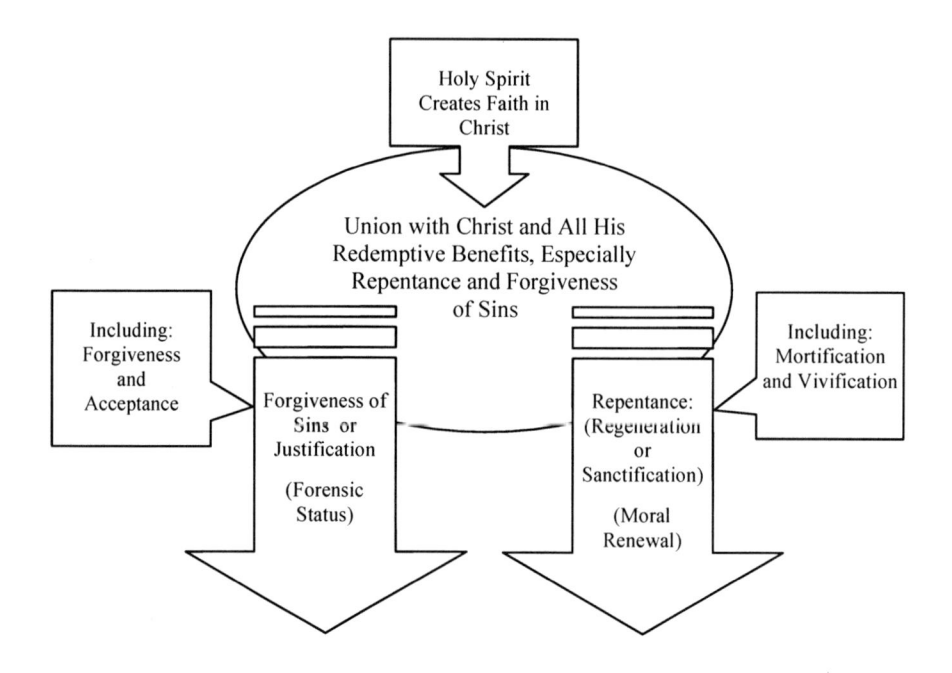

Figure 1. Calvin's *ordo salutis*.

---

[31]*Inst.* 3:1:4 [*OS* 4:1-6].
[32]*Inst.* 3:1:1 [*OS* 4:1-24]; 3:2:1 [*OS* 4:6-9]; 3:3:1 [*OS* 4:55-56].
[33]*Inst.* 3:3:1 [*OS* 4:55-56]; 3:11:1 [*OS* 4:181-182].
[34]*Inst.* 3:3:1 [*OS* 4:55-56]; 3:3:9 [*OS* 4:63-65]; 3:3:19 [*OS* 4:76-77]; 3:11:1 [*OS* 4:181-182]. Note the references cited in his chapter on Victor A. Shepherd, "Sanctification and Faith" in *The Nature and Function of Faith in the Theology of John Calvin* (Macon, GA: Mercer University Press, 1983), 35-38.
[35]*Inst.* 3:3:8 [*OS* 4:62-63].
[36]*Inst.* 3:11:1 [*OS* 4:181-82].

Though it is treated second in order, it is "the main hinge on which religion turns."[37] Justification itself has two sides or aspects. It is both forgiveness of sins and a gracious acceptance of our persons by God.[38] While justification is forensic and has to do with our status or standing before God, repentance (also called regeneration or sanctification) has to do with moral renewal.[39] To paraphrase an old proverb, one diagram may be worth more than an extended exposition. Note Figure 1 in previous page.

Figure 1 diagrams Calvin's structuring of the application of the redemption found in Christ. It shows clearly the important distinction that he made between faith and repentance. Faith is unto union with Christ. Repentance is a consequence of union with Christ. Though this is not a chronological distinction, since faith, union with Christ, and repentance are inseparable, it is a logical and sequential distinction. The work of the Holy Spirit in creating faith in Christ, on the one hand, and in morally renewing (giving repentance to) the believer are distinguished. Though the moral renewal (repentance) of the believer is the work of the Holy Spirit, "faith is the principal work of the Spirit."[40] It is not difficult to collect statements from this part of the *Institutes* to support the distinction between the work of the Spirit in creating faith and the work of the Spirit in moral renewal. The statement of 3:3:1 is both clear and exemplary. Chapter Three is entitled, "Our Regeneration by Faith: Repentance." This statement of Calvin makes explicit a number of the important structures or thoughts in Calvin's presentation of the way of salvation or the application of redemption. Faith in Christ confers both repentance and forgiveness of sins. Repentance is equated with "newness of life" and "actual holiness of life." Forgiveness of sins—"the free imputation of righteousness"—is carefully distinguished from newness of life. Calvin explicitly denies that repentance precedes faith, but affirms the opposite. Repentance is the fruit of faith.

> Even though we have taught in part how faith possesses Christ, and how through it we enjoy his benefits, this would still remain obscure if we did not add an explanation of the effects we feel. With good reason, the sum of the gospel is held to consist in repentance and forgiveness of sins. Any discussion of faith that omitted these topics would be barren

---

[37] Ibid.
[38] *Inst.* 3:11:4 [*OS* 4:184-85].
[39] *Inst.* 3:11:2-4 [*OS* 4:182-185].
[40] *Inst.* 3:1:4 [*OS* 4:5-6].

and mutilated and well-nigh useless. Now, both repentance and forgiveness of sins—that is, newness of life and free reconciliation—are conferred on us by Christ, and both are obtained by us through faith. As a consequence, reason and the order of teaching demand that I begin to discuss both at this point. However, our immediate transition will be from faith to repentance. For when this topic is rightly understood it will better appear how man is justified by faith alone, and simple pardon; nevertheless actual holiness of life, so to speak, is not separated from free imputation of righteousness. Now it ought to be a fact beyond controversy that repentance not only constantly follows faith, but is born of faith. For since pardon and forgiveness are offered through the preaching of the gospel in order that the sinner, freed from the tyranny of Satan, the yoke of sin, and the miserable bondage of vices, may cross over into the Kingdom of God, surely no one can embrace the grace of the gospel without betaking himself from the errors of his past life into the right way, and applying his whole effort to the practice of repentance. There are some, however, who suppose that repentance precedes faith, rather than flows from it, or is produced by it as fruit from a tree. Such persons have never known the power of repentance, and are moved to feel this way by an unduly slight argument.[41]

It is true that Calvin elsewhere occasionally makes statements that seem at variance with his teaching here. Specifically, two difficulties may be noted. On the one hand, occasionally he seems to speak of regeneration as producing faith. On the other hand, occasionally he speaks of repentance as preceding faith. One may see the first difficulty in Calvin's comments on John 1:13. His exact words require quotation:

> It may be thought that the Evangelist reverses the natural order by making regeneration to precede faith, whereas, on the contrary, it is an effect of faith, and therefore ought to be placed later. I reply, that both statements perfectly agree . . . the illumination of our minds by the Holy Spirit belongs to our renewal, and thus faith flows from regeneration as from its source; but since it is by the same faith that we receive Christ, who sanctifies us by his Spirit, on that account it is said to be the beginning of our adoption.
> Another solution, still more plain and easy, may be offered; for when the Lord breathes faith into us, he regenerates us by some method that

---

[41]*Inst.* 3:3:1 [*OS* 4:55-56]. For many more references to the distinction and relation between faith and repentance see *Inst.* 3:3:2-25 [*OS* 4:56-84]. See also 3:11:14 [*OS* 4:198], where Calvin remarks, "From this it follows that not even the spiritual works come into account when the power of justifying is ascribed to faith."

is hidden and unknown to us; but after we have received faith, we perceive, by a lively feeling of conscience, not only the grace of adoption, but also newness of life and the other gifts of the Holy Spirit.[42]

One may note the second difficulty in Calvin's careful comments on Acts 20:21. He says there:

> He doth not, therefore, name repentance in the former place, as if it did wholly go before faith, forasmuch as a part thereof proceedeth from faith, and is an effect thereof; but because the beginning of repentance is a preparation unto faith. I call the displeasing of ourselves the beginning, which doth enforce us, after we be thoroughly touched with the fear of the wrath of God, to seek some remedy.[43]

These two difficulties are really just one. Repentance and regeneration, as we have noted already, designate the same reality for Calvin, only from two distinct viewpoints. Repentance views the matter from the viewpoint of human responsibility and activity. Regeneration views it from the standpoint of divine power and agency.[44]

The underlying problem is that repentance and regeneration seem both to precede and succeed faith and, thus, suggest that moral renewal precedes faith. The problem may be resolved, however, when several things are recalled. *First*, Calvin is not really confused. His statements make clear that he is aware of the seeming contradiction involved in his statements and that he thinks it is capable of resolution. *Second*, the structure of Calvin's applied soteriology noted above already indicates that the Holy Spirit's work precedes faith. The question only concerns whether and in what sense this work of the Holy Spirit may be called regeneration. *Third*, and most importantly for my thesis, Calvin maintains even in the statements made above the distinction between faith and repentance. In other words, even if repentance and regeneration are in some well-qualified sense prior to faith, they are still clearly distinguished from faith. The statements cited make clear that in so far as repentance and regeneration precede faith they do not convey "newness of life." Regeneration creates faith in and union with Christ. It is in union with Christ that newness of life comes. Repentance in so far as it

---

[42]*Comm.* John 1:13 [*CR* 75:12-13].
[43]*Comm.* Acts 20:21 [*CR* 76:462-464].
[44]The treatments of Stuermann, *A Critical Study*, 199 and Shepherd, *The Nature and Function of Faith*, 35-38, touch on this difficulty and provide helpful discussions of it.

precedes faith is not newness of life, but simply displeasure with ourselves and the fear of God's judgment that makes us seek help. Thus, there is maintained a clear distinction between faith and repentance. Calvin's comments on Psalm 130:4 make this point.

> When a man is awakened with a lively sense of the judgment of God, he cannot fail to be humbled with shame and fear. Such self-dissatisfaction would not however suffice, unless at the same time there were added faith, whose office it is to raise up the hearts which were cast down with fear, and to encourage them to pray for forgiveness. David then acted as he ought to have done when, in order to his attaining genuine repentance, he first summons himself before God's judgment; but to preserve his confidence from falling under the overpowering influence of fear, he presently adds the hope which there was of obtaining pardon.[45]

According to Calvin, the repentance that precedes faith is dissatisfaction, shame, and fear—not newness of life. It is clearly distinguished from the faith that must be *added* in order that forgiveness might be sought and attained. There is no danger, then, that the ambiguity in the order of faith and repentance in Calvin should lead to a confusion of faith and repentance or moral renewal. Even, then, in Calvin's "variant" presentation of the order of faith and repentance, they remain quite distinct. Faith continues to be clearly distinguished from repentance and regeneration.

Generally, the terms, repentance, regeneration, and sanctification, describe the process of moral renewal that takes place in the Christian as a result of union with Christ. As we have seen, even where they occasionally do not, the distinction between faith and repentance is maintained. Repentance when it precedes faith does not refer to moral renewal, but to a wholly negative view of oneself variously described as displeasure, dissatisfaction, shame, and fear.

This process of moral renewal is understood in Calvin as increasing obedience to and conformity to the law of God.[46] This is the point of the so-called *third use of the law* that is distinctive of Calvin's theology. Of

---

[45]*Comm.* Psa 130:4 [*CR* 60:334-336]. Shepherd, *The Nature and Function of Faith*, 37, also points to Luke 24:46 [*CR* 73:817-818]; Acts 11:18 [*CR* 76:257-258]; and Acts 17:31 [*CR* 76:421-427] with regard to this.

[46]Shepherd, *The Nature and Function of Faith*, 156-164, asserts faith's need of law and avers that the law reflects God's intention for the shape of the existence of faith. Cf. *Inst.* 3:19:2-3 [*OS* 4:283-284]; *Comm.* 2 Pet. 2:19 [*CR* 83:469-470].

course, Calvin sees an inseparable connection between this process of moral renewal defined in terms of conformity to God's law and justification by faith alone. Calvin, however, by making faith in Christ the gift of the Holy Spirit *unto* union with Christ, posits a plain distinction between faith on the one hand, and repentance, regeneration, and sanctification, on the other. Faith leads to union with Christ. Repentance etc. flows out of union with Christ. The connection is clear, and the distinction could not be plainer. In this sense too, then, evangelical obedience is not included in faith itself. Or to put the matter more precisely, it is not in its character as obedience (or as producing moral renewal) that faith justifies. Calvin maintains a strict distinction between faith and repentance conceived as moral renewal.

- **Law and Grace in Calvin**

A third telling consideration which points to the fact that faith does not justify as obedience in Calvin is the contrast between law and grace to be found in his writings.

As noted previously, Calvin asserts that faith is knowledge of God's benevolence toward us, founded upon the truth of the freely given promise in Christ. "Now we shall possess a right definition of faith if we call it a firm and certain knowledge of God's benevolence toward us, founded upon the truth of the freely given promise in Christ, both revealed to our minds and sealed upon our hearts through the Holy Spirit."[47]

Calvin pervasively describes faith in relation to and as formed by the freely given promise in Christ. To add to the evidence already cited in this essay, one may point to several things. Though faith respects the whole Word of God, it is not the Word of God in its undifferentiated entirety that creates faith. It is the promise of mercy. "Accordingly we need the promise of grace, which can testify to us that the Father is merciful, since we can approach him in no other way, and upon grace alone the heart of man can rest."[48] Faith is an empty vessel. "We compare faith to a kind of vessel; for unless we come empty with the mouth of our vessel open to seek Christ's grace, we are not capable of receiving Christ."[49] As we have seen, faith is therefore passive. It is "something merely passive, bringing nothing of ours to the recovering of

---

[47]*Inst.* 3:2:7 [*OS* 4:15-16].
[48]Ibid.
[49]*Inst.* 3:11:7 [*OS* 4:188-189]; 3:11:10 [*OS* 4:191-192].

God's favour but receiving from Christ that which we lack."[50] Faith justifies as receiving and embracing the promise in Christ. "For faith is said to justify because it receives and embraces the righteousness offered in the gospel."[51] Faith, then, is only the instrumental cause of justification—not its efficient, material, or meritorious cause.[52]

The above is certainly an impressive array of evidence for faith being the response to the freely given promise in Christ. Yet the presentation of this subject would be wholly inadequate in bringing out the nature of justifying faith as response to grace in Calvin if it did not also bring out the contrast between law and grace (or gospel) in Calvin. This distinction means that faith is a response to grace in contrast to law.

Calvin begins his extended treatment of faith in the third chapter of Book Three of the *Institutes* by underscoring the distinction between law and grace.

> Secondly, it is not only hard, but above our strength and beyond our abilities, to fulfill the law to the letter; thus, if we look to ourselves only, and ponder what condition we deserve no trace of good hope will remain; but cast away by God, we shall lie under eternal death. Thirdly, it has been explained that there is but one means of liberation that can rescue us from such miserable calamity; the appearance of Christ the redeemer, through whose hand the Heavenly Father, pitying us out of his infinite goodness and mercy, willed to help us; if, indeed, with firm faith we embrace this mercy and rest in it with steadfast hope.[53]

Throughout his treatment of justification this distinction remains crucial. Note the important distinction Calvin makes between the promises of the law and the promises of the gospel.

> Now, to be sure, the law itself has its own promises. Therefore, in the promises of the gospel there must be something distinct and different unless we would admit that the comparison is inept. But what sort of difference will this be, other than the gospel promises are free and dependent solely upon God's mercy, while the promises of the law depend upon the condition of works?[54]

---

[50]*Inst.* 3:13:5 [*OS* 4:219-220].
[51]*Inst.* 3:11:17 [*OS* 4:200-201]. *Comm.* Gen. 15:6 [*CR* 51:211-214].
[52]*Comm.* Rom. 3:22 and 24 [*CR* 77:57-62].
[53]*Inst.* 3:3:1 [*OS* 4:55-56].
[54]*Inst.* 3:11:17 [*OS* 4:200-201].

Calvin distinguishes the three uses of the law in Book Two, Chapter Seven of the *Institutes* where he mentions the first, second, and third uses of the law explicitly.[55] The treatment of the first use of the law—condemnation—in paragraphs 6-9 makes the contrast between the gracious promises of the gospel, on the one hand, and those of the law, on the other, explicit.[56]

The comparatively brief comments just made (with regard to justifying faith being for Calvin a response to grace in contrast to law) raises the much debated issue of law and gospel in Calvin. Those comments make clear that this contrast is crucial for understanding the meaning of *sola fide* for Calvin.

It has, however, been frequently claimed that in his understanding of law and gospel Calvin's views are much different than those of Luther. The contrast between law and gospel is crucial for the meaning of *sola fide*. The thesis of this study involves the contention that substantial unity existed between Luther and Calvin and in the Reformation tradition with regard to justification *sola fide*. Thus, this claim is potentially quite problematic for this thesis. It must, therefore, be examined.

The differences between Calvin and Luther on the subject of the law have frequently been stated quite strongly. Such strong statements of the differences between Calvin and Luther have sometimes been made by way of criticism of Calvin from the Lutheran side. I. John Hesselink notes:

> Calvin's stress on the unity of the two Testaments is well known. For scholars of a past generation, when the accent was on the diversity of the Testaments, this was frequently a stumbling block. A rather common complaint was that Calvin so stressed the unity of the Testaments that their alleged differences were of no real significance.

---

[55]See especially *Inst.* 2:7:6 [*OS* 3:332], 10 [*OS* 3:335-336], 12 [*OS* 3:337-338].

[56]Shepherd, *The Nature and Function of Faith*, 227, argues that for Calvin "Jesus Christ is the substance of the God-given law." Throughout his treatment of the subject of the law in Calvin, Shepherd betrays the Barthian tendency to subsume law under grace and to cloud the sharp distinction between law and gracious promise in Calvin. His lengthy argument on the subject notwithstanding, it is simply impossible to read Calvin this way. Of course, from one standpoint Calvin views the law as an administration of grace and as revealing or containing the gospel. The Old Testament—the law—did reveal Christ for Calvin. In this sense the promise of God's mercy does always precede the claim of God's law (See Shepherd, *The Nature and Function of Faith*, 154). Yet, the effect of Shepherd's treatment is to obscure or minimize the other side of Calvin's balanced treatment of the subject in which he sees the law as the antithesis of grace so that the law condemns while the promise of grace justifies.

Seeberg, for example, maintains that "Calvin's legalism results in a tendency to blur the boundaries between Old and New Testaments." Wernle likewise alleges that "Calvin in his moral zeal actually denies the difference between the Old and New testaments, closes his eyes to all of the new values (*Werten*) which Jesus brought into the world, and lowers him to the level of a correct interpreter of the old Moses. How much clearer the Anabaptists were on this point!"[57]

On the other hand, such pointed contrasts between Luther and Calvin have often been made in favor of Calvin and against Luther. Edward A. Dowey, for example, remarks:

> Despite agreement between them on many denotations and designations for law, and upon a doctrine of justification by faith alone to the exclusion of all merit, Luther and Calvin do differ profoundly on the role, function, or use of the law for the Christian.[58]

Dowey's remark that, despite their differences on the use of the law for the Christian, Luther and Calvin agree about justification by faith alone seems overly complacent. If the contrast between law and gospel is crucial for the understanding of *sola fide*, then differences with regard to this cannot be insulated from the doctrine of justification.[59]

As a matter of fact, this very connection may be emerging in contemporary contrasts being drawn between Calvin and the Reformed tradition, on the one hand, and Luther and Lutheranism, on the other. Some in the Reformed tradition today, but influenced by the new perspective on Paul with its re-formulations of justification *sola fide*, have thought it helpful to their viewpoint to stress the contrast between Reformed and Lutheran on the subject of law and gospel. Andrew Sandlin argues this case in his article, "Lutheranized Calvinism: *Gospel* or *Law*, or *Gospel* and *Law*."[60] Douglas Wilson strives to accentuate the

---

[57] I. John Hesselink, *Calvin's Concept of the Law* (Allison Park, PA: Pickwick Publications, 1992), 155, 211.

[58] Edward A. Dowey, Jr., "Law in Luther and Calvin," *Theology Today* 41 (July 1984): 153. See also Edward A. Dowey Jr. *The Knowledge of God in Calvin's Theology* (Grand Rapids: William B. Eerdmans, 1994), 221-242.

[59] To be fair, Dowey's focus in these remarks is on the slightly different issue of the uses of the law—and not precisely the contrast between law and gospel.

[60] Andrew Sandlin, "Lutheranized Calvinism: *Gospel* or *Law*, or *Gospel* and *Law*," *The Reformation and Revival Journal* 11, no. 2 (Spring, 2002): 123-135. This entire issue of *The Reformation and Revival Journal* is dedicated to justification and an appreciative assessment of the new perspective and N.T. Wright.

Sola Fide in Calvin

same contrast between Calvinist and Lutheran in "A Pauline Take on the New Perspective." Wilson notes six concerns of "the Old Perspective that the New Perspective wants to deny." The third of these is "that law stands in opposition to grace." Wilson then straightforwardly remarks that he with Calvin and the Reformed also deny this.[61]

Wilson later defends this thesis by asserting that for the Reformed (and Calvin assumedly) the contrast between law and grace is merely psychological—not hermeneutical. In other words, for Wilson the difference between Calvin and Luther is that the distinction between law and gospel was only in how Scripture subjectively struck a person depending on his own spiritual condition. It was not an objective or hermeneutical quality of certain portions of Scripture. Thus, Wilson argues:

> Before proceeding further, it is important to note that there is agreement between the Lutheran and historic Reformed position *if the discussion involves the psychology of individual conversion*. In other words, the Bible does contain moral imperatives and commandments which reveal and increase sin (Rom. 3:20; 5:20). And the Bible also contains words of peace in the gospel explicitly stated as such. Consequently, when a man in rebellion is convicted by the moral demands of the law, reflects on his position before God, hears the gospel preached, and repents and believes, it is fully appropriate to discuss this transition in terms of law and grace, law and gospel. But the psychology of conversion ought not to be transformed into a hermeneutic. Suppose a man is an adulterer. He has his attention drawn to the words of Scripture—the command to not commit adultery. He hears that God will judge him for his disobedience (Heb. 13:4). He comes under conviction of sin and repents. This is wonderful, but none of it changes the fact that exegetically the Ten Commandments (including the prohibition of adultery which convicted this man of his sin) are presented to the people of Israel *as gospel*. The preamble of the Decalogue is a declaration that God is the One who delivered us from the land of Egypt, *out of the house of bondage*. That is good news—gospel.[62]

---

[61] Ibid., 5-20. Wilson here remarks, "In line with the New Perspective, I also deny the first three points as stated above. But this is simply because I hold to the historic Reformed faith, over against contemporary dispensationalism or historic Lutheranism. Does this make Calvin or Turretin advocates of the New Perspective also?"(5).

[62] Ibid., 9-10.

Wilson is at liberty to disagree with Calvin, but he is not at liberty to misrepresent him. It simply cannot be denied that in distinguishing between the promises of the law and the promises of the gospel—as we have seen Calvin do—he posits an objective or hermeneutical distinction between law and gospel. The distinction between Calvin and Luther that Wilson posits is both wishful thinking and a drastic misrepresentation of Calvin and the Reformed tradition after him.

Nevertheless, it is true that, if one limits his view of Calvin to the *Institutes* and especially the treatments of the law in Book Two, one may come away with a skewed and imbalanced view of Calvin's view of the law. Andrew J. Bandstra remarks:

> Thus Calvin himself may have to shoulder some of the blame for the fact that his views on law and gospel have often been only partially presented. His position on law and gospel has been presented most frequently only under the two rubrics of unity of substance and difference of form. The rubric of antithesis of letter and Spirit has hardly received a hearing; no doubt this is in part due to the fact that this aspect is not so clearly represented in the *Institutes*.
>
> On the other hand, the *Institutes,* no matter how important, do not represent Calvin's total view. Calvin the exegete is as important as Calvin the theologian. Surely the commentary materials need to be taken seriously in attempting to assess the whole of Calvin's view on the law-gospel motif. When this is done, it is clear that the antithesis of law and gospel, properly defined, is a necessary and important part of his total perspective.[63]

Indeed, massive evidence for the "Lutheran" perspective, the contrast between law and gospel, may be gleaned from Calvin's commentaries.[64] Here Bandstra helpfully suggests the three rubrics he mentions in the quotation above: unity of substance, difference of form,

---

[63] Andrew J. Bandstra, "Law and Gospel," in *Exploring the Heritage of John Calvin*, ed. David E. Holwerda (Grand Rapids: Baker, 1976), 38. Bandstra remarks in a footnote that the dichotomy between law and gospel is, however, present in the *Institutes* in muted form in 2:11 [*OS* 3:423-436] and in more explicit fashion in 3:17:6 [*OS* 30:594-595].

[64] Here is a partial listing of the major passages in his commentaries where he contrasts law and grace: *Comm.* Exod. 19:1 [*CR* 52:192-194]; Deut. 30:11 [*CR* 52:257-258]; Psa. 19:7 [*CR* 59:198-200]; John 1:17 [*CR* 75:18-19]; Rom. 4:15 [*CR* 77:78-79]; 5:20 [*CR* 77:102]; 8:15 [*CR* 77:147-150]; 10:5 [*CR* 77:197-198]; 2 Cor. 3:6 [*CR* 78:39-41]; Gal. 2:19 [*CR* 78:197-199]; 3:19-20 [*CR* 78:214-217]. Also to be noted in this regard are Calvin's comments on the so-called first use of the law in *Sermons on the Ten Commandments* (from Deuteronomy), ed. and trans. Benjamin W. Farley (Grand Rapids: Baker, 1980), 25-26, 219-236, and 255-308.

and antithesis of letter and Spirit. The last, he argues, represents Calvin's emphasis on the antithesis of law and gospel. Hesselink and Bandstra cite massive evidence for this emphasis in Calvin's commentaries.[65] The following comments by Calvin on Romans 8:15 are representative:

> Although the covenant of grace is contained in the law, yet Paul removes it from there, for in opposing Gospel to the law he regards only what was peculiar to the law itself, viz., command and prohibition, and the restraining of transgressors by the threat of death. He assigns to the law its own quality, by which it differs from the Gospel. . . . Finally, the law, considered in itself, can do nothing but bind those who are subject to its wretched bondage by the horror of death as well, for it promises not blessing except on condition, and pronounces death on all transgressors. As, therefore, under the law there was the spirit of bondage which oppressed the conscience with fear, so under the Gospel there is the spirit of adoption, which gladdens our souls with the testimony of our salvation.[66]

No doubt there are differences in emphasis between Luther and Calvin on the law. If, however, substantive differences exist between them, it is not by way of Calvin's subtraction from Luther's antithesis between law and gospel, but by way of Calvin's addition of an emphasis on the third use of the law.[67] Calvin certainly held both the first use of the law and the objective antithesis of law and gospel. At this point Calvin was and remained Luther's debtor and student.

It is clear in light of the above discussion that the unique, peculiar, and justifying quality or property of faith is not obedience to the law. Faith may be obedience, but it is obedience to the gospel and to grace as distinguished from the law. Faith may be obedience, but it is not in this character that its unique or justifying property resides. Faith may result in

---

[65]Hesselink, *Calvin's Concept of the Law*, 155-215; Bandstra, "Law and Gospel," 11-39. See also Francois Wendel, *Calvin: Origins and Development of His Religious Thought*, trans. Philip Mairet (Grand Rapids: Baker, 2002), 185-214; Dowey, *The Knowledge of God in Calvin's Theology*, 221-242.

[66]*Comm.* Rom. 8:15 [*CR* 77:147-150].

[67]I do not intend here to take sides in the debate over whether Luther held the so-called third use of the law. Whether or not Luther held it, the third use of the law was certainly emphasized and given a prominence by Calvin that it did not have for Luther. This variation at least in emphasis becomes plainly visible in the sometimes vehement debates in the traditions descending from each respectively. What must be emphasized is that, however the descendants of Calvin and Luther may feel about the matter, Calvin did not see a strong emphasis on the third use of the law as contrary to the first use of the law or the antithesis of law and gospel.

obedience to the law of God, but it is not at all because of this that it occupies the place in the doctrine of justification that it does for Calvin. It is not because of this that it has power to justify or is the instrumental cause of justification. Faith justifies as and only as the trustful, resting, and reposing response to gratuitous promise. Faith justifies because by this repose on Christ it joins the person to Christ.

Conclusion

For all these reasons we must reach the conclusion that, though faith possesses the character of obedience for Calvin, it is not as obedience that it justifies. It is rather in its quality as resting and reposing on the gratuitous promises of the gospel of Christ. Thus, we reach the same conclusion already reached by W. Stanford Reid in his fine article, "Justification by Faith according to John Calvin."

> In his own day and ever since, those opposed to his doctrine have cited the terms of Galatians 5:6 "faith working by love" as showing that love plays a part in justification. While Calvin is prepared to recognize that faith does work by love, he also insists that "it does not take its power to justify from that working of love. Indeed, it justifies by no other means than by leading us into fellowship with the righteousness of Christ. . . . And then that faith is reckoned as righteousness solely where righteousness is given through a grace not owed." In his commentary on Galatians, he ends his exposition of this verse by pointing out that when he is speaking of justification, he sets aside all works and this theme characterizes his exegesis of the whole epistle.[68]

The emerging tendency of theologians in the Reformation tradition to unify faith and obedience in such a way as to identify them, to speak of being justified by faith working through love, to erase the distinction between law and grace, and to define justifying faith partly in terms of faithfulness (i.e., faithful obedience to God's commands) is troubling in itself. But not only so, it is profoundly contrary to the classic view of *sola fide* enunciated by Luther and Calvin. Such phraseology as *sola fide*, if it is to be defined meaningfully and fairly, must be defined in terms of its classic, historical articulation by Luther and Calvin. The question is certainly raised whether modern evangelicals who speak in the ways described above may fairly say that they believe in *sola fide*.

---

[68]Reid, "Justification by Faith according to John Calvin," 300.

It may be that Calvin's definition of faith, relating of faith and repentance, and contrast between law and gospel are in need of some recasting. Evangelicals should be aware, however, that if they engage in *extensive* and *basic* revisions of Calvin's theology at these points, their claims to believe in justification *sola fide* become historically inaccurate and misleading.

CHAPTER 4
SOLA FIDE IN THE REFORMATION CONFESSIONS
Thesis, Argument, and Approach

The previous chapters of this study attempted to clarify the meaning of *sola fide* for Martin Luther and John Calvin. Through an examination of the Reformation breakthrough in the pioneering work of Martin Luther and the careful articulation of that insight in the systematic labors of John Calvin, a nuanced but clear understanding of the meaning of *sola fide* for Luther and Calvin in relation to the much discussed issues of faith, obedience, and justification has been attained. Though the respective, religious movements originated by the two great reformers would later diverge in many respects, in the matter of justification *sola fide* Calvin's view was substantially identical with that of Luther. Both maintained a definition of justifying faith that was passive or receptive. Both, though asserting the inseparability of justifying faith and evangelical obedience, distinguished justifying faith from evangelical obedience. Both understood the meaning of justifying faith in terms of a fundamental dichotomy between law and gospel. Justifying faith was, therefore, viewed as a response to the promises of the gospel and not the precepts of the law.

The question to be addressed in this chapter is whether this view of *sola fide* was maintained in the Reformation tradition following Luther and Calvin. The classic articulation of justification *sola fide* emerged in the Reformation and was its characteristic and cardinal doctrine. If it can be established that substantially the same definition, distinction, and dichotomy characterize the affirmation of *sola fide* in the subsequent decades and century as characterized it in Luther and Calvin, it will be clear that this view of justification *sola fide* has unified support in the Reformation tradition that was the womb of most evangelicals today. Thus, if only this understanding of justification *sola fide* has historical warrant in the movement that both defined this doctrine and was defined by it, then *sola fide* has a unified and identifiable meaning. If evangelicals today deviate from this *historic* view of justification *sola fide*, both their affirmation of *sola fide* and their claim to be evangelicals are historically misleading.

How can it be ascertained whether the vast, international movement associated with Luther and Calvin maintained their views of the cardinal doctrine of the Reformation? So massive would be the task of surveying even the main theologians in this tradition and even simply through the seventeenth century and even on this one issue, that such a survey becomes impracticable. Thankfully, such a practically impossible task is unnecessary. The various segments of the international Reformation movement were not slow to articulate their views in carefully crafted Creeds and Confessions. In these Confessions—not the potentially eccentric views of individual theologians, but—the great unifying truths which were the common faith of the various, Reformation churches were articulated. Many of these confessional symbols have stood the test of time and remain the confessional standards of the descendants of these churches until today. A survey of such Confessions provides a more practicable, more accurate, and, thus, more satisfactory method of ascertaining whether the views of the Reformers regarding justification *sola fide* were maintained by their theological descendants.

This analysis of these Confessions has, of course, been limited to the "major" Confessions (and Catechisms) of the Reformation movement of the sixteenth and seventeenth centuries.[1] In order to provide some objective standard as to what constitutes such a "major" Confession and avoid the appearance of a subjective, slanted, or biased selection, I have with a few exceptions (shortly to be noted) surveyed those Confessions and Catechisms presented in volume 3 of *The Creeds of Christendom* by Philip Schaff under *Part First: The Creeds of the Evangelical Lutheran Church* and *Part Second: The Creeds of the Evangelical Reformed Churches*.[2] It is reasonable to assume that Schaff's selection of the major Reformation Confessions was not biased with regard to the present issue. At any rate, the use of Schaff's standard presentation, *The Creeds of Christendom*, provides some check on the subjectivity of the present author.[3]

---

[1]These time limitations seem necessary generally in order not to drift too far from the genuine sources of the Reformation. More specifically, these limitations are necessary in order to prevent the alien influences of "Enlightenment," "modernist," and "rationalist" tendencies that arose from distorting our view of the original Protestantism.

[2]*The Creeds of Christendom with a History and Critical Notes*, vol. 3, ed. Philip Schaff, rev. David S. Schaff (Grand Rapids: Baker Book House, 1983). Parallel to Schaff in the material it covers and more contemporary is *Creeds and Confessions of Faith in the Christian Tradition*, vol. 3, ed. J. Pelikan, V. Hotchkiss (New Haven: Yale University Press, 2003). It is abbreviated in this chapter as *CC*.

[3]Perhaps it should be noted that the following survey covers (in all) 15 of the most important Reformation Confessions and Catechisms. I also summarize nine more doctrinal statements in the paragraph that follows. I am not aware of any significant Creed or Catechism that is neglected in this survey. I am not aware of any Reformation (Lutheran or Reformed) Catechism or Creed that is at variance from the conclusions from

The analysis which follows covers all the Confessions and Catechisms presented by Schaff with the following exceptions. *Luther's Small Catechism* has nothing relevant to the question.[4] *The Saxon Visitation Articles* contain nothing directly relevant to the issue being investigated. *The Sixty-Seven Articles of Ulrich Zwingli* were written in 1523 and so precede both the mature statements of Luther and systematic work of Calvin. They contain little of relevance to our subject. Additionally, *The Ten Theses of Berne* were written in 1528 and also precede the systematic work of Calvin. Additionally, they contain nothing directly relevant to the issue at hand. *The First Helvetic (or Second Basle) Confession* written in 1536 precedes the work of Calvin in Geneva. Additionally, its statements about faith, obedience, and justification are quite rudimentary and contain nothing definitive on the subject. *The Second Scottish Confession* of 1581 primarily addresses national issues peculiar to Scotland and has little of relevance to the issue. *The Anglican Catechism* of 1549 and 1662 has nothing directly relevant. *The Lambeth Articles* of 1595 "are a Calvinistic Appendix to the Thirty-nine Articles."[5] There is nothing specifically relevant to the issue here. *The Arminian Articles* that provoked the Synod of Dort in 1619 have nothing directly relevant and do not specifically challenge the Reformed view of justification *sola fide*.

The final Confession to be considered in this survey will be the *Westminster Confession*. This Confession is part of what I will call the Westminster "complex" of documents. Several Creeds and Catechisms that are part of this "complex" will be considered in connection with the survey of the *Westminster Confession*. Schaff does not include *The Westminster Larger Catechism* in his survey, but I will include it as a part of the Westminster complex and because it clarifies the statements of the *Westminster Confession*. The *Westminster Shorter Catechism* (which is included by Schaff) will also be treated in connection with the *Westminster Confession*. The *Savoy Declaration* (1658) of the English Congregationalists and the *1689 Baptist Confession* will also be surveyed in connection with the *Westminster Confession*. These revisions of the *Westminster* are of special interest to the "congregational" and "free

---

this survey. If such existed, its variant doctrine of justification would only prove its eccentricity and—in the face of the evidence offered here—its "non-Reformational" character.

[4]Luther's *Large Catechism* does, of course, contain an interesting understanding of faith as the true fulfillment of the First Commandment, but I deal with this in chap. 2.

[5]*The Creeds of Christendom*, 3:523. CC 2:545-546.

church" wings of Protestantism of which I am part. Schaff does present these two "daughter" Confessions of the *Westminster*, but in a later division of his work.[6]

My method in this study will be, first, to provide a brief historical introduction to each of the Confessions and Catechisms discussed. Then, I will consider whether the definition of justifying faith, the distinction between justifying faith and evangelical obedience, and the dichotomy between law and gospel critical to Luther's insight and Calvin's articulation of justification *sola fide* is maintained or contradicted in each of the creedal symbols discussed.

The Augsburg Confession, A. D. 1530

- **Historical Introduction**

The Augsburg Confession was occasioned by the command of Emperor Charles V to the Lutheran princes to present to him a statement of their faith. Schaff remarks, however, that its "deeper cause must be sought in the inner necessity and impulse to confess and formularize the evangelical faith" in the hearts of the Reformation leaders.[7] It is the joint production of Luther and Melanchthon. Quoting Schaff:

> Luther thus produced the doctrinal matter of the Confession, while Melanchthon's scholarly and methodical mind freely produced and elaborated it into its final shape and form, and his gentle, peaceful, compromising spirit breathed into a moderate, conservative tone. In other words, Luther was the primary, Melanchthon the secondary author, of the contents, and the sole author of the style and temper of the Confession.[8]

Melanchthon was revising the text of this Confession until the last days before its presentation to the Emperor. He seems to have continued revising it afterwards with no sense of impropriety. Eventually (after 1540) this led to a distinction between the text of the Confession *invariata* and *variata*. The *variata* incorporated some of Melanchthon's own distinctives with regard to the Lord's Supper and the doctrine of sin

---

[6]Ibid., 3:707-729, 738-745. Unaccountably and, I think, inexcusably there is no treatment of the *1689 Baptist Confession* either by this name or by its American name, *The Philadelphia Confession of Faith*, in CC.
[7]Ibid., 1:225-226.
[8]Ibid., 1:229.

and grace. Though the original copies of *The Augsburg Confession* presented to the Emperor are not extant, the 1530 *invariata* text of the Confession may be sufficiently recovered from early translations and publications of it and will be used here.[9]

The Augsburg Confession, as the first of the great Reformation confessions, is of great importance for this study. Schaff remarks:

> The Augsburg Confession is the fundamental and generally received symbol of the Lutheran Church . . . . But its influence extends far beyond the Lutheran Church. It struck the key-note to other evangelical confessions, and strengthened the cause of the Reformation everywhere.[10]

With this brief introduction, we come now to examine the doctrine of justification *sola fide* taught within the Augsburg Confession.[11]

- **The Definition of Justifying Faith**

The definition of faith with which the Augsburg Confession is working first comes to light in its article on justification.

> Also they teach that men can not be justified [obtain forgiveness of sins and righteousness] before God by their own powers, merits, or works, but are justified freely [of grace] for Christ's sake through faith, when they believe that they are received into favor, and their sins forgiven for Christ's sake, who by his death hath satisfied for our sins. This faith doth God impute for righteousness before him. Rom. iii and iv.[12]

The key words here are "but are justified freely [of grace] for Christ's sake through faith, when they believe that they are received into favor, and their sins forgiven for Christ's sake." Faith is here described as a confidence or assurance that the gospel promises apply to us personally. Specifically, faith justifies *when it believes that one is received into favor and forgiven for Christ's sake*. This articulates the

---

[9]None of the changes Melanchthon introduced alter the doctrine of justification itself.

[10]*The Creeds of Christendom*, 1:234-235.

[11]The English translation cited here is that given by Schaff and introduced by him, *The Creeds of Christendom*, 1:3. The phrase *faith alone* occurs in Article VI and XX. *Faith only* also occurs in Article XX.

[12]*The Creeds of Christendom*, 3:10. Augsburg Confession, Part First, Article IV. [*CC* 2:60-61].

view of faith as a passive assurance of God's favor that we have seen in both Luther and Calvin.

This understanding of faith recurs frequently through the Augsburg Confession.

> Now repentance consisteth properly of these two parts: One is contrition, or terrors stricken into the conscience through the acknowledgment of sin; the other is faith, which is conceived by the Gospel, or absolution, and doth believe that for Christ's sake sins be forgiven.[13]

> Wherefore they condemn those that teach that the Sacraments do justify by the work done and do not teach that faith which believes the remission of sin.[14]

> ... our works cannot reconcile God or deserve remission of sins, grace, and justification at his hands, but that these we obtain by faith only, when we believe that we are received into favor for Christ's sake.[15]

> Faith is taken in Scriptures, not for such knowledge as is in the wicked, but for a trust, which doth comfort and lift up disquieted minds.[16]

> So it cometh to pass that all lusts and human counsels bear sway in the heart so long as faith and trust in God are absent.[17]

> The Scripture also teacheth that we are justified before God through faith in Christ, when we believe that our sins are forgiven for Christ's sake.[18]

It is important to note that faith is not viewed only or merely as assurance that God's promises are true for us. It is also viewed (to borrow Calvin's wonderful phrase) as a *passive work* in which we receive or apprehend God's promises for ourselves.

> For remission of sins and justification is apprehended by faith....[19]

---

[13] Ibid., 3:14. *Augsburg Confession*, Part First, Article XII. [*CC* 2:64-65].
[14] Ibid., 3:15. *Augsburg Confession*, Part First, Article XIII. [*CC* 2:65].
[15] Ibid., 3:21. *Augsburg Confession*, Part First, Article XX. [*CC* 2:71].
[16] Ibid., 3:25. *Augsburg Confession*, Part First, Article XX. [*CC* 2:73].
[17] Ibid., 3:25. *Augsburg Confession*, Part First, Article XX. [*CC* 2:74].
[18] Ibid., 3:37. *Augsburg Confession*, Part Second, Article III. [*CC* 2:86].
[19] Ibid., 3:11. *Augsburg Confession*, Part First, Article VI. [*CC* 2:62].

Sola Fide in the Reformation Confessions

> ... to the end that fearful consciences ... might know that grace, and forgiveness of sins are received by faith in Christ.[20]

> By faith alone is apprehended remission of sins and grace and because the Holy Spirit is received by faith, our hearts are now renewed, and so put on new affections, so that they are able to bring forth good works.[21]

Whether described intellectually as assurance that God's promises are true for us or more volitionally as the apprehension and reception of Christ and His benefits in the gospel, the same definition of faith is displayed. It is the passive definition of justifying faith we have found in Luther and Calvin. It is not as active obedience to God's commands that faith justifies, but passively as assurance of our forgiveness for Christ's sake and as reception of Christ.

- **The Distinction between Faith and Obedience**

The statement on justification also contrasts faith and any works we might do in order to be justified.

> Also they teach that men can not be justified [obtain forgiveness of sins and righteousness] before God by their own powers, merits, or works, but are justified freely [of grace] for Christ's sake through faith, when they believe that they are received into favor, and their sins forgiven for Christ's sake, who by his death hath satisfied for our sins. This faith doth God impute for righteousness before him. Rom. iii and iv.[22]

The contrast instituted between faith and "their own powers, merits, or works" clearly implies a distinction between faith and obedience. This distinction is confirmed in the article on new obedience.

> Also they teach this faith should bring forth good fruits ..., because it is God's will, and not on any confidence of meriting justification by their works. For remission of sins and justification is apprehended by faith. ...[23]

---

[20] Ibid., 3:23. *Augsburg Confession*, Part First, Article XX. [*CC* 2:73].
[21] Ibid., 3:24. *Augsburg Confession*, Part First, Article XX. [*CC* 2:74].
[22] Ibid., 3:10. *Augsburg Confession*, Part First, Article IV. [*CC* 2:60-61].
[23] Ibid., 3:11. *Augsburg Confession*, Part First, Article VI. [*CC* 2:62-63].

There is here a comparatively mild response to the concern of Roman Catholicism that the Protestants were minimizing the importance of good works. There is no statement to the effect that good works or new obedience is the essential evidence of justifying faith. Good works should be done, "because it is God's will." Later in Article XX a stronger assertion will be made. What is clear here, however, is that "good fruits" are the result of faith. What is also clear here is that "justification is apprehended by faith." This faith is clearly distinguished from the *good fruits* of our *works*.

The stronger response to the importance of good works found in Article XX also makes clear the distinction between faith and obedience or good works.

> Moreover, ours teach that it is necessary to do good works; not that we may trust that we deserve grace by them, but because it is the will of God that we should do them. By faith alone is apprehended remission of sins and grace and because the Holy Spirit is received by faith, our hearts are now renewed, and so put on new affections, so that they are able to bring forth good works.

The structure of this paragraph is similar to the one we have seen in Calvin's *Institutes of the Christian Religion*.[24] Faith alone receives both remission of sins and the Holy Spirit. As a result of the reception of the Spirit, our hearts are renewed and we "bring forth good works." The distinction between faith alone—justifying faith—and good works is patent. Faith alone receives the Holy Spirit and as a result of this reception brings forth good works. Thus, the distinction between faith and obedience is very clear in *The Augsburg Confession*.

- **The Dichotomy between Law and Gospel**

It is no surprise to find the contrast between law and gospel in the Lutheran Confession *par excellence*. This contrast is crucial to its presentation of justification *sola fide*.

Article XII concerns repentance and strongly implies this contrast between law and gospel. It also specifically relates the origin of faith to the gospel. By contrasting faith with contrition and then making the pointed statement that faith is conceived by the gospel, the dichotomy

---

[24]*Inst.* 3:1-11. [*OS* 4:55-67].

Sola Fide in the Reformation Confessions

between the law (producing terrors) and the gospel (giving birth to faith) is directly implied.

> Now repentance consisteth properly of these two parts: One is contrition, or terrors stricken into the conscience through the acknowledgment of sin; the other is faith, which is conceived by the Gospel, or absolution, and doth believe that for Christ's sake sins be forgiven.[25]

This dichotomy between law and gospel is also clearly implicit in many references to the righteousness of faith. The righteousness of faith is said to consist—not in our obedience to the law, nor in faith itself, but—in the forgiveness of our sins and reception into God's favor for Christ's sake alone through the *instrumentality* of faith.

> And Paul doth everywhere teach that righteousness is not to be sought of our own observances, and services which are devised by men; but that it cometh by faith to those that believe that they are received into favor by God for Christ's sake.
> But it is evident that the monks teach that these counterfeited religions satisfy for sins, and merit grace and justification. What else is this than to detract from the glory of Christ, and to obscure and deny the righteousness of faith?
> Or is this not attributing justification to works? . . . to teach that such a service doth justify men; because that the righteousness of faith, which ought especially to be taught in the church, is obscured when those marvelous religions of angels, the pretense of poverty, and humility, and of celibacy, are cast before men's eyes.[26]

No doubt need remain that the peculiar signs of the doctrine of *sola fide* taught by Luther may be found in the Augsburg Confession. Not surprisingly, a seamless transition is made from his teaching to that of the first, great Reformation Confession.

---

[25]*The Creeds of Christendom*, 3:14. *Augsburg Confession*, Part First, Article XII. [*CC* 2:12-13].

[26]Ibid., 3:55-56. *Augsburg Confession*, Part Second, Article VI. [*CC* 2:61-62].

The Formula of Concord, A. D. 1576

- **Historical Introduction**

The Formula of Concord was so named from its aim to bring peace to the Lutherans after the numerous and bitter controversies of especially the decades following the death of Luther. These controversies were caused, firstly, by the escalating theological differences between Luther and Melanchthon in their later years and, secondly, by the centrifugal force of tensions with Romanism and Calvinism.[27] Many of these controversies are of no direct importance for the interests of this study. Three of these controversies are, however, important to consider briefly.

The "Osiandric Controversy" (as Schaff calls it) derives its name from Andrew Osiander who confounded justification and sanctification and taught that Christ's people are righteous through their union with the righteous, divine nature of Christ.

> He assailed the forensic conception of justification, and taught instead a medicinal and creative act, whereby the sinner is *made* just by an *infusion* of the *divine nature* of Christ, which is our righteousness.[28]

The result of this controversy is that *The Formula of Concord* teaches that Christ's obedience unto death as the God-man is imputed to us as our righteousness.[29]

The controversy over predestination was carried on more broadly, but was epitomized by the dispute between Jerome Zanchius and John Marbach in Strasburg.[30] The result for *The Formula of Concord* was, according to Schaff, to introduce into it "an obvious and irreconcilable antagonism"[31] between Article II and Article XI. Schaff argues that Article II teaches in the most extreme language total depravity and inability, while Article XI denies the corollary of this doctrine, irresistible grace.[32]

Schaff's assessment seems, however, too severe. There is no denial of irresistible grace in Article XI. This is not to say that there is no

---

[27]Ibid., 1:258-259.
[28]Ibid., 1:272.
[29]Ibid., 1:274.
[30]Ibid., 1:302-307.
[31]Ibid., 1:314.
[32]Ibid., 1:314-315.

problem. Article XI does not affirm irresistible grace and leaves us completely in the dark with regard to the means by which divine election brings about the salvation of the elect. The interest of Article XI is only to affirm a sincere and indiscriminate call of the gospel. This, of course, does not need to be read as contrary to the doctrine of irresistible grace. The Canons of Dort themselves affirm such a call.

> THIRD AND FOURTH HEAD: ARTICLE 8. As many as are called by the gospel are unfeignedly called. For God hath most earnestly and truly declared in His Word what will be acceptable to Him, namely, that all who are called should comply with the invitation. He, moreover, seriously promises eternal life and rest to as many as shall come to Him, and believe on him.[33]

Though Schaff is too severe, there is, nevertheless, a recession from a clear assertion of the strict Augustinian view of predestination and irresistible grace in Article XI of *The Formula of Concord*. What is interesting for our purposes is that this recession does not result in a withdrawal from justification *sola fide*. *Faith alone* is not simply equivalent to *grace alone*. Luther's insight into justification is not merely the rediscovery of the Augustinian doctrines of sin and grace. It may be that where the Augustinian doctrines of sin and grace are lost, the foundation of Luther's doctrine of justification by faith alone has eroded and *sola fide* cannot long survive. The implication, however, of *The Formula of Concord* is that Luther and Augustine (and, thus, *faith alone* and *grace alone*) cannot be simply equated as some today assume.

The "Majoristic Controversy" owes its name to Georg Major who declared that "good works are *necessary* to salvation."[34] In principle this was not inconsistent with the Reformers' insistence on the living and productive nature of faith. Yet it seemed to contradict *sola fide*. Not surprisingly, Major's formula was vehemently opposed. Even Melanchthon "felt that the necessity of good works for salvation might imply their meritoriousness."[35] Major himself consented to drop the phrase. Schaff concludes, "The 'Form of Concord' settled the controversy by separating good works both from justification and salvation, yet declaring them necessary as effects of justifying faith."[36]

---

[33] Ibid., 3:522. [*CC* 2:585].
[34] Ibid., 1:275.
[35] Ibid., 1:276.
[36] Ibid., 1:277.

If Schaff's conclusion is borne out by our study of the Formula of Concord, nothing could more loudly insist on the distinction between justifying faith and evangelical obedience. The insistence on completely distinguishing good works from both justification and salvation and viewing them simply as the effects of justifying faith makes very clear the maintenance of Luther's *sola fide* in Lutheranism.[37]

The Formula of Concord, sadly, did not live up to its name or aim. It did not bring an end to the discord of the Lutherans. Schaff remarks:

> The Form of Concord, as it is the last, is also the most disputed of the Lutheran symbols. It never attained general authority, like the Augsburg Confession or Luther's Catechism, although far greater exertions were made for its introduction.[38]

- **The Definition of Justifying Faith**

In its article entitled, "Of the Righteousness of Faith before God," the definition of justifying faith is clearly revealed.

> We believe, moreover, teach, and confess that this justifying faith is not a bare knowledge of the history of Christ, but such and so great a gift of God as that by it we rightly recognize Christ our Redeemer in the word of the gospel, and confide in Him: to wit, that for his obedience' sake alone we have by grace the remission of sins, are accounted holy and righteous before God the Father, and attain eternal salvation.[39]

Faith is here described as that grace by which "we rightly recognize Christ our Redeemer in the word of the gospel, and confide in Him." Both *recognizing* and *confiding* define justifying faith passively.

The following quotation will also come up for attention later. Though it does not use the word faith explicitly, it certainly implies that faith as a response to a gospel that is "nothing else than a certain and

---

[37] *The Formula of Concord* twice asserts "faith alone": *The Creeds of Christendom*, 3:116, 118, 159. [*CC* 2:176, 177, 195]. *The Formula of Concord*, Article III and Article IX. Notice especially the statement found on p. 118: "We believe, teach, and confess that, for the preserving of the pure doctrine of the righteousness of faith before God, it is necessary that the exclusive particles . . . should be most diligently retained . . . *By faith in Christ alone are we justified and saved.*"

[38] *The Creeds of Christendom*, 1:331.

[39] Ibid., 3:116. [*CC* 2:177]. *The Formula of Concord*, Article III.

most joyful message" must be defined in passive terms. Faith must be assurance, confidence, resting, and receiving.

> But when the Law and the Gospel are compared together, as well as Moses himself, the teacher of the Law, and Christ the teacher of the Gospel, we believe, teach, and confess that the Gospel is not a preaching of repentance, convicting of sins, but that it is properly nothing else than a certain and most joyful message and preaching full of consolation, not convicting or terrifying, inasmuch as it comforts the conscience against the terrors of the Law, and bids it look at the merit of Christ alone, and by a most sweet preaching of the grace and favor of God, obtained through Christ, lifts it up again.[40]

- **The Distinction between Faith and Obedience**

> By unanimous consent . . . it is taught in our churches that we most wretched sinners are justified before God and saved alone by faith in Christ, so that Christ alone is our righteousness.[41]

This affirmation close to the beginning of *The Formula of Concord* already implies the distinction between faith and obedience. It sets "faith in Christ" in juxtaposition with "we most wretched sinners." This strongly implies that faith is not viewed as obedience, but as consistent with being a wretched sinner. Similar is the following statement in which the "justification of faith" is distinguished from "the renewing of man."

> We believe, teach, and confess that the word *justify* in this article, conformably to the usage of Holy Scripture signifies the same as to absolve from sin . . . . And if at any time for the word Justification the words Regeneration and Vivification are used (as is done in the Apology of the Augsburg Confession) these words are to be taken in the above-stated signification. For elsewhere these words are to be understood of the renewing of man, which is rightly distinguished from the justification of faith.[42]

Similar to the statement that juxtaposed wretched sinners with those who have faith is the following. It affirms that those who believe in Christ are yet "obnoxious to many infirmities and stains," but still ought

---

[40]Ibid., 3:128. [*CC* 2:182]. *The Formula of Concord*, Article V.
[41]Ibid., 3:114. [*CC* 2:176]. *The Formula of Concord*, Article III.
[42]Ibid., 3:116-117. [*CC* 2:177]. *The Formula of Concord*, Article III.

to believe in Christ and rest on imputed righteousness in the midst of that sin even in the hour of death. This rather clearly implies that neither faith itself *considered as a virtue*, nor the obedience it engenders, is the essence of justifying faith. Justifying faith is passive and distinct from obedience.

> We believe, teach, and confess, moreover, that, although they that truly believe in Christ and are born again are even to the hour of death obnoxious to many infirmities and stains, yet they ought not to doubt either of the righteousness which is imputed to them through faith or concerning their eternal salvation, but rather are they firmly to be convinced that, for Christ's sake, according to the promise and unshaken word of the gospel, they have God reconciled to them.[43]

The next citation distinguishes faith from obedience by making faith precede and be the source of good works. Hence, good works and faith are not equivalent.

> But after that man is justified by faith, then that true and living faith works by love . . . and good works always follow justifying faith, and are most certainly found together with it, provided only it be a true and living faith. For true faith is never alone, but hath always charity and hope in its train.[44]

The final quotation on this point is perhaps the most explicit of all. Some thought apparently that faith justified as the commencement of the renewal God graciously was working in us. *The Formula of Concord* rejects the notion that faith

> bestows salvation upon us for the reason that that renewal which consists in love towards God and our neighbour commences in us through faith. . . . That believers in Christ are righteous and saved before God, both through the imputed righteousness of Christ and through the new obedience which is begun in them . . . . That faith does not justify without good works, that therefore good works are necessarily required for righteousness, and that independently of their being present man can not be justified.[45]

---

[43] Ibid., 3:117. [*CC* 2:177]. *The Formula of Concord*, Article III.
[44] Ibid., 3:118. [*CC* 2:177]. *The Formula of Concord*, Article III.
[45] Ibid., 3:120. [*CC* 2:178]. *The Formula of Concord*, Article III.

Sola Fide in the Reformation Confessions 87

- **The Dichotomy between Law and Gospel**

The witness borne to the Lutheran distinction between law and gospel is much more extensive in *The Formula of Concord* than in *The Augsburg Confession*. Thus, its testimony to the meaning of *sola fide* is also more extensive. We have already noted this statement above:

> But when the Law and the Gospel are compared together, as well as Moses himself, the teacher of the Law, and Christ the teacher of the Gospel, we believe, teach, and confess that the Gospel is not a preaching of repentance, convicting of sins, but that it is properly nothing else than a certain and most joyful message and preaching full of consolation, not convicting or terrifying, inasmuch as it comforts the conscience against the terrors of the Law, and bids it look at the merit of Christ alone, and by a most sweet preaching of the grace and favor of God, obtained through Christ, lifts it up again.[46]

Faith as the subjective response to the objective gospel understood as *not a preaching of repentance, convicting of sins, but . . . a certain and most joyful message and preaching full of consolation* must be distinguished from obedience and defined in passive terms. This is confirmed in other previously cited quotations:

> We believe, moreover, teach, and confess that this justifying faith is not a bare knowledge of the history of Christ, but such and so great a gift of God as that by it we rightly recognize Christ our Redeemer in the word of the gospel, and confide in Him: to wit, that for his obedience' sake alone we have by grace the remission of sins, are accounted holy and righteous before God the Father, and attain eternal salvation.[47]

Very clearly, *The Formula of Concord* bears witness to the meaning of justification *sola fide* found in both Luther and Calvin. Having concluded our review of Lutheran Confessions, however, we now move on to the Reformed Confessions. Here we come to a different tradition and one which some in our day regard as deviating from the Lutheran presentation of *sola fide*.[48]

---

[46]Ibid., 3:128. [*CC* 2:182]. *The Formula of Concord*, Article V.

[47]Ibid., 3:116. [*CC* 2:177]. *The Formula of Concord*, Article III.

[48]For Schaff's introduction to the Reformed Confessions, see *The Creeds of Christendom*, 1:354-359.

The Second Helvetic Confession, A. D. 1566

- **Historical Introduction**

The Second Helvetic Confession was primarily the work of Henry Bullinger, the successor of Zwingli in Zurich. Originally written as a part of his will and as a testimony to his own faith, it was met with the approval of a number of Reformed leaders. Through a series of providences, and after being subjected to scrutiny and some revision by (among others) Beza, Calvin's successor at Geneva, it was pressed into duty as a Confession of various continental Reformed churches.[49] Schaff remarks:

> The Helvetic Confession is the most widely adopted, and hence the most authoritative of all the Continental Reformed symbols, with the exception of the Heidelberg Catechism.[50]

Schaff does not provide a full English translation of *The Second Helvetic Confession*.[51] The quotations below are taken from *The Constitution of the Presbyterian Church (U.S.A.)*.[52]

- **The Definition of Faith**

Though *The Second Helvetic Confession* verbally asserts justification by *faith alone* only once,[53] its testimony is much more expansive to the meaning of *sola fide* than this might seem to imply. Brief early allusions to justifying faith hint at its definition. We are "ingrafted into Christ by faith."[54] "Now there only remains for all of us to give all glory to Christ, believe in him, rest in him alone, despising and rejecting all other aids in

---

[49] For a more detailed introduction to the *Second Helvetic Confession*, see Schaff's *Creeds of Christendom*, 1:390-420.

[50] *The Creeds of Christendom*, 1:394.

[51] He does provide in vol. 1 of the *Creeds of Christendom* what he calls "a condensed translation of the original." See *The Creeds of Christendom*, 1:396. For Schaff's condensed translation, see *The Creeds of Christendom*, 1:396-420.

[52] *The Constitution of the Presbyterian Church (U.S.A.), Part I, Book of Confessions* (Louisville: Geneva Press, 1996). To facilitate the location of these quotations from other sources, they will be cited in terms of the chapter of the *Second Helvetic Confession* in which they occur.

[53] *Second Helvetic Confession*, ch. 15. [CC 2:487].

[54] Ibid., ch. 10. [CC 2:473].

life."⁵⁵ These brief statements imply that the essence and efficacy of faith is resting in and so ingrafting us into Christ. These hints are, however, expanded in some of the most clear and emphatic language to be found anywhere in the Reformation Confessions.

Bullinger reflects deeply on the meaning of *sola fide* shortly after saying "that sinful man is justified by faith alone in Christ, not by the law or any works." This incisive reflection comes by way of explaining the rationale for justification *sola fide*.

> Therefore, because faith receives Christ our righteousness and attributes everything to the grace of God in Christ, on that account justification is attributed to faith, chiefly because of Christ and not therefore because it is our work. For it is the gift of God.⁵⁶

This remarkable and pointed assertion makes absolutely clear the significance of *sola fide*. The rationale and, therefore, the meaning of faith alone justifying is that it, first, "receives Christ our righteousness," and second, "attributes everything to the grace of God in Christ." Then Bullinger says explicitly and emphatically that "on that account justification is attributed to faith." Justifying faith is, therefore, emphatically passive in that it is receptive and attributes everything to grace.

This clear explanation is supplemented by a pointed definition of faith provided in the chapter entitled, "Of Faith and Good Works, and of Their Reward, and of Man's Merit."

> Christian faith is not an opinion or human conviction, but a most firm trust and a clear and steadfast assent of the mind, and then a most certain apprehension of the truth of God presented in the Scriptures and in the Apostles' Creed, and thus also of God himself, the greatest good, and especially of God's promise and of Christ who is the fulfilment of all promises.⁵⁷

Faith is again here defined in emphatically passive terms. It is a "firm trust," "a clear and steadfast assent of mind," and "a most certain apprehension of the truth." Furthermore, this trust, assent, and apprehension is directed "especially" to "God's promise and Christ."

---

⁵⁵Ibid., ch. 11. [*CC* 2:479].
⁵⁶Ibid., ch. 15. [*CC* 2:487].
⁵⁷Ibid., ch. 16. [*CC* 2:488].

It may be supposed that by making the object of faith here "the truth of God presented in the Scriptures" generally and not solely the gospel of Christ that the passive character of justifying faith has been compromised. This supposition is not true for two reasons. *First*, this statement does not alter the passive terms in which faith is here defined. *Second*, this entire statement is not a specific definition of justifying faith, but of faith more generally. In other words, it does not purport to explain or define justifying faith. That has already been addressed in the previously cited place.

- **The Distinction between Faith and Obedience**

This clear definition of faith is matched by an equally clear distinction between faith and obedience.

> Therefore, we do not share in the benefit of justification partly because of the grace of God or Christ, and partly because of ourselves, our love, works or merit, but we attribute it wholly to the grace of God in Christ through faith. For our love and our works could not please God if performed by unrighteous men. Therefore, it is necessary for us to be righteous before we may love and do good works. We are made truly righteous, as we have said, by faith in Christ purely by the grace of God, who does not impute to us our sins, but the righteousness of Christ, or rather, he imputes faith in Christ to us for righteousness. Moreover, the apostle very clearly derives love from faith when he says: "The aim of our command is love that issues from a pure heart, a good conscience, and a sincere faith" (I Tim. 1:5).[58]

The preceding quotation is very clear. Our works are rejected as relevant for justification not merely because they are done to "merit" justification or as a way of earning justification. Not just as merit, but in every respect, faith is distinguished from obedience: "we do not share in the benefit of justification partly because of the grace of God or Christ, and partly because of ourselves, our love, works or merit." Not just our merit or works, but even our evangelical love have nothing to do with our being justified. Rather, "we attribute it wholly to the grace of God in Christ through faith." Faith is, thus, distinguished not just from merit or works, but even love in its role as justifying.

---

[58]Ibid., ch. 15. [*CC* 2:487].

Sola Fide in the Reformation Confessions

This view of faith is also implied in Bullinger's understanding of the relation of James and Paul.

> Wherefore, in this matter we are not speaking of a fictitious, empty, lazy and dead faith, but of a living, quickening faith. It is and is called a living faith because it apprehends Christ who is life and makes alive, and shows that it is alive by living works. And so James does not contradict anything in this doctrine of ours. For he speaks of an empty, dead faith of which some boasted but who did not have Christ living in them by faith (James 2:14 ff.). James said that works justify, yet without contradicting the apostle (otherwise he would have to be rejected) but showing that Abraham proved his living and justifying faith by works. This all the pious do, but they trust in Christ alone and not in their own works.[59]

Bullinger makes very clear that works justify only in the sense of *showing* and *proving* that our faith is not an empty, dead faith. Works are not somehow equivalent to justifying faith for James. The righteous do good works not as their faith, but as the proof of their faith. "This all the pious do, but they trust in Christ alone and not in their own works."

All of this emphasis on the passivity of faith and the distinction between faith and obedience might seem to be undermined by the next statement of Bullinger.

> The same apostle calls faith efficacious and active through love (Gal. 5:6). It also quiets the conscience and opens a free access to God, so that we may draw near to him with confidence and may obtain from him what is useful and necessary. The same [faith] keeps us in the service we owe to God and our neighbor, strengthens our patience in adversity, fashions and makes a true confession, and in a word, brings forth good fruit of all kinds, and good works.[60]

Such a statement might seem to raise questions about the view of faith previously expounded by Bullinger himself. It is to be noticed, however, that this statement occurs in the chapter on good works (entitled "Of Faith and Good Works, and of Their Reward, and of Man's Merit")—not in the chapter on justification. It is also followed by the words: "These same works ought not to be done in order that we may earn eternal life

---

[59] Ibid., ch. 15. [*CC* 2:488].
[60] Ibid., ch. 16. [*CC* 2:489].

by them, for, as the apostle says, eternal life is the gift of God."[61] They are also followed by this paragraph.

> Nevertheless, as was said above, we do not think that we are saved by good works, and that they are so necessary for salvation that no one was ever saved without them. For we are saved by grace and the favor of Christ alone. Works necessarily proceed from faith. And salvation is improperly attributed to them, but is most properly ascribed to grace. The apostle's sentence is well known: "If it is by grace, then it is no longer of works; otherwise grace would no longer be grace. But if it is of works, then it is no longer grace, because otherwise work is no longer work" (Rom. 11:6).[62]

It is not justifying faith, then, that is described in the above paragraph, but the works that proceed from such faith. All the activities mentioned in the preceding paragraph are not justifying faith, but the works that proceed from it.

- **The Dichotomy between Law and Gospel**

In light of contemporary attempts to contrast the Reformed and Lutheran traditions on the dichotomy between law and gospel,[63] it is striking that no great distinction is found between the view of law and gospel in the Lutheran Confessions and that found in the *Second Helvetic Confession*. In the following quotations, Bullinger makes crystal clear that he held substantially the same contrast or dichotomy that is presented in the Lutheran documents already considered.

> We teach that this law was not given to men that they might be justified by keeping it, but that rather from what it teaches we may know (our) weakness, sin and condemnation, and, despairing of our strength, might be converted to Christ in faith. For the letter, which is opposed to the Spirit, signifies everything external, but especially the doctrine of the law which, without the Spirit and faith, works wrath and provokes sin in the minds of those who do not have a living faith. The law was not

---

[61] Ibid., ch. 16. [*CC* 2:489].
[62] Ibid., ch. 16. [*CC* 2:490].
[63] See Doug Wilson, "A Pauline Take on the New Perspective," *Credenda Agenda* 15, no. 5 (Winter 2003), 5-21; Norman Shepherd, "Justification by Faith Alone," *Reformation and Revival Journal* 2, no. 2 (Spring 2002), 75-89; and Andrew Sandlin, "Lutheranized Calvinism: *Gospel* or *Law*, or *Gospel* and *Law*," *The Reformation and Revival Journal* 11, no. 2 (Spring 2002), 123-135.

given that by keeping it we might be justified. It is the letter which works wrath . . . For no flesh could or can satisfy the law of God and fulfill it, because of the weakness in our flesh which adheres and remains in us until our last breath. For the apostle says again: "God has done what the law, weakened by the flesh, could not do: sending his own Son in the likeness of sinful flesh and for sin" (Rom. 8:3). Therefore, Christ is the perfecting of the law and our fulfilment of it (Rom. 10:4), who, in order to take away the curse of the law, was made a curse for us (Gal. 3:13). Thus he imparts to us through faith his fulfillment of the law, and his righteousness and obedience are imputed to us.[64]

That same preaching of the Gospel is also called by the apostle "the spirit" and "the ministry of the spirit" because by faith it becomes effectual and living in the ears, nay more, in the hearts of believers through the illumination of the Holy Spirit (II Cor. 3:6). For the letter, which is opposed to the Spirit, signifies everything external, but especially the doctrine of the law which, without the Spirit and faith, works wrath and provokes sin in the minds of those who do not have a living faith. For this reason the apostle calls it "the ministry of death." In this connection the saying of the apostle is pertinent: "The letter kills, but the Spirit gives life." And false apostles preached a corrupted Gospel, having combined it with the law, as if Christ could not save without the law.[65]

In the paragraphs just cited the dichotomy between the righteousness of the law and the righteousness of the gospel by imputed righteousness is also stated. The contrast between these two righteousnesses can only be maintained by means of some dichotomy between law and gospel. It is reiterated in several clear statements about imputed righteousness in the Confession's chapter on justification. We learn from the following quotations that the righteousness of the law consists in our obedience to it. The righteousness of justification consists in our being forgiven for our sins against it and in having the obedience of Christ to it imputed to us. Here again is a clear contrast between law and gospel.

According to the apostle in his treatment of justification, to justify means to remit sins, to absolve from guilt and punishment, to receive into favor, and to pronounce a man just. . .

---

[64] *Second Helvetic Confession*, ch. 12. [*CC* 2:480].
[65] Ibid., ch. 13. [*CC* 2:482].

Now it is most certain that all of us are by nature sinners and godless, and before God's judgment-seat are convicted of godlessness and are guilty of death, but that, solely by the grace of Christ and not from any merit of ours or consideration for us, we are justified, that is, absolved from sin and death by God the Judge. . . .

For Christ took upon himself and bore the sins of the world, and satisfied divine justice. Therefore, solely on account of Christ's sufferings and resurrection God is propitious with respect to our sins and does not impute them to us, but imputes Christ's righteousness to us as our own (II Cor. 5:19 ff.; Rom. 4:25), so that now we are not only cleansed and purged from sins or are holy, but also, granted the righteousness of Christ, and so absolved from sin, death and condemnation, are at last righteous and heirs of eternal life. Properly speaking, therefore, God alone justifies us, and justifies only on account of Christ, not imputing sins to us but imputing his righteousness to us. . . .[66]

The Second Helvetic Confession clearly continues the view of justification *sola fide* taught by the Reformers and in the Lutheran Confessions.

The Gallican Confession, A. D. 1559

- **Historical Introduction**

In coming to *The Gallican Confession*, we make a slight regression in time, but a slight progression in the development of Reformation thought. This is justification enough, perhaps, for the order of its treatment. Here we meet for the first time the decisive influence of Calvin. Though Bullinger and *The Second Helvetic Confession* show the influence of Calvin, they nevertheless owe Zwingli and the Lutheran Reformation a great debt. In *The French Confession of Faith* (*Confessio Fidei Gallicana*) we come to Calvin's homeland and the church beloved to him, over which he exercised so much influence.

The Gallican Confession is the work of John Calvin, who prepared the first draft, and of his pupil, Antonie de la Roche Chandieu, who, with the Synod of Paris in 1559, brought it into its present enlarged shape.[67]

---

[66]Ibid., ch. 15. [*CC* 2:486-487].
[67]Ibid.,, 1:493.

The Gallican Confession explicitly affirms justification *sola fide* in paragraph 20.[68] The English translation given here is that provided by Schaff.[69]

- **The Definition of Justifying Faith**

A number of testimonies can be brought forward to illustrate the passive view of justifying faith assumed by Calvin throughout this Confession. In the following quotations the favorite synonym for justifying faith is resting. (See the first and third quotations below.) Calvin's emphasis on faith as a "passive work"—a human activity that, though volitional, is passive in its essence—is interestingly brought out by the language of the first quotation ("till we resolve to be loved in Jesus Christ."). This same volitional emphasis may be found in the language of *appropriating the promises of life* "when we accept them" in the second quotation. The same quotation has Calvin's most characteristic language when it describes faith as assurance ("being assured that we are established by the Word of God and shall not be deceived."). In the last of the four quotations cited below, faith is likened to an empty vessel that is filled with Christ at the Lord's Table.

> We therefore reject all other means of justification before God, and without claiming any virtue or merit, we rest simply in the obedience of Jesus Christ, which is imputed to us as much to blot out all our sins as to make us find grace and favor in the sight of God. And, in fact, we believe that in falling away from this foundation, however slightly, we could not find rest elsewhere, but should always be troubled. Forasmuch as we are never at peace with God till we resolve to be loved in Jesus Christ, for of ourselves we are worthy of hatred.[70]

> And this is done inasmuch as we appropriate to our use the promises of life which are given to us through him, and feel their effect when we accept them, being assured that we are established by the Word of God and shall not be deceived. Thus our justification through faith depends upon the free promises by which God declares and testifies his love to us.[71]

---

[68] Ibid., 3:370. [*CC* 2:380]. *The Gallican Confession*, Paragraph XX.
[69] Ibid., 3:356, where this translation is introduced. The English translation occurs in parallel with the French original.
[70] *The Creeds of Christendom*, 3:370. [*CC* 2:380]. *The Gallican Confession*, Paragraph XVIII.
[71] Ibid., 3:371. [*CC* 2:380]. *The Gallican Confession*, Paragraph XX.

> . . . for we should always be doubting and restless in our hearts, if we did not rest upon the atonement by which Jesus Christ has acquitted us.[72]

> And thus all who bring a pure faith, like a vessel, to the sacred table of Christ, receive truly that of which it is a sign; for the body and the blood of Jesus Christ give food and drink to the soul, no less than bread and wine nourish the body.[73]

- **The Distinction between Justifying Faith and Evangelical Obedience**

Faith is clearly distinguished from obedience in *The Gallican Confession*.

> We therefore reject all other means of justification before God, and without claiming any virtue or merit, we rest simply in the obedience of Jesus Christ, which is imputed to us as much to blot out all our sins as to make us find grace and favor in the sight of God.[74]

Here faith is contrasted with claiming "any virtue or merit." Note that it is not just merit with which resting on Christ is contrasted, but also *any virtue*. This distinction between faith and even "the newness of life" wrought by regeneration is patent in the following citation as well. If "by this faith we are regenerated in newness of life," then justifying faith is clearly not viewed as simply the commencement of evangelical obedience.

> We believe that by this faith we are regenerated in newness of life, being by nature subject to sin. Now we receive by faith grace to live holily and in the fear of God, in accepting the promise which is given to us by the Gospel, namely: that God will give us his Holy Spirit. This faith not only does not hinder us from holy living, or turn us from the love of righteousness, but of necessity begets in us all good works.[75]

---

[72] Ibid., 3:372. [*CC* 2:381]. *The Gallican Confession*, Paragraph XXII.
[73] Ibid., 3:381. [*CC* 2:385]. *The Gallican Confession*, Paragraph XXXVII.
[74] Ibid., 3:370. [*CC* 2:380]. *The Gallican Confession*, Paragraph XVIII.
[75] Ibid., 3:372. [*CC* 2:381]. *The Gallican Confession*, Paragraph XXII.

- **The Dichotomy between Law and Gospel**

There are no extensive statements of the dichotomy between the law and gospel in *The Gallican Confession*.[76] The contrast between the righteousness of the law and the righteousness of the gospel is, however, suggested when Calvin insists that the righteousness of the gospel consists—not in our obedience to the law, but—in the forgiveness of our sins against it.

> We believe that all our justification rests upon the remission of our sins, in which also is our only blessedness, as says the Psalmist (Psa. 32:2). We therefore reject all other means of justification before God, and without claiming any virtue or merit, we rest simply in the obedience of Jesus Christ, which is imputed to us as much to blot out all our sins as to make us find grace and favor in the sight of God.[77]

The same view of *faith alone* as in the previous Confessions we have examined is held forth in *The Gallican Confession*. Though there is perhaps a briefer statement of the dichotomy between law and gospel, there is the same definition of justifying faith and distinction between justifying faith and evangelical obedience that we have observed before.

The Heidelberg Catechism, A. D. 1563

- **Historical Introduction**

The Heidelberg Catechism was the product of the dual authorship of Zacharius Ursinus and Caspar Olevianus. It combines dogmatic precision and spiritual warmth. Perhaps for this reason, it is one of the most widely regarded Reformed symbols. Says Schaff:

> As a standard of public doctrine the Heidelberg Catechism is the most catholic and popular of all the Reformed symbols. The German Reformed church acknowledges no other.[78]

---

[76]There is found, however, a typically Calvinistic assertion of the third use of the law for the ruling of our lives: *The Creeds of Christendom*, 3:372-73. [CC 2:381]. *The Gallican Confession*, Paragraph XXIII.

[77]*The Creeds of Christendom*, 3:370. [CC 2:380]. *The Gallican Confession*, Paragraph XVIII.

[78]Ibid., 1:540. See Schaff's extensive and extolling introduction on pp. 529-554 of the same volume.

Both in Question and Answer 61 and in Question and Answer 65 *The Heidelberg Catechism* affirms *sola fide* in so many words. The text used below is from the Christian Classics Ethereal Library.[79]

- **The Definition of Justifying Faith**

Faith is directly defined and in terms familiar to us from Calvin's formal definition in the *Institutes*.

> Question 21. What is true faith? Answer: True faith is not only a certain knowledge, whereby I hold for truth all that God has revealed to us in his word, but also an assured confidence, which the Holy Ghost works by the gospel in my heart; that not only to others, but to me also, remission of sin, everlasting righteousness and salvation, are freely given by God, merely of grace, only for the sake of Christ's merits.[80]

This more formal definition of faith in terms of assurance of our salvation through God's promises is supplemented by the description of faith given in the question intended to define the meaning of justification by faith alone. Justifying faith is again in the following citation described in passive, though more volitional, terms as receiving and applying Christ to ourselves.

> Question 61. Why sayest thou, that thou art righteous by faith only? Answer: Not that I am acceptable to God, on account of the worthiness of my faith; but because only the satisfaction, righteousness, and holiness of Christ, is my righteousness before God; and that I cannot receive and apply the same to myself any other way than by faith only.[81]

---

[79]*The Heidelberg Catechism*. [on-line]; accessed 1 November 2004; available from www.reformed.org/documents/heidelberg.html. This is an HTML adaptation of the e-text version provided by "The Christian Classsics Ethereal Library" (CCEL). The text version is located at www.ccel.org/creeds/heidelberg-cat-ext.txt. See www.reformed.org/documents/heidelberg.html. *The Creeds of Christendom*, 3:307-355, contains an introduction to Schaff's text and also an English translation in parallel with the original German.

[80]*The Heidelberg Catechism*, Question and Answer 21. [*CC* 2:432].

[81]Ibid., Question and Answer 61. [*CC* 2:440].

- **The Distinction between Justifying Faith and Evangelical Obedience**

The distinction between faith and obedience is made clear first in Question and Answer 60. Faith is juxtaposed with an accusing conscience. Both may exist at the same time. If it coexists with a consciousness of disobedience to the commands of God, justifying faith is clearly not equivalent to obedience to the commands of God.

Furthermore, this question and answer attribute to faith such a righteousness "as if I had fully accomplished all that obedience which Christ has accomplished for me." Faith never renders personally such a perfect obedience and cannot be, therefore, equivalent to obedience. It must be distinct from obedience.

> Question 60. How are thou righteous before God? Answer: Only by a true faith in Jesus Christ; so that, though my conscience accuse me, that I have grossly transgressed all the commandments of God, and kept none of them, and am still inclined to all evil; notwithstanding, God, without any merit of mine, but only of mere grace, grants and imputes to me, the perfect satisfaction, righteousness and holiness of Christ; even so, as if I never had had, nor committed any sin: yea, as if I had fully accomplished all that obedience which Christ has accomplished for me; inasmuch as I embrace such benefit with a believing heart.

This distinction between faith and obedience is confirmed by Question and Answer 64. Here we meet the typical objection that justification by faith must make men careless and profane. If justifying faith were equivalent to obedience, such an objection could never arise. Here we also meet the typical Protestant response to such an objection. Faith, though distinct from obedience, by implanting men in Christ results in evangelical obedience.

> Question 64. But does not this doctrine make men careless and profane? Answer: By no means: for it is impossible that those, who are implanted into Christ by a true faith, should not bring forth fruits of thankfulness.

- **The Dichotomy between Law and Gospel**

The dichotomy between law and gospel becomes visible, first, in the Catechism's contrast between our corrupt nature "against which I have to struggle all my life long" and "the righteousness of Christ." Since the

Catechism clearly requires a perfect righteousness to be justified before God,[82] this righteousness cannot be the imperfect righteousness that results from the righteousness infused into us through regeneration. Clearly, also, there is a contrast instituted between the perfect righteousness required by the law which we lack in ourselves and the perfect righteousness provided by the gospel which we have by faith in Christ.

> Question 56. What believest thou concerning "the forgiveness of sins"? Answer: That God, for the sake of Christ's satisfaction, will no more remember my sins, neither my corrupt nature, against which I have to struggle all my life long; but will graciously impute[83] to me the righteousness of Christ, that I may never be condemned before the tribunal of God.[84]

> Question 62. But why cannot our good works be the whole, or part of our righteousness before God? Answer: Because, that the righteousness, which can be approved of before the tribunal of God, must be absolutely perfect, and in all respects conformable to the divine law; and also, that our best works in this life are all imperfect and defiled with sin.[85]

---

[82]Ibid., Questions and Answers 5, 10, and 62. [*CC* 2:430, 431, 441].

[83]In place of *will graciously impute* the English text given by Schaff has *graciously imparts*. *CC* 2:439 also reads *graciously imparts*. Both *impute* and *impart* are theologically loaded words within the context of the debate between Roman Catholics and Protestants over justification. They have starkly different implications. Thus, the difference in translation is quite significant. The German word here translated in such divergent ways is *schenket* from the verb, *schenken* which means to give, bestow, or award. Thus, the Catechism actually speaks of God giving or bestowing the righteousness of Christ. One can see from this how the two variant translations arose. Yet both translations, *impute* and *impart*, are misleading and defective. *Impute*, though it correctly represents the intention of the language, gives a too specific meaning for a word that simply means *give*. *Impart* may convey the idea of infused righteousness to theologically sensitive minds. Since the idea intended is likely the gift of imputed righteousness, the translation *impart* is also misleading. A better translation would avoid both *impute* and *impart* and simply translate with the word *give*.

[84]*The Heidelberg Catechism*, Question and Answer 56. [*CC* 2:439].

[85]Ibid., Question and Answer 62. [*CC* 2:441].

The Belgic Confession, A. D. 1561

- **Historical Introduction**

Guido de Bres constructed *The Belgic Confession* in 1561 with the assistance of several others. It became the acknowledged Confession of the Reformed Churches of Holland and Belgium, being adopted several times by national synods in the later sixteenth and early seventeenth century, including the Synod of Dort in 1619. Schaff judges, "It is, upon the whole, the best symbolical statement of the Calvinistic system of doctrine, with the exception of *The Westminster Confession*."[86]

The textual history of *The Belgic Confession* is helpfully discussed by Schaff,[87] but the variants and developments of the text do not seem to effect the conclusions of this study. The English text used here is the one provided by Schaff. *The Belgic Confession* clearly affirms justification by faith alone, but only uses these exact words one time.[88]

- **The Definition of Justifying Faith**

The following testimonies speak to the definition of faith found in this Confession.

The passive character of justifying faith is clearly indicated by the descriptive words used of it in these citations. Justifying faith according to these paragraphs *embraces, appropriates, relies on, rests in, receives*, and *takes refuge in* Christ. Though these words certainly speak of faith as volitional (and in that sense a human activity), they clearly indicate as well that the core *activity* of faith is passive in character. Supplementing these descriptions of faith is the characterization of faith as the instrument of justification. It "is only an instrument with which we embrace Christ our Righteousness. . . . And faith is an instrument that keeps us in communion with him in all his benefits." The effect of describing faith as an *instrument* is to make clear that the role of faith in justification is only to connect us with Christ and His righteousness and bring nothing else to justification. It is not faith as virtue, merit, or incipient obedience, but only as an *instrument* bringing us into union with Christ that faith has any significance for our justification.[89]

---

[86] *The Creeds of Christendom*, 1:506.
[87] Ibid., 1:506-508; 3:383. See *CC* 2:405-406.
[88] Ibid., 3:408. [*CC* 2:416]. *The Belgic Confession*, Article XXII.
[89] So far as I can tell, this is the first place in the Reformed Confessions that faith is

We believe that, to attain the true knowledge of this great mystery, the Holy Ghost kindleth in our hearts an upright faith, which embraces Jesus Christ, with all his merits, appropriates him, and seeks nothing more besides him. . . . Therefore we justly say with Paul, that we are justified by faith alone, or by faith without works. However, to speak more clearly, we do not mean, that faith itself justifies us, for it is only an instrument with which we embrace Christ our Righteousness. But Jesus Christ, imputing to us all his merits and so many holy works which he has done for us, and in our stead, is our Righteousness. And faith is an instrument that keeps us in communion with him in all his benefits, which, when become ours, are more than sufficient to acquit us of our sins.[90]

And therefore we always hold fast this foundation, ascribing all the glory to God, humbling ourselves before him, and acknowledging ourselves to be such as we really are, without presuming to trust in any thing in ourselves, or in any merit of ours, relying and resting upon the obedience of Christ crucified alone, which becomes ours, when we believe in him.[91]

With respect to those, who are members of the Church, they may be known by the marks of Christians: namely, by faith; and when they have received Jesus Christ the only Saviour. . . . But this is not to be understood, as if there did not remain in them great infirmities; but they fight against them through the Spirit, all the days of their life, continually taking their refuge in the blood, death, passion and obedience of our Lord Jesus Christ.[92]

- **The Distinction between Justifying Faith and Evangelical Obedience**

Article XXIV of *The Belgic Confession* entitled, "Of Man's Sanctification and Good Works," repeats many of the themes with which we are now familiar from this survey. Good works are the inevitable result and mark of justifying faith. Thus, it is not true that justification *sola fide* makes men negligent to lead a holy life. Such works are only

---

characterized as an instrument. The French is *l'instrument*. *The Westminster Confession* (11:2) and Larger Catechism (Question 73) also utilize this term. *The Formula of Concord* uses the term in Article III. See *Creeds of Christendom*, 3:116; *CC* 2:176.

[90]*The Creeds of Christendom*, 3:407-408. [*CC* 2:416]. *The Belgic Confession*, Article XXII.

[91]Ibid., 3:409. [*CC* 2:416-417]. *The Belgic Confession*, Article XXIII.

[92]Ibid., 3:420. [*CC* 2:420]. *The Belgic Confession*, Article XXIX.

acceptable to God because they proceed from faith and are purified by grace. We do good works not to merit something by them, but because God works them in us. God rewards good works, but it is only grace crowning His own gifts. In all this the distinction between faith and obedience is certainly implied. In one statement, however, this distinction rings out as clear as a bell.

> For it is by faith in Christ that we are justified, even before we do good works; otherwise they could not be good works, any more than the fruit of a tree can be good, before the tree itself is good.[93]

Clearly, if we are justified by faith before we do good works, faith is here viewed as distinct from good works. No statement could more emphatically express the difference between faith and good works in Reformation theology.

- **The Dichotomy between Law and Gospel**

In conformity with what we have observed in the Reformed Confessions flowing from Calvin's influence[94] considered so far, there is no explicit or programmatic assertion of the contrast between law and gospel like that found, for instance, in *The Formula of Concord*. In Article XXV, "Of the Abolishing of the Ceremonial Law," there is merely the notation of the third use of the law to "regulate our life."[95]

Nevertheless, the clear emphasis on the necessity of an imputed righteousness provided by Christ is everywhere in implicit contrast to that righteousness of the law that we are unable to provide. Thus, the article on justification begins with the words:

> We believe that our salvation consists in the remission of our sins for Jesus Christ's sake, and that therein our righteousness before God is implied: as David and Paul teach us, declaring this to be the happiness of man, that God imputes righteousness to him without works.[96]

---

[93] Ibid., 3:411. [*CC* 2:417]. *The Belgic Confession*, Article XXIV.

[94] As noted previously, the *Second Helvetic Confession* was written by Bullinger, shows a strong Lutheran influence, and is substantially pre-Calvin in character, if not in date. Thus, the fact that this "Reformed" Confession has a more explicit statement of the law-gospel dichotomy is consistent with what we have observed here about the relatively low profile this dichotomy has in the Reformed Confessions flowing from Calvin.

[95] Ibid., 3:413. [*CC* 2:417-418]. *The Belgic Confession*, Article XXV.

[96] Ibid., 3:409. [*CC* 2:416-417]. *The Belgic Confession*, Article XXIII.

It is interesting to note a reference to Adam later in this paragraph that is at least suggestive with regard to the development of the idea of the covenant of works that will become visible in later Reformed Confessions.

> This is sufficient to cover our iniquities, and to give us confidence in approaching to God; freeing the conscience of fear, terror and dread, without following the example of our first father, Adam, who, trembling, attempted to cover himself with fig-leaves. And verily if we should appear before God, relying on ourselves, or on any other creature, though ever so little, we should, alas! be consumed. And therefore every one must pray with David: O Lord, enter not into judgment with thy servant: for in thy sight shall no man living be justified.[97]

Thus, in *The Belgic Confession* the same themes that mark the Reformers' understanding of *sola fide* continue unabated and unaltered.

The First Scottish Confession, A. D. 1560

- **Historical Introduction**

Dating from almost the same period as all the Reformed Confessions we have so far considered is the *First Scottish Confession*. It was penned somewhat hastily by John Knox and his compatriots at the urgent request of the Scottish Parliament. Through Knox it bears the impress of Calvin's thought. It does not expressly or verbally affirm *sola fide*, but there is no reason to doubt (as we will see from the evidence) that Knox held this doctrine. It must be acknowledged, however, that he and his fellow-workers seem most concerned to emphasize the sovereignty of God in salvation and the necessity of good works as the indispensable mark of saving faith. Thus, the testimony of this Confession to justification *sola fide* is relatively brief in most respects. The text used here is an updated English text based word-for-word on the old English of the text given in Schaff.[98]

---

[97]Ibid., 3:409. [*CC* 2:416-417]. *The Belgic Confession*, Article XXIII.
[98]Ibid., 3:437-479. The updated English version I will cite is *The Scottish Confession of Faith* (Dallas: Presbyterian Heritage Publications, 1993 and 1995), accessed 12 November, 2004, www.swrb.com/newslett/actualNLs/ScotConf.html

Sola Fide in the Reformation Confessions

- **The Definition of Justifying Faith**

In terms that are quite familiar by now, justifying faith is described as being given "grace to acknowledge and embrace him[99] as our only Mediator."[100] Similarly, we read, "Our faith and its assurance do not proceed from flesh and blood."[101] Faith is here closely related to assurance. It is also identified as a receiving of Christ.

> For as soon as the Spirit of the Lord Jesus, whom God's chosen children receive by true faith, takes possession of the heart of any man, so soon does he regenerate and renew him.[102]

- **The Distinction between Justifying Faith and Evangelical Obedience**

While implied (as the immediately foregoing quotation makes clear) and certainly not denied, the distinction between faith and obedience is somewhat obscured by the urgency with which Knox and his fellows argue the inseparability of faith and sanctification. In the following quotation, there is perhaps the strongest affirmation of this that we have so far discovered.

> The cause of good works, we confess, is not our free will, but the Spirit of the Lord Jesus, who dwells in our hearts by true faith, brings forth such works as God has prepared for us to walk in. *For we most boldly affirm that it is blasphemy to say that Christ abides in the hearts of those in whom is no spirit of sanctification.* Therefore we do not hesitate to affirm that murderers, oppressors, cruel persecutors, adulterers, filthy persons, idolaters, drunkards, thieves, and all workers of iniquity, have neither true faith nor anything of the Spirit of the Lord Jesus, so long as they obstinately continue in wickedness.[103]

Even in this clear and bold statement of the necessity of a godly life in order to be thought to have faith, the evangelical order remains clear. "The cause of good works, we confess, is not our free will, but the Spirit of the Lord Jesus, who dwells in our hearts by true faith, brings forth

---

[99]The antecedent of "him" is Christ.
[100]*The Scottish Confession of Faith*, Article VIII. [*CC* 2:392].
[101]Ibid., Article XII. [*CC* 2:394].
[102]Ibid., Article XIII. [*CC* 2:395].
[103]Ibid., Article XIII. [*CC* 2:395]. The emphasis is mine.

such works." The Spirit (first) produces faith which (second) unites us to Christ who by His Spirit now (third) dwells in our hearts and as a consequence (fourth) produces good works.

- **The Dichotomy between Law and Gospel**

A bit surprisingly, considering what we have seen so far in Confessions that bear the influence of Calvin, the contrast between law and gospel is laid out at great length and with great clarity. It is true that a handle for misunderstanding may be found in the words, "he accepts our imperfect obedience as if it were perfect," but the framers of the Confession do not mean that our justifying righteousness is found in this *imperfect obedience*—even when it is cleansed by the blood of Christ. The point of the framers is clearly that, because we are already perfectly clean and righteous in Christ, God *also* graciously accepts our attempts to obey Him. Article 15, "The Perfection of the Law and The Imperfection of Man," is here quoted in its entirety.

> We confess and acknowledge that the law of God is most just, equal, holy, and perfect, commanding those things which, when perfectly done, can give life and bring man to eternal felicity; but our nature is so corrupt, weak, and imperfect, that we are never able perfectly to fulfill the works of the law. Even after we are reborn, if we say that we have no sin, we deceive ourselves and the truth of God is not in us. It is therefore essential for us to lay hold on Christ Jesus, in his righteousness and his atonement, since he is the end and consummation of the Law and since it is by him that we are set at liberty so that the curse of God may not fall upon us, even though we do not fulfill the Law in all points. For as God the Father beholds us in the body of his Son Christ Jesus, he accepts our imperfect obedience as if it were perfect, and covers our works, which are defiled with many stains, with the righteousness of his Son. We do not mean that we are so set at liberty that we owe no obedience to the Law—for we have already acknowledged its place—but we affirm that no man on earth, with the sole exception of Christ Jesus, has given, gives, or shall give in action that obedience to the Law which the Law requires. When we have done all things we must fall down and unfeignedly confess that we are unprofitable servants. Therefore, whoever boasts of the merits of his own works or puts his trust in works of supererogation, boasts of what does not exist, and puts his trust in damnable idolatry.[104]

---

[104] Ibid., Article XV. [*CC* 2:396-397].

The Thirty-nine Articles of the Church of England, A. D. 1563

- **Historical Introduction**

The Thirty-nine Articles of the Church of England remains to this day its formal doctrinal standard. It dates from the same period as the previously considered Reformed Confessions and maintains (as we will see) the same views with regard to justification by faith alone. Schaff provides in his third column the text of the 1801 American Revision of these articles.[105] Since it has modern English spellings and contains no changes that alter its meaning for our purposes,[106] it is that text which will be cited. *Sola fide* is explicitly affirmed in Article XI.[107]

The relevant statements are quite brief and are found in Articles XI and XII which I now quote in their entirety.

> XI. Of the Justification of Man.
> We are accounted righteous before God, only for the merit of our Lord and Saviour Jesus Christ by Faith, and not for our own works or deservings. Wherefore, that we are justified by Faith only, is a most wholesome Doctrine, and very full of comfort, as more largely is expressed in the Homily of Justification.
>
> XII. Of Good Works.
> Albeit that Good Works, which are the fruits of Faith, and follow after Justification, cannot put away our sins, and endure the severity of God's judgment; yet are they pleasing and acceptable to God in Christ, and do spring out necessarily of a true and lively Faith insomuch that by them a lively Faith may be as evidently known as a tree discerned by the fruit.

These two brief articles are in perfect alignment with what we have seen. They do not contradict the Reformed views with which we have become familiar in this study. Little is said directly about the definition of justifying faith, except that it forms no part of the ground of our justification. Little is said about the dichotomy between law and gospel, though this contrast is certainly in the background of Article XI. A clear distinction is asserted between justifying faith and evangelical obedience.

---

[105] *The Creeds of Christendom*, 3:486-516.

[106] Schaff, *The Creeds of Christendom*, 1:649-654, discusses these revisions.

[107] *The Creeds of Christendom*, 3:494. *The Scottish Confession of Faith*, Article XIII. [CC 2:531]. *The Thirty-nine Articles*, Article XI.

Faith is said to logically precede justification and good works to succeed it. We "are justified *by* Faith only." "Good works . . . are the *fruits* of Faith, and *follow after* Justification." (Emphasis mine.)

With *The Thirty-nine Articles* we conclude our survey of the intense period of Reformed confessional development that coincided with the close of Calvin's life and ministry. The remaining Reformed Confessions take us forward 50-100 years.

The Irish Articles, A. D. 1615

- **Historical Introduction**

The so-called *Irish Articles of Religion* were adopted in 1615 by the Protestant clergy of Ireland as the doctrinal basis of the Protestant church of that island. Their author was one of the most renowned scholars of his day and later the Archbishop of Armagh, James Ussher, who is best known today for his chronology of the Bible. Ussher was, in fact, elected to serve in the Westminster Assembly, but refrained because of his commitment to the cause of crown and episcopacy. In character, these Articles reflect Calvinism and Puritanism with the exception of their support of the ecclesiastical supremacy of the crown. The importance of the *Irish Articles* (which because of the reaction against Puritanism led by Archbishop Laud were short-lived as the doctrinal basis of the Irish Protestant church) is the way in which they anticipate the climactic expression of Reformed confessionalism found in *The Westminster Confession*. Says Schaff:

> They were the chief basis of the Westminster Confession, as is evident from the general order, the headings of chapters and subdivisions, and the almost literal agreement of language in the statement of several of the most important doctrines.[108]

The Irish Articles are arranged in 104 consecutively numbered articles under 19 headings.[109] They explicitly affirm that we are justified by faith alone twice.[110]

---

[108] Ibid., 1:665.
[109] The text used here is the one given by Schaff. *The Creeds of Christendom*, 3:526-544. For the sake of simplicity I will cite the volume and page numbers in Schaff and the number of the article being cited without giving the heading number.
[110] *The Creeds of Christendom*, 3:533. [CC 2:558-559]. Both occurrences are in the

The Definition of Justifying Faith

The Irish Articles provide clear and repeated testimonies to justifying faith as a passive work. In the following paragraph faith is described as *applying, receiving,* and *embracing* Christ. It is not in itself, nor as a matter of its own virtue or obedience, that it justifies.

> We are accounted righteous before God, only for the merit of our Lord and Saviour Jesus Christ, applied by faith; and not for our own works or merits. And this righteousness, which we so receive of God's mercy and Christ's merits, embraced by faith, is taken, accepted, and allowed of God for our perfect and full justification.[111]

The nature of justifying faith is addressed specifically later in these Articles. In the article about to be quoted both the intellectual and volitional character of faith is stressed, but it remains a "passive work" that has for its core activity not only *belief, persuasion,* and *assurance,* but also *particular application of the gratuitous promises of the Gospel, laying hold of Christ,* and *an earnest trust and confidence.*

> By justifying Faith we understand not only the common belief of the Articles of Christian Religion, and a persuasion of the truth of God's word in general: but also a particular application of the gratuitous promises of the Gospel, to the comfort of our own souls: whereby we lay hold on Christ with all his benefits, having an earnest trust and confidence in God that he will be merciful unto us for his only Son's sake. So that a true believer may be certain, by the assurance of faith, of the forgiveness of his sins, and of his everlasting salvation by Christ.[112]

The Distinction between Justifying Faith and Evangelical Obedience

This definition of faith as essentially passive is exhibited with unusual clarity in the distinction between faith and obedience found in *The Irish Articles*. At the simplest level, this distinction is found in the assertion that "All that are justified are likewise sanctified: their faith being always accompanied with true Repentance and good Works."[113] Faith is

---

same article, *Irish Articles*, Article 36.
[111] Ibid., 3:532. [*CC* 2:558]. *Irish Articles*, Article 34.
[112] Ibid., 3:533-34. [*CC* 2:559]. *Irish Articles*, Article 37.
[113] Ibid., 3:534. [*CC* 2:559]. *Irish Articles*, Article 39.

accompanied by good works and is, therefore, not identical with or equivalent to such acts of obedience.

This distinction is also clear from the now familiar assertion that good works are the fruits of faith and justification. Since faith is *unto* justification and good works *follow* justification, they are clearly distinct.

> Albeit that good works, which are the fruits of faith and follow after justification, cannot make satisfaction for our sins, and endure the severity of God's judgement: yet are they pleasing to God, and accepted of him in Christ, and do spring from a true and lively faith, which by them is to be discerned as a tree by the fruit.[114]

The clearest assertion of this distinction is, however, not yet before us. This is found in Article 36. Though the Article is lengthy, it deserves quotation in its entirety.

> When we say that we are justified by faith only, we do not mean that the said justifying faith is alone in man, without true Repentance, Hope, Charity, and the fear of God (for such a faith is dead, and cannot justify), neither do we mean that this our act to believe in Christ, nor this our faith in Christ, which is within us, doth of itself justifie us, nor deserve our justification unto us (for that were to account ourselves to be justified by the virtue or dignity of some thing that is within ourselves): but the true understanding and meaning thereof is that although we have Faith, Hope, Charitie, Repentance, and the fear of God within us and add never so many good works thereunto: yet we must renounce the merit of all our said virtues, of Faith, Hope, Charitie, and all our other virtues, and good deeds, which we either have done, shall do, or can do, as things that be far too weak and imperfect, and insufficient to deserve remission of our sins, and our justification: and therefore we must trust only in God's mercy, and the merits of his most dearly beloved Son, our only Redeemer, Saviour, and Justifier, Jesus Christ. Nevertheless, because Faith doth directly send us to Christ for our justification, and that by faith given us of God we embrace the promise of God's mercy, and the remission of our sin (which thing none other of our virtues or works properly doth): therefore the Scripture saith, that Faith without works; and the ancient fathers of the Church to the same purpose, that only Faith doth justify us.[115]

---

[114] Ibid., 3:534. [*CC* 2:559-560]. *Irish Articles*, Article 41.
[115] Ibid., 3:533. [*CC* 2:558-559]. *Irish Articles*, Article 36.

This is a remarkable statement of the distinction maintained by the Reformers between faith and obedience. As we will see, current evangelicals sometimes argue that, while the idea of merit has no place in the doctrinal system of the Bible, other kinds of works may be thought as justifying. They go on to assert that, when faith is set against merit in Reformation theology, a false dichotomy is set up because the Bible never considers that men can merit anything from God. Whether this is true or not, statements like the one just quoted show that faith is not just set over against meritorious works. Faith is also distinguished from "the virtue or dignity of some thing that is within ourselves." Faith does not justify because of its inherently virtuous character or because of its dignity as a moral act. Faith only justifies as directly sending us to Christ for our justification. We will see that there are modern tendencies that so equate or combine faith and obedience that this distinction is destroyed.

Also important to note in the above quotation is the explicit definition of the quality in faith which makes it justifying:

> ... because Faith doth directly send us to Christ for our justification, and that by faith ... we embrace the promise of God's mercy, and the remission of our sin (which thing none other of our virtues or works properly doth): therefore the Scripture saith ... that only Faith doth justify us.[116]

- **The Dichotomy between Law and Gospel**

In the introduction to *The Irish Articles*, Schaff's comments that the *Irish Articles* prepare the way for the *Westminster Confession* and are in some sense a transitional development for it were noted. We have also noted portents of a recasting of the contrast between law and gospel in the Confessions more directly influenced by Calvin. That recasting comes to clear expression in these Articles.

> Man being at the beginning created according to the image of God (which consisted especially in the Wisdom of his mind and the true Holiness of his free will) had the covenant of the law ingrafted in his heart: whereby God did promise unto him everlasting life, upon condition that he performed entire and perfect obedience unto his Commandments, according to that measure of strength wherewith he

---

[116]Ibid., 3:533. [*CC* 2:558-559]. *Irish Articles*, Article 36.

was endued in his creation, and threatened death unto him if he did not perform the same.[117]

In this remarkable statement the contrast between law and gospel is cast in terms of a contrast between the "covenant of the law" made with man in creation and (implicitly) with the covenant of the gospel made with Christ. This contrast is made explicit in the only other use of the term, covenant, in the *Irish Articles*. This use is found in the heading that precedes Articles 29 and 30. It reads: *Of Christ, The Mediator of the Second Covenant*. It is this contrast that lies behind the teaching of imputed righteousness in these Articles[118] and that also lies behind the statement that faith is peculiarly a response to "the gratuitous promises of the Gospel."[119]

The *Irish Articles* come from a later period in Reformation confessional development. Yet it is clear that their testimony to the Reformers' view of *sola fide* is not at all diminishing. Rather than deviating from their views, the testimony to justification by faith alone is becoming fuller and clearer in each of the three perspectives that we are surveying.

The Canons of the Synod of Dort, A. D. 1619

- **Historical Introduction**

The Synod of Dort was an international gathering of Reformed leaders and has for this reason commanded wide respect. Schaff remarks:

> The Synod of Dort is the only Synod of a quasi-ecumenical character in the history of the Reformed Churches. In this respect it is even more important than the Westminster Assembly of Divines.[120]

The Canons of the Synod of Dort in 1619 were, of course, the response to (what Schaff calls) The Five Arminian Articles put forth in 1610 by the followers of Arminius. This "Remonstrance" was not directed against the doctrine of justification by faith alone, but against the Calvinistic (and Augustinian) understanding of salvation by grace

---

[117]Ibid., 3:530. [*CC* 2:556]. *Irish Articles*, Article 21.
[118]Ibid., 3:532-33. [*CC* 2:558-559]. *Irish Articles*, Article 34-36.
[119]Ibid., 3:533-534. [*CC* 2:559]. *Irish Articles*, Article 37.
[120]Ibid., 1:514.

Sola Fide in the Reformation Confessions

alone. The five articles presented the Arminian alternatives to the Reformed doctrines of absolute predestination (Article I), limited atonement (Article II), irresistible grace (Article III and IV), and the certain perseverance of true believers (Article V).[121]

We have seen that Luther's doctrine of justification by faith alone arose under the influence and in the context of his meditations on Augustine's doctrine of grace alone. At the same time, we have seen that Luther's doctrine of faith alone cannot be reduced to the Augustinian doctrine of grace alone, but embodies an advancement over Augustine and a breakthrough not plain to Augustine or clear in Augustine's doctrine of justification.

In light of this, it is not surprising that Arminianism did not lead immediately to the denial of Luther's doctrine of faith alone. At the same time, one might expect that it would *incipiently* undermine and *eventually* overthrow faith alone by its rejection of its logical foundation and historical womb–Augustine's views of grace alone. These two expectations are borne out by an examination of the documents involved.

Arminius does not seem to have rejected justification by faith alone. Nevertheless, there are constant references to and disputations about the subject in his works. These references certainly show that he used expressions that raised questions about his views of this matter.[122]

That Arminianism would exhibit an almost inevitable tendency to decline from Reformation views of justification by faith alone is not unexpected. As one of its defenders, Frederic Platt, remarks, "Theologically, Arminianism is a mediating system throughout. Its most characteristic feature is conditionalism . . . . The supreme principle of Arminianism is conditionalism."[123] This condition in Arminianism is faith (and its fruits, good works and perseverance) and is ultimately supplied by human free will. If the term 'condition' is properly defined, faith may be described as a condition of justification in Reformed

---

[121] Ibid., 3:545-549.

[122] James Arminius, *The Writings of James Arminius*, trans. James Nichols and W. R. Bagnall (Grand Rapids: Baker Book House, 1956), 1:262-263, 355-364, 595-600; 2:116-118, 499-500, 504-505. Much of the controversy surrounded Arminius' confusing statements about the meaning of "faith being counted as righteousness" in Rom 4:5. See James Buchanan, *The Doctrine of Justification* (Grand Rapids: Baker Book House, 1977), 460-461. In this classic exposition of the Reformation doctrine of justification Buchanan agrees with the above assessment: "That his sentiments were, to a large extent, in accordance with those of the Reformers, will appear from the following extracts."

[123] Platt, "Arminianism," 1:811, in *Encyclopedia of Religion and Ethics*, ed. James Hastings (New York: Charles Scribner's Sons, 1922).

theology.[124] Arminianism, however, constructs a radically different context for the understanding of faith as a condition. As we have seen at several points, the whole meaning of faith alone in Reformation theology was to exalt and protect grace alone. We noted previously the statement of the early Reformed creed, *The Second Helvetic Confession*.

> Therefore, because faith receives Christ our righteousness and attributes everything to the grace of God in Christ, on that account justification is attributed to faith, chiefly because of Christ and not therefore because it is our work. For it is the gift of God.[125]

Within the radically different system of Arminianism it was, therefore, inevitable that faith should become something more and something different than it was in the Reformed context of the sovereignty of grace.[126]

Also leading in the direction of an erosion of justification by faith alone was the Arminian view of universal atonement. There was a clear tension involved in holding at one and the same time that (1) salvation was not universal, (2) the atonement was universal, and (3) the atonement was strictly penal and substitutionary. How could some go to hell for their sins, if Christ had given a strict, penal substitution for their sins on the cross? This tension soon was resolved by the Arminian, Grotius, by the development of the governmental theory of the atonement.[127] With the jettisoning of the penal substitutionary view of the atonement, the path was smoothed toward a view that treated the evangelical obedience of faith as a graciously accepted substitute for perfect obedience to the law.

All of this being said, it is not surprising that in and around Arminianism unorthodox views of justification by faith developed. It is, furthermore, not unexpected that *The Canons of Dort* would address such developments. Note the following paragraphs in which it rejects those:

> Who teach: That the new covenant of grace, which God the Father, through the mediation of the death of Christ, made with man, does not

---

[124]Buchanan, *The Doctrine of Justification*, 380.

[125]*Second Helvetic Confession*, ch. 15.

[126]Frederic Platt, "Arminianism," shows that the tendency to deny *faith alone* is not simply logical, but actual and historical. He remarks that Dutch Arminianism later led to "the virtual rejection of the doctrines of Original Sin and imputed righteousness," 1:811.

[127]G.C. Joyce, "Grotius," in *Encyclopedia of Religion and Ethics*, ed. James Hastings (New York: Charles Scribner's Sons, 1922), 6:441-442.

herein consist that we by faith, in as much as it accepts the merits of Christ, are justified before God and saved, but in the fact that God, having revoked the demand of perfect obedience of faith, regards faith itself and the obedience of faith, although imperfect, as the perfect obedience of the law, and does esteem it worthy of the reward of eternal life through grace. For these contradict the Scriptures, being: "justified freely by his grace through the redemption that came by Christ Jesus. God presented him as a sacrifice of atonement, through faith in his blood (Rom 3:24-25)." And these proclaim, as did the wicked Socinus, a new and strange justification of man before God, against the consensus of the whole Church.[128]

These two paragraphs reaffirm the three perspectives on *sola fide* that we have been considering against incipient Arminian tendencies. *First*, the traditional definition of justifying faith as simply accepting the merits of Christ is affirmed. *Second*, the traditional distinction between justifying faith and evangelical obedience is also affirmed by denying that God "regards faith itself and the obedience of faith, although imperfect, as the perfect obedience of the law, and does esteem it worthy of the reward of eternal life through grace." The view rejected is strikingly similar to that of some, contemporary evangelicals which we will later review in this study. *Third*, in the preceding two points the dichotomy between law and gospel is implicitly affirmed.

The Canons of Dort are relevant to the subject at hand in both a general and a specific respect. Generally, they reaffirm the Augustinian view of grace alone for salvation within which context the doctrine of justification by faith alone arose. Specifically, the emergent tendency of Arminianism to characterize faith as "a new work" graciously accepted in place of obedience to the law is rejected.

The Westminster Confession of Faith, A. D. 1647 and Related Confessions and Catechisms till A. D. 1689

- **Historical Introduction**

Reformation confessional development reached its climax in the framing and promulgation of *The Westminster Confession of Faith*. The central

---

[128]*Crisis in the Reformed Churches*, ed. by Peter Y. Dejong (Grand Rapids: Reformed Fellowship Inc., 1968), 243. The statement is the Second Head, Paragraph Four. *The Canons of Dort* cited in this volume follows the official English text adopted by the Christian Reformed Church (230).

importance and doctrinal status of *The Westminster Confession* for those in the tradition of Reformation thought scarcely needs proving. Schaff eloquently states the undeniable historical fact as follows:

> It was after such antecedents, and in such surroundings, that the Westminster Assembly of Divines was called to legislate for Christian doctrine, worship, and discipline in three kingdoms. It forms the most important chapter in the ecclesiastical history of England during the seventeenth century. Whether we look at the extent or ability of the labors, or its influence upon future generations, it stands first among Protestant Councils. The Synod of Dort was indeed fully equal to it in learning and moral weight, and was more general in its composition, since it embraced delegates from nearly all Reformed Churches; while the Westminster Assembly was purely English and Scotch, and its standards even today are little known on the Continent of Europe. But the doctrinal legislation of the Synod of Dort was confined to five points at issue between Calvinism and Arminianism; the Assembly of Westminster embraced the whole field of theology, from the eternal decrees of God to the final judgment. The Canons of Dort have lost their hold upon the mother country; the Confession and Shorter Catechism of Westminster are as much used now in Anglo-Presbyterian Churches as ever, and have more vitality and influence than any other Calvinistic Confession.[129]

The historical backdrop of the calling of the Westminster Assembly in the Puritan conflict in Britain is well-known and need not be recounted here. The Assembly was composed of Puritans—all of whom embraced the Calvinistic system of doctrine. Says Schaff:

> As to doctrine, there was no serious difference among the members. They all held the Calvinistic system with more or less rigor. There were no Arminians, Pelagians, or Antinomians among them.[130]

The exception to their doctrinal unity—if it is to be counted as an exception—was in their ecclesiology. Parliament intended the Assembly to represent all phases of the Puritan movement in England. Archbishop Laud and the Arminians were, of course, excluded because they were the source of England's current turmoil. Episcopalians, Presbyterians, and Independents were invited, but many of the Episcopalians would not attend out of loyalty to the crown. The substantial result was that the

---

[129]Ibid., 1:728.
[130]Ibid., 1:732.

opinion of the vast majority of the Assembly was Presbyterian with a small minority representing Independent views.[131] These divergent views make little difference, of course, to the subject at hand. They did, however, forecast the later revisions of *The Westminster Confession* by Congregationalists and Baptists.

The Westminster Assembly sat for over five years (1643-1649).[132] The Confession was completed in the final days of 1646 and submitted to Parliament. It is variously dated from 1646-1648, depending on which of several events is chosen to mark its origin.[133]

The Westminster Assembly also constructed a Shorter and Larger Catechism. *The Westminster Shorter Catechism* exercised an influence equal or superior to *The Heidelberg Catechism*.

The growth of Calvinistic Independency in England led to two revisions of *The Westminster Confession*. *The Savoy Declaration of Faith* is a revision of *The Westminster Confession* that had great, though brief, authority among English Congregationalists. It was promulgated in 1658. Its authority was enhanced by the fact that John Owen was involved in this revision and is thought to have written its lengthy preface.[134] Though the areas of revision concern primarily issues of church and state, Owen and the other revisers also introduced expansions relevant to the issue at hand.

Of greater historical importance is *The 1689 Baptist Confession of Faith*. This Baptist revision of *The Savoy Declaration* and *Westminster Confession* was (probably) originally framed in 1677. It was, however, adopted in London in 1689 by representatives of perhaps 100 Calvinistic Baptist churches. It also became the vastly influential Confession of the American Reformed Baptists in 1742, when it was adopted with two small revisions (irrelevant to our subject) by the Philadelphia Association and became known as the *Philadelphia Confession of Faith*.[135] It differs from the *Westminster* on issues of church, state, covenant, and baptism primarily, but also contains expansions interesting for the subject at hand. We will discuss primarily the statements of *The Westminster*

---

[131]Ibid., 1:732-740.
[132]Ibid., 1:753.
[133]Ibid., 1:754-760.
[134]*The Creeds and Platforms of Congregationalism*, ed. Williston Walker (New York: Pilgrim Press, 1991), 340-353.
[135]Sam Waldron, *A Modern Exposition of The 1689 Baptist Confession of Faith* (Darlington, England: Evangelical Press, 1999), 425-432.

Confession. We will then supplement this discussion where necessary with the statements of the Catechisms and the later Confessions.[136]

- **The Definition of Justifying Faith**

Three references to the definition of justifying faith may be isolated in *The Westminster Confession of Faith.* The relevant statements are in italics below. They are repeated verbatim in *The Savoy Declaration* and *1689 Baptist Confession.*[137]

> Those whom God effectually calleth, he also freely justifieth: not by infusing righteousness into them, but by pardoning their sins, and by accounting and accepting their persons as righteous; not for anything wrought in them, or done by them, but for Christ's sake alone; nor by imputing faith itself, the act of believing, or any other evangelical obedience to them, as their righteousness; but by imputing the obedience and satisfaction of Christ unto them, *they receiving and resting on him* and his righteousness, by faith; which faith they have not of themselves, it is the gift of God.[138]

> *Faith, thus receiving and resting on Christ and his righteousness,* is the alone instrument of justification: yet is it not alone in the person justified, but is ever accompanied with all other saving graces, and is no dead faith, but worketh by love.[139]

> *By this faith, a Christian believeth to be true whatsoever is revealed in the Word,* for the authority of God himself speaking therein; and acteth differently upon that which each particular passage thereof containeth; yielding obedience to the commands, trembling at the threatenings, and

---

[136] The standard text of *The Westminster Confession* presented in Schaff will be used here. *The Creeds of Christendom*, 3:600-673. Later revisions on issues of church and state made by American Presbyterians do not alter its statements with regard to the subject of justification by faith alone. *The Westminster Confession* affirms justification by faith alone verbally and explicitly once. *The Creeds of Christendom*, 3:626. [CC 2:621]. *The Westminster Confession of Faith*, 11:2. In the famous words, "Faith, thus receiving and resting on Christ and his righteousness, is the *alone* instrument of justification." (Emphasis mine.)

[137] James M. Renihan, "A Theological Family Tree: The 2nd London Baptist Confession and Its Source Documents," unpublished paper (Institute of Reformed Baptist Studies, Westminster Seminary, Escondido, CA, 2000), 32, 36, 37. The emphasis is mine.

[138] *The Creeds of Christendom*, 3:626. [CC 2:620]. *The Westminster Confession of Faith*, 11:1. The emphasis is mine.

[139] Ibid., 3:626. [CC 2:621]. *The Westminster Confession of Faith*, 11:2.

embracing the promises of God for this life, and that which is to come. But *the principal acts of saving faith are accepting, receiving, and resting upon Christ alone* for justification, sanctification, and eternal life, by virtue of the covenant of grace.[140]

Several observations are important here. *First*, the repetition of the verbs *receive* and *rest* and also the use of the verb *accept* clearly indicate the passive essence of justifying faith. These same verbs are, however, also clearly volitional rather than intellectual. Justifying faith is described here, then, in volitional but passive terms.

Second, the description of saving faith in 14:2 distinguishes between its secondary and principal acts. The secondary acts of saving faith are its response to the Word of God generally. These secondary acts are described as believing to be true whatever it reveals and giving different responses as appropriate to what is revealed. The Confession includes *obedience, trembling, and embracing* in such *acts*. The principal acts of saving faith are, however, described in the passive terms noticed before: *accepting, receiving, and resting upon Christ alone for justification*. Clearly, justifying faith is defined passively.

Third, the statement of 14:2 also describes faith in intellectual terms— *By this faith, a Christian believeth to be true whatsoever is revealed in the Word*. Even here it is added that faith also *acts*—responding appropriately to the different aspects of the Word. Thus, these descriptions of saving faith possess a distinctly volitional character. This leads us to note that *The Westminster Confession* maintains a passive definition of justifying faith in spite of the fact that it avoids the tendency of Luther and Calvin and some early Reformation Confessions to speak of faith as assurance of salvation or, in other words, to speak as if assurance of salvation is of the essence of faith.[141]

---

[140]Ibid., 3:630-631. [*CC* 2:623]. *The Westminster Confession of Faith*, 14:2. The *1689 Baptist Confession* has a lengthy addition to 14:2 which, however, does not change its meaning significantly for our purposes. See Renihan, *A Theological Family Tree*, 36.

[141]*The Westminster Confession* specifically rejects this notion. Speaking specifically of the assurance of grace and salvation, the title of the chapter from which the following quotation is taken, it says: "This infallible assurance doth not so belong to the essence of faith, but that a true believer may wait long, and conflict with many difficulties before he be partaker of it . . ." *The Creeds of Christendom*, 3:638. [*CC* 2:628]. *The Westminster Confession of Faith*, 18:3. The parallel statements of both the Savoy and 1689 are identical. See Renihan, *A Theological Family Tree*, 45. The statement of the Westminster Larger Catechism (Question and Answer 81), *The Confession of Faith, The Larger and Shorter Catechisms with the Scripture Proofs at Large, Together with the Sum of Saving Knowledge* (Ross-shire, Scotland: The Publications Committee of the Free Presbyterian

- **The Distinction between Justifying Faith and Evangelical Obedience**

The Westminster Confession emphasizes the distinction between justifying faith and evangelical obedience by first making clear that faith itself is no part of the righteousness on the ground of which we are justified.

> Those whom God effectually calleth, he also freely justifieth: not by infusing righteousness into them, but by pardoning their sins, and by accounting and accepting their persons as righteous; not for anything wrought in them, or done by them, but for Christ's sake alone; nor by imputing faith itself, the act of believing, or any other evangelical obedience to them, as their righteousness.[142]

The Westminster Larger Catechism expands this statement by asking the question:

> Q. 73. How doth faith justify a sinner in the sight of God?
> A. Faith justifies a sinner in the sight of God, not because of those other graces which do always accompany it, or of good works that are the fruits of it, nor as if the grace of faith, or any act thereof, were imputed to him for his justification; but only as it is an instrument by which he receiveth and applieth Christ and his righteousness.[143]

The thrust of this answer is almost laborious in its clarity. Faith does not justify as being in itself or in any of its acts a good work, nor as accompanied by other graces, nor as giving birth to evangelical obedience, but only in its capacity as "an instrument by which he receiveth and applieth Christ and his righteousness."

The language which describes faith as the instrument of justification is striking. This means that faith is to be viewed as the instrumental cause

---

Church of Scotland, 1970), 171-172, is even more clear on the distinction between saving faith and the assurance of salvation: "Assurance of grace and salvation not being of the essence of faith, true believers may wait long before they obtain it." My point is that a passive definition of justifying faith does not depend on or assume the notion that assurance of salvation is of the essence of faith. *Westminster* maintains a passive definition of justifying faith, while rejecting this notion.

[142] *The Creeds of Christendom*, 3:626. [CC 2:620]. *The Westminster Confession of Faith*, 11:1.

[143] *The Confession of Faith, The Larger and Shorter Catechisms*, 165-166. The Westminster Larger Catechism, Question and Answer 73.

of justification—language that may be traced back to Calvin himself.[144] The assertion that faith is the instrumental cause of justification is interesting when compared to the statement of the Confession with regard to repentance. Repentance, in contrast, is denied an instrumental function in the cause of pardon.

> Although repentance be not to be rested in, as any satisfaction for sin, or any cause of the pardon thereof, which is the act of God's free grace in Christ; yet it is of such necessity to all sinners, that none may expect pardon without it.[145]

If this interpretation of the comparison between 11:2 and 15:3 of *Westminster* is correct, it again bears witness to the jealousy with which it distinguished faith and obedience. Not even repentance was to be allowed as a cause (an instrumental cause) of justification in the way that justifying faith was.[146]

- **The Dichotomy between Law and Gospel**

The dichotomy between law and gospel is expressed with special fullness in the Westminster complex of documents. Two matters call for particular attention: *first*, its contrast between the covenant of works and the covenant of grace; and *second*, its doctrine of imputed righteousness.

---

[144]This thought is strengthened by the comments of Calvin himself on the causes of justification: John Calvin, *Calvin's Commentaries*, 22 vols. (Grand Rapids: Baker Book House, 1981). On Rom 3:22 Calvin comments: "When therefore we are justified, the efficient cause is the mercy of God, the meritorious is Christ, the instrumental is the word in connection with faith. Hence faith is said to justify, because it is the instrument by which we receive Christ, in whom righteousness is conveyed to us." See also his comments on Rom 3:24.

[145]*The Creeds of Christendom*, 3:632. [CC 2:624]. *The Westminster Confession of Faith*, 15:3.

[146]William Cunningham, *Historical Theology* (London: Banner of Truth Trust, 1969), 2:74-76, has an extensive treatment of this subject in which he asserts among other things: "On all these accounts, the expressions instrument, or instrumental cause, are those which have most generally commended themselves to orthodox divines, as indicating most correctly the place and influence assigned in Scripture to faith in the matter of a sinner's justification." If this is a correct assessment, then the construction I have placed on the matter under discussion seems to be correct. In the parlance of the orthodox, Reformed theologians, faith was the instrumental cause of justification, but repentance was not the instrumental cause of pardon—a constituent element of justification.

In the first of the key statements on the definition cited above, *Westminster Confession* 14:2, the relationship of justifying faith to the covenant of grace is explicit.

> By this faith, a Christian believeth to be true whatsoever is revealed in the Word, for the authority of God himself speaking therein; and acteth differently upon that which each particular passage thereof containeth; yielding obedience to the commands, trembling at the threatenings, and embracing the promises of God for this life, and that which is to come. But the principal acts of saving faith are accepting, receiving, and resting upon Christ alone for justification, sanctification, and eternal life, by virtue of the covenant of grace.[147]

The relationship between the covenant of grace and faith is also made explicit in Chapter 7 of the Confession.

> Man, by his fall, having made himself incapable of life by that covenant, the Lord was pleased to make a second, commonly called the covenant of grace; wherein he freely offereth unto sinners life and salvation by Jesus Christ; requiring of them faith in him, that they may be saved, and promising to give unto all those that are ordained unto eternal life his Holy Spirit, to make them willing, and able to believe.[148]

The significant aspect of this embedding of saving faith in the covenant of grace for present purposes is the contrast between the covenant of grace and the covenant of works that is present in both paragraphs. This contrast is explicit at 7:3 in its description of the covenant of grace as "a second" covenant. The preceding paragraph reads, "The first covenant made with man was a covenant of works, wherein life was promised to Adam; and in him to his posterity, upon condition of perfect and personal obedience."[149]

---

[147] *The Creeds of Christendom*, 3:630-631. [CC 2:623]. *The Westminster Confession of Faith*, 14:2. *The 1689 Baptist Confession* has a lengthy addition to 14:2 which, however, does not seem to change its meaning significantly for our purposes. See Renihan, *A Theological Family Tree*, 36.

[148] Ibid., 3:617. [CC 2:615]. *The Westminster Confession of Faith*, 7:3. *The Savoy Declaration* is identical in this paragraph. The same language occurs in the considerably reshaped Chapter 7 of *The 1689 Baptist Confession* in its paragraph 2. See Renihan, *A Theological Family Tree*, 21.

[149] *The Creeds of Christendom*, 3:616-617. [CC 2:615]. *The Westminster Confession of Faith*, 7:2.

It is implicitly present in 14:2. *The Westminster Confession* maintains throughout the contrast between the covenant of works and the covenant of grace it teaches in Chapter 7.[150]

The significance of this is manifold. In this contrast, the dichotomy between law and gospel is clearly maintained. For *The Westminster Confession* the covenant of works was "the law." If this needs proof, it is provided by the statement found in 19:1 and 2.

> God gave to Adam a law, as a covenant of works, by which he bound him and all his posterity to personal, entire, exact, and perpetual obedience, promised life upon the fulfilling, and threatened death upon the breach of it, and endued him with power and ability to keep it. This law, after his fall, continued to be a perfect rule of righteousness; and, as such, was delivered by God upon Mount Sinai, in ten commandments, and written in two tables: the first four commandments containing our duty towards God; and the other six, our duty to man.

In its contrast between the covenant of works and the covenant of grace the dichotomy between law and gospel found in Luther and Calvin is refined and clarified. The dichotomy between law and gospel too easily implied that the Mosaic covenant was exclusively "law" in the sense of being a covenant of works. *The Westminster Confession* evades this implication by speaking of a covenant of life or works made with Adam. Thus, justification *sola fide* is delivered from dependence on a very controversial view of the Old Covenant.

In its contrast between the covenant of works and the covenant of grace the meaning of justification *sola fide* is clarified. Saving faith is not primarily trembling at the threats of the law or obedience to the commands of the law. It is resting in the provisions of the covenant of grace. Thus, the definition of justifying faith as passive is confirmed, and the distinction between justifying faith and evangelical obedience is

---

[150] *The 1689 Baptist Confession* removes the reference to the covenant of works in its reshaped chapter 7. It introduces the language about the covenant of grace and faith with the words: "Moreover, man having brought himself under the curse of the law by his fall, it pleased the Lord to make a covenant of grace." The removal of references to the covenant of works found in *The Westminster Confession of Faith* and *The Savoy Declaration* at several points in *The 1689 Baptist Confession* might seem to suggest some discomfort with the concept. The fact that it retains references to the covenant of works in 19:6 and 20:1 requires, however, a different explanation. See my discussion of this problem in Waldron, *A Modern Exposition*, 95-96. At any rate, the dichotomy between law and gospel in *The 1689 Baptist Confession* is unambiguous even in the revised language quoted above.

evinced. Saving faith in its justifying office or quality is a restful and receptive response to the provisions of the covenant of grace. It is not as obedience to law—even as that law is taken up in the covenant of grace—that faith justifies.[151]

Within the structure of the covenantal contrast *The Westminster Confession* teaches justification by the imputed righteousness of Christ. Note the following statements:

> Those whom God effectually calleth, he also freely justifieth: not by infusing righteousness into them, but by pardoning their sins, and by accounting and accepting their persons as righteous; not for anything wrought in them, or done by them, but for Christ's sake alone; nor by imputing faith itself, the act of believing, or any other evangelical obedience to them, as their righteousness; but by imputing the obedience and satisfaction of Christ unto them . . .[152]

> Christ, by his obedience and death, did fully discharge the debt of all those that are thus justified, and did make a proper, real, and full satisfaction to his Father's justice in their behalf. Yet, inasmuch as he was given by the Father for them; and his obedience and satisfaction accepted in their stead; and both, freely, not for anything in them; their justification is only of free grace; that both the exact justice and rich grace of God might be glorified in the justification of sinners.[153]

> Q. 33. What is justification?
> A. Justification is an act of God's free grace, wherein he pardoneth all our sins, and accepteth us as righteous in his sight, only for the righteousness of Christ imputed to us, and received by faith alone.[154]

The Independent revisers of *The Westminster Confession* did not apparently find even such clear statements of justification by imputed righteousness satisfactory. They add in the text of 11:1 this clarification,

---

[151] The requirements of the law are taken up within the covenant of grace according to *The Westminster Confession*, 19:7: "Neither are the forementioned uses of the law contrary to the grace of the gospel, but do sweetly comply with it; the Spirit of Christ subduing and enabling the will of man to do that freely, and cheerfully, which the will of God, revealed in the law, requireth to be done" (*The Creeds of Christendom*, 3:643; *CC* 2:630).

[152] *The Creeds of Christendom*, 3:626. [*CC* 2:620]. *The Westminster Confession of Faith*, 11:1.

[153] Ibid., 3:626-627. [*CC* 2:621]. *The Westminster Confession of Faith*, 11:3.

[154] Ibid., 3:683. [*CC* 2:655]. *The Westminster Shorter Catechism*, Question and Answer 33.

"Christ's active obedience unto the whole Law, and passive obedience in his death, for their whole and sole righteousness."[155]

In this detail we discover again that there was no deviation from the doctrine of justification by faith alone. There was rather—if anything—a tightening and crystallization of the doctrine. The office of justifying faith was in no sense to be (or add to) the righteousness at the basis of God's justifying verdict. It was only to receive and rest on as its sole (justifying) righteousness the active and passive obedience of Christ.

Conclusion

This survey of the ten most important Reformation Confessions shows beyond dispute that a single, unified understanding of the *sola fide* of justification was maintained throughout the Reformed and Lutheran traditions in the sixteenth and seventeenth centuries. There was no deviation or detraction from the views of Luther and Calvin on this central issue. This survey of their Confessions and Catechisms is the best window into the actual views of the descendants of Luther and Calvin. In spite of the differences that developed between Lutherans and Calvinists, their understanding of justification by faith alone remained one.

This is not to deny, of course, that the views of Luther and Calvin were refined. The tendency of both Luther and Calvin to speak sometimes of justifying faith in terms that seemed to make its essence merely intellectual and to consist in assurance of salvation ultimately is clarified by *The Westminster Confession*. *The Confession* distinguishes saving faith and assurance of salvation. It also consistently speaks of faith in clearly volitional terms. Nevertheless, the essentially passive definition of justifying faith is maintained. It is resting on and receiving Christ and the provisions of the covenant of grace.

Similarly, the dichotomy between law and gospel was open to the objection that it understood the Mosaic covenant to be a covenant of works. This view of the Mosaic covenant is gradually modified and refined. In the later Reformed Confessions it is presented in terms of a contrast not between Moses and Christ, but between Adam and Christ and between the covenant of works (or life) with Adam and covenant of grace made in Christ.

---

[155]Both *The Savoy Declaration* and *The 1689 Baptist Confession* contain these additional words. See Renihan, *A Theological Family Tree*, 36.

Finally, the doctrine of imputed righteousness is clear throughout these confessional documents. Even this doctrine, however, undergoes clarification at the hands of the Calvinistic Independents who insist on language that makes an explicit doctrine of the double imputation of Christ's active and passive obedience to the believer indisputable. These clarifications take nothing from the Reformers' *sola fide*. They only clarify the doctrine, tighten it, and situate it in a more biblically defensible position.

Sola fide designates a doctrine that in the Reformation tradition was both clearly defined and universally held. It was in this tradition that it was first embraced and clearly articulated by the Christian church. If theological terminology is to maintain its ability to communicate meaningfully, it is to this Reformation doctrine that justification *by faith alone* must refer.

When justification by faith alone is affirmed, it is, therefore, misleading for some other or contradictory meaning to be attached to the words. This study now turns, therefore, to the question of whether certain, current, evangelical thinkers have this classically articulated meaning in mind when they affirm their faith in justification *sola fide*.

CHAPTER 5
SOLA FIDE IN DANIEL FULLER
An Introduction to Daniel Fuller

Daniel P. Fuller is the son of the quintessential evangelical evangelist, Charles Fuller, who founded the quintessential evangelical seminary, Fuller Seminary, where Daniel Fuller taught for many years.[1] All this is important because, when one examines Fuller's views of justification *sola fide*, there should be no confusion as to his evangelical pedigree or profession.

Two major influences on Fuller from outside the precincts of American evangelicalism also significantly impacted Fuller. In *The Unity of the Bible* Fuller cites Karl Barth with regard to the question of the purpose of creation. Though he prefers Jonathan Edwards to Barth on this issue, it is nevertheless clear that he regards Barth as an important conversation partner.

> A good place to begin this task is to consider briefly how the Swiss theologian Karl Barth (1886-1968), under whom I studied for three years, and the early American theologian Jonathan Edwards understood God's motive in creating the world. Their quite opposite answers to this question pinpoint the pitfalls to be avoided.[2]

The citation of Barth in the early pages of *Gospel and Law: Contrast or Continuum* has to do expressly with the issue at stake in this study. It is noteworthy that the title of Fuller's book begins with the same words and in the same peculiar order as the article of Barth cited by Fuller. Barth's article is entitled, "Gospel and Law," not law and gospel, the traditional order.[3] The change Barth has made in this order is both very

---

[1] Daniel P. Fuller, *Give the Winds a Mighty Voice* (n.p.: Word, 1972), recounts the life of his famous father and at the same time provides a considerable amount of biographical detail with regard to himself. Dr. Daniel P. Fuller, "Another Reply to *Counted Righteous in Christ*," *Reformation and Revival Journal* 2, no. 2 (Spring 2002): 119-120, is according to the blurb attached to his latest article "emeritus professor of hermeneutics, Fuller Theological Seminary. He received the B.D. and Th.M. degrees from Fuller Seminary and earned a Th.D. (1957) at Northern Baptist Seminary and a D.Theol. (1965) from the University of Basel."

[2] Daniel P. Fuller, *The Unity of the Bible* (Grand Rapids: Zondervan, 1992), 130.

[3] Karl Barth, "Gospel and Law," in *Community, State, and Church* (Garden City, NY: Doubleday, 1960), 72, remarks, "The gospel is not Law, just as the Law is not

deliberate and highly significant—as is the fact that Fuller has followed his order in the title of his own book.[4] As we shall see, Fuller is insistent that God's relationship with Adam was gracious and the identical requirement of God both before and after the fall was "the obedience of faith."

Also profoundly influencing Fuller's views is Oscar Cullmann. Fuller remarks:

> Further insights came in the 1960s during my studies in Switzerland. There in lecture after lecture, as well as in his prolific writings, Oscar Cullmann emphasized the need to summarize the whole Bible along the timeline of redemptive history, instead of reverting to the timeless categories of God, humankind, Christ, church, and last things that has characterized the organization of systematic theology down through the ages.[5]

From Cullmann, Fuller gleaned an intense conviction of the importance of salvation history and biblical theology. This led him to the conviction that systematic theology should be organized in a more salvation-historical fashion.[6] This emphasis on salvation history is also probably related to his conviction that the analogy of faith hermeneutic characteristic of traditional systematics must be rejected or, at least, significantly adjusted.[7]

It is not difficult to see how Barth's reversal of the traditional order of law and gospel and Cullmann's emphasis on salvation history as the unifying principle of the Bible impacted Fuller. These two perspectives led to his organization of the Bible around the concept of "the obedience of faith."[8]

Gospel; but because the Law is in the Gospel, from the Gospel, and points to the Gospel, we must first of all know about the Gospel in order to know about the Law, and not vice versa."

[4]Daniel P. Fuller, *Gospel & Law: Contrast or Continuum* (Grand Rapids: Eerdmans, 1980), 4-5.

[5]Fuller, *The Unity of the Bible*, xv.

[6]Ibid., 102.

[7]Daniel P. Fuller, "Biblical Theology and the Analogy of Faith," in *Unity and Diversity in New Testament Theology: Essays in Honor of George E. Ladd*, ed. Robert A. Guelich (Grand Rapids: William B. Eerdmans, 1978), 195-213.

[8]Wayne Strickland, "Preunderstanding and Daniel Fuller's Law-Gospel Continuum," *Bibliotheca Sacra* (April-June 1987), 184-185, notes that the unifying and organizing principle for the unity of the Bible for Cullmann, Fuller, and the *Heilsgeschichte* model. He says, "Obedience of faith as the method of salvation in the *Heilsgeschichte* model is rejected by others as the basis of the Bible's unity."

From the inside of American evangelicalism Fuller (who was raised as a Dispensationalist) came under the influence of "covenant theology." This influence is visible as early as 1957 when he wrote his doctoral dissertation for Northern Baptist Theological Seminary. It was entitled, "The Hermeneutics of Dispensationalism,"[9] and sought to critique the hermeneutical fallacies of Classic Dispensationalism.[10] It is clear that Fuller is driven to no small degree by a reaction against the divorce and separation of law and grace prevalent in Dispensationalism. Especially odious to Fuller is the separation of justification by faith alone and sanctification in this view. Fuller argues that Dispensationalism is guilty of the Galatian heresy. For Fuller this means that it sees something in addition to justifying faith as necessary to produce sanctification.[11] He also rejects the separation of faith and obedience often associated with (and he probably saw as rooted in) Dispensationalism.[12]

Fuller's reaction against the reigning paradigms of evangelicalism did not stop with his rejection of Dispensationalism. *Gospel & Law* also chronicles Fuller's growing dissatisfaction with the hermeneutics of covenant theology, because it too posits a hermeneutical contrast between law and gospel.[13] Nevertheless, it cannot be denied that Fuller was and remained greatly influenced by covenant theology.

Evidence for this is not difficult to find. In the footnotes of *The Unity of the Bible* Fuller affirms the typically Reformed view of limited atonement.[14] Despite his critique of Calvin and other covenant theologians because of their insistence on an antithesis between law and gospel (and his rather unaccountable preference for Luther), it remains true that it was covenant theology that emphasized most clearly the unity of the old and new covenants.[15] Thus, even in his emphasis on the

---

[9] Fuller, "The Hermeneutics of Dispensationalism" (Th.D. diss.: Northern Baptist Theological Seminary, 1957).

[10] Fuller, *Gospel & Law*, ix. On p. x of the same work he speaks of "the notes of the *Scofield Reference Bible* upon which I had been raised."

[11] Ibid., 115-117, accuses Dispensationalism of the Galatian heresy.

[12] Fuller, *The Unity of the Bible*, 315, rejects the idea that a faith that does not persevere can justify. W. Robert Godfrey, "Back to Basics," *Presbyterion* 9, nos. 1-2 (Spring-Fall 1983), 83, comments on Fuller's practical motivations.

[13] Fuller, *Gospel & Law*, 1-64. Thus, in this book he also accuses Calvin of the Galatian heresy, 117.

[14] Fuller, *The Unity of the Bible*, 221.

[15] Charles P. Huckaby, "A Modern Evangelical Dialogue with Martin Luther: Interaction with the German Reformer in Daniel P. Fuller's *The Unity of the Bible*," *Reformation & Revival* 8 (Winter 1999), 217. Huckaby remarks, "Fuller claims that Calvin's exegesis of key Pauline passages has set the law and gospel at odds. Calvin has

continuity of the two covenants he is (historically speaking) closest to covenant theology. This suggests the influence on him of covenant theology. The importance of this influence situates Fuller in terms of his background as in some sense a Reformed evangelical.

Fuller seems to have addressed the issue we are exploring, "Faith, Obedience, and Justification," in three longer and four shorter writings.[16] The first was his doctoral dissertation entitled, "The Hermeneutics of Dispensationalism." This dissertation was later refined and expanded in the most important of his books for our purposes, *Gospel & Law: Contrast or Continuum*, published in 1980. Also important for our purposes is his other major work, *The Unity of the Bible*, published in 1992.

The first of the four shorter publications is an article published in the *Westminster Theological Journal* in 1975 entitled, "Paul and 'The Works of the Law'."[17] The remaining three are articles in response to criticism of the views expounded in *Gospel & Law* and *Unity of the Bible*. Most recently, Fuller responded critically to John Piper's *Counted Righteous in Christ* in "Another Reply to *Counted Righteous in Christ*."[18] More than 20 years ago, Fuller responded to the criticisms of O. Palmer Robertson in an article entitled, "A Response on the Subjects of Works and

---

positioned law and gospel as a *contrast* when in reality they are a continuum . . . . This is a humorously unexpected accusation in some ways because when moderns consider Calvin and Luther, it is Calvin who is normally said to stress the continuity between the Old and New Testaments to the point where he is said to make the Bible a 'flat book'! Usually it is Luther who is portrayed as separating law and gospel. One might expect to see Fuller likewise discount the German Reformer." Huckaby goes on to show, however, that Fuller rather seems to take Luther as one of his heroes. Reformed reviewers of Fuller have frequently suggested that he has seriously misrepresented Calvin and covenant theology. See O. Palmer Robertson, "Daniel P. Fuller's *Gospel & Law: Contrast or Continuum*: a Review Article," *Presbyterion* 8, no. 1 (Spring, 1982), 86; Mark Karlberg, "Legitimate Discontinuities between the Testaments," *JETS* 28, no. 1 (March, 1985), 11-12; Anthony A. Hoekema, "*Gospel & Law*: A Review," *Calvin Theological Journal* 17 (April, 1982), 11-12.

[16]Fuller has published a considerable amount of other material. Some of the most well-known publications are Daniel P. Fuller, "The Holy Spirit's Role in Biblical Interpretation," in *Scripture, Tradition, and Interpretation*, ed. W. Ward Gasque and William Sanford LaSor (Grand Rapids: Eerdmans, 1978) and "Biblical Theology and the Analogy of Faith." Two full-length books on other subjects may be mentioned here. They are his biography of his father, Charles Fuller, *Give the Winds a Mighty Voice* (1972) and *Easter Faith and History*, (1965).

[17]Daniel P. Fuller, "Paul and 'The Works of the Law'," *Westminster Theological Journal* 38 (1975-76), 28-42.

[18]Daniel P. Fuller, "Another Reply to *Counted Righteous in Christ*," *Reformation and Revival Journal* 2, no. 2 (Spring 2002), 115-120.

Grace."[19] At about the same time, he authored an article entitled, "Daniel P. Fuller's Reply to Paul Feinberg's Critique of *Gospel & Law: Contrast or Continuum*."[20]

The foregoing introduction to Daniel Fuller's biography and writings should leave no doubt that he occupies a place close to the center of the evangelical world. If his views of justification *sola fide* should prove to be substantially deviant, Fuller's prominence would clearly accentuate the seriousness of this departure.

A number of his protégés and students are prominent evangelicals.[21] One prominent evangelical whose views seem to be profoundly influenced by Fuller is Scott Hafemann. His book, *The God of Promise and the Life of Faith*, contains repeated references to Fuller,[22] echoes faithfully Fuller's emphasis on "the obedience of faith" and his tendency to identify faith and obedience,[23] and opens with this tribute to Fuller: "My first word of thanks thus goes to my three most formative professors, Drs. John Piper, Daniel Fuller, and Peter Stuhlmacher."[24]

The mention of John Piper in the foregoing quotation leads us to a necessary (albeit brief) discussion of Fuller's relation to his most important student, John Piper. At first face, there might seem to be significant reason to conclude that Piper's popularity implies the

---

[19]Daniel P. Fuller, "A Response on the Subjects of Works and Grace," *Presbyterion* 9, nos. 1-2 (Spring-Fall 1983), 72-79. About this time (1982-83) a number of interactions with Fuller's views on gospel and law appeared in this journal. They are written by Wilber B. Wallis, O. Palmer Robertson, Meredith G. Kline, and W. Robert Godfrey.

[20]Daniel P. Fuller, "Daniel P. Fuller's Reply to Paul Feinberg's Critique of *Gospel & Law: Contrast or Continuum*" (paper presented at the annual meeting of the Evangelical Theological Society, Toronto, ON, 28 December, 1981). Paul Feinberg, "Critique of *Gospel & Law: Contrast or Continuum*," (audiocassette of session held at the annual meeting of the Evangelical Theological Society, Toronto, ON, 28 December, 1981). It is apparently not available in paper form. I am informed that the only copy of this cassette is available and held by The Assemblies of God Theological Seminary in Missouri.

[21]Godfrey, "Back to Basics," 83, ponders the similarities between Norman Shepherd and Daniel Fuller and sees both some differences and significant similarities. There is, however, no suggestion of dependence in either direction by Godfrey.

[22]Scott J. Hafemann, *The God of Promise and the Life of Faith* (Wheaton, IL: Crossway Books, 2001), 247.

[23]Ibid., 103. In fairness to Hafemann, it must be noted that he does seem to define faith as trusting in God's promises (84, 87), but all of the emphasis is on the unity of faith and obedience and not on their distinctive characteristics. My concern is that the distinction between faith and obedience is disappearing. See also the statements he makes on 216 and 217, where denying that the law and the gospel are two different messages, he says that the obedience of faith (which is, as he says, faith expressing itself in obedience) is both the means and the result of being saved. The similarity to Fuller is clear.

[24]Ibid., 13.

increasing popularity of Fuller's views. Piper provides a strong endorsement of *Gospel & Law* on the back-cover of my copy of this book.[25] He is mentioned as one of those whose questions moved Fuller to adopt the thesis of this book.[26] A glowing foreword to *The Unity of the Bible* is provided by Piper.[27] *The Unity of the Bible* contains many themes that Piper emphasizes.[28]

Nevertheless, all is not as this account might make it seem between Fuller and Piper. Even in *Future Grace* Piper adopts a more positive attitude towards the Reformed tradition than does Fuller and nuances his views much more carefully than Fuller with regard to the traditional doctrine of justification.[29] The publication by Piper of *Counted Righteous in Christ*, in which he upholds the doctrine of the positive imputation of Christ's righteousness, is a manifestation of Piper's growing, public support of the traditional doctrine of justification.[30] This trend has brought overt criticism from Fuller and indicates a growing difference between them on the doctrine of justification.[31]

Discussions of deviations from the traditional, Reformation doctrine of justification perforce raise questions today about whether Fuller has been influenced by "the new perspective on Paul." He does not appear to have been so influenced. There seems, in other words, to be no evidence of any direct connection between Fuller and "the new perspective" *in the origination of his views*. No doubt, Fuller was influenced by the same theological winds that produced Sanders, Dunn, and Wright, but Fuller's views seem to have developed independently of their influence. This is shown by the publication date of *Gospel & Law* in 1980 and the fact that Fuller's views had clearly been developing along these lines for some

---

[25]Fuller, *Gospel & Law: Contrast or Continuum*, back cover.

[26]Ibid., ix, x, xii.

[27]Fuller, *The Unity of the Bible*, x-xii.

[28]John Piper, *Future Grace* (Sisters, OR: Multnomah Publishers, 1995). Note the debt Piper owes Fuller, cf. chaps. 6, 10, 13, 17, 21, 24, 27 of *Future Grace* with 281-297 of *The Unity of the Bible*. Piper intersperses these chapters on the same evils (with one or two exceptions) and how they are solved by faith in future grace as Fuller summarizes on the pages noted of *The Unity of the Bible*.

[29]Piper, *Future Grace*, 21-25, does this and adopts the position that in the Protestant tradition faith is the instrumental cause of good works and sanctification, a view which Fuller says that tradition denies when, for instance, he remarks that Calvin held the Galatian heresy. See Fuller, *Gospel & Law*, 115-117.

[30]Piper, *Counted Righteous in Christ* (Wheaton, IL: Crossway Books, 2002).

[31]Fuller, "Another Reply to *Counted Righteous in Christ*," 115-120. Because Piper distinguishes justifying and sanctifying faith, Fuller suggests that Piper is also flirting with the Galatian heresy (119).

time.[32] Furthermore, in *The Unity of the Bible* Fuller takes a position regarding inter-testamental Judaism that is out of accord with the usual views of "the new perspective."[33] Finally, Fuller seems to be motivated by much more "evangelical" themes than "the new perspective."[34]

The focus of this critique is on his views of *sola fide*. Fuller often affirms not only justification by faith alone, but even sanctification by faith alone.[35] The concern of this chapter is to examine whether Fuller's affirmation of *sola fide* is historically meaningful. In other words, when he affirms *sola fide*, does he mean by it what the Reformation tradition (as exemplified in Luther, Calvin, and the Reformation Confessions) that first clearly and consistently articulated this doctrine meant?

Fuller and the Dichotomy between Law and Gospel

- **Introduction**

The starting-point for this discussion of Fuller's views of justification *sola fide* must be the thesis of *Gospel & Law: Contrast or Continuum*. He argues there that the relationship between the gospel and law is not one of contrast, but of continuum or continuity. His critique of a contrast between law and gospel is stated with blunt clarity.

> I then had to accept the very drastic conclusion that the antithesis between law and gospel established by Luther, Calvin, and the covenant theologians could no longer stand up under the scrutiny of biblical theology.[36]

---

[32] E.P. Sanders' ground-breaking work, *Paul and Palestinian Judaism* (Minneapolis: Fortress Press, 1977), was published in 1977—a mere three years before *Gospel & Law*. Sanders, Dunn, and Wright are not mentioned in the bibliography and indices of Fuller's *Gospel & Law*. Only a short article by Dunn is mentioned by Fuller in *The Unity of the Bible*.

[33] Fuller, *The Unity of the Bible*, 256, assumes that the Jews placed a legalistic interpretation on Gen. 15:6. Fuller, *Gospel & Law*, 87, also refers to "the legalistic misunderstanding of the law which the majority of the Jews have espoused since the time of Moses."

[34] The "new perspective on Paul" does not appear primarily concerned about the Galatian heresy, nor with the "easy-believism" that has infected evangelicals.

[35] The following is a partial listing of those places where Fuller affirms *sola fide*: in *The Unity of the Bible* see 146, 270; in *Gospel & Law* xi, 105, 115, 117, 119; in "A Response on the Subjects of Works and Grace," 77.

[36] Fuller, *Gospel & Law*, xi.

> Thus dispensationalism joins with Lutheranism and with the covenant theology of Calvinism in seeking to draw a sharp distinction between the law and gospel.[37]

> So it is from the vantage point of the obedience of faith and not works in which men can boast that Leviticus 18:5 and the rest of the Mosaic law are to be understood.[38]

> . . . Christ and the Mosaic law . . . are in such a continuum that to repudiate one is to repudiate the other. Just as the law became the righteousness of God only for whose who responded to it in faith rather than works (cf. Rom. 9:31-32a), so Christ becomes the righteousness of God for all who, rather than stumbling at him (cf. Rom. 9:32b-33), submit to him in faith and thus are not ashamed.[39]

> It is therefore clear that in placing outside the law the reason for its inability to make people good, Paul was necessarily implying that the law itself, both in its content and its thought structure, was as capable of making people righteous as was the gospel.[40]

We have argued previously, and it certainly ought not to be questioned, that for the Reformation tradition the subjective response to the gospel—faith alone—is shaped by the objective character of the gospel. As Fuller himself admits in the above quotations, he has significantly altered the objective character of the message that shapes faith in denying the dichotomy between law and gospel held by Dispensationalist, Reformed, and Lutheran alike. The question is whether a gospel so altered still calls for a response that may be described as *sola fide*.

- **The Overview of Fuller's Continuum**

The continuum or continuity that Fuller posits between gospel and law must be examined in terms of the two historic contrasts of covenant theology that Fuller denies. He rejects the contrast between the old covenant as law and the new covenant as gospel. He also rejects the characterization of God's relation with Adam as a covenant of works to be contrasted with a covenant of grace made in Christ. Thus, he posits a

---

[37] Ibid., 17.
[38] Ibid., 81.
[39] Ibid., 85.
[40] Ibid., 346.

continuum between the Old and New Covenants and between the Covenant of Works and the Covenant of Grace.

Fuller scrutinizes the idea that the Old and New Covenants are related as law to gospel in several ways. He remarks that the idea that the Old Covenant was conditional, while the Abrahamic and New Covenants are unconditional is misguided and argues that, while the Noahic and Davidic Covenants were unconditional, all other biblical covenants were conditional. Thus, there is no contrast between the Old and New at this point.

> ... Calvin (thought that) ... there are unconditional promises (in the gospel) in distinction from conditional ones (in the law). ... all biblical promises (except those in the Noahic and Davidic Covenants) are unconditional promises ... [41]
>
> The passage definitely teaches that Abraham's posterity must keep the way of the Lord, *so that* "the Lord may bring to Abraham what he has promised him."[42]
>
> In any event, dispensationalists draw the strongest possible contrast between the Abrahamic and Mosaic eras. Sometimes they have perceived the difference to be so great that they have charged Israel with making a grave blunder by promising God, through Moses, that "all that the Lord has spoken [in giving the law] we will do" (Exod. 19:8).[43]
>
> The condition Abraham met in order to be forgiven and thus be blessed was simply to believe the promise that his posterity would constitute a large nation that would be protected by God and eventually impart its divine blessings to all other nations.[44]
>
> The conclusion, then, is that instead of two sets of promises in the Bible—conditional and unconditional—there is only one kind of promise throughout Scripture, and the realization of its promises is dependent upon compliance with conditions which are well characterized as "the obedience of faith" ... [45]

---

[41] Ibid., 121.
[42] Ibid., 137.
[43] Ibid., 139.
[44] Fuller, *The Unity of the Bible*, 256.
[45] Fuller, *Gospel & Law*, 105.

The only difference between the Old and New Covenants was that in the Old God did not supply the condition of the covenant promises to the vast majority of Israelites.

> The only difference between the new covenant and the old Mosaic covenant which it replaces is that the people under the new covenant are given a new heart which has the inclination, or the predisposition, to want to keep God's laws.[46]

> The revelatory law was only deficient in that it lacked the power to make a man righteous. "If a law had been given," Paul says, "which could make alive, then righteousness would indeed by the law." This means that, in general, the recipients of the Mosaic law did not receive along with it the supernatural, regenerative power of the Holy Spirit to keep the law.[47]

> It is therefore clear that in placing outside the law the reason for its inability to make people good, Paul was necessarily implying that the law itself, both in its content and its thought structure, was as capable of making people righteous as was the gospel.[48]

> A third reason for regarding the law and the gospel as similar is that in those passages speaking of the new covenant as replacing the old, the only change that occurs is that the heart is regenerated by the Holy Spirit.[49]

But what of the evidence often cited to show that there is a contrast between the law and the gospel? Fuller's methodology is to examine two of the major texts that in Calvin's opinion taught such a contrast between the law and the gospel–Romans 10:5-8 and Galatians 3:10-12.

> Our purpose in this chapter is to reexamine Paul's teaching on this matter by focusing on the two passages in Paul which Calvin thought "most clearly" set forth the distinction between the "faith righteousness and the law righteousness" (*Inst.* III, 11, 17).[50]

---

[46]Ibid., 144.
[47]Ibid., 202.
[48]Fuller, *The Unity of the Bible*, 346.
[49]Ibid., 349.
[50]Fuller, *Gospel & Law*, 65.

It is not necessary for our purposes to go into all the nuances of Fuller's attempt carefully to exegete these two passages. With regard to Romans 10:5-8, he concludes that a right understanding of the passage and especially the particle, δέ, in Romans 10:6 does not lead to the conclusion that there is a contrast between law and gospel. He considers the possibility put forward by John Murray and E.H. Gifford that Romans 10:5 and its allusion to Leviticus 18:5 is intended to represent "a Pharisaic misinterpretation" of the law rather than the original meaning of Leviticus 18:5, but prefers Felix Fluckiger's view that the δέ of verse 5 is continuative rather than contrastive. Thus, the righteousness required by the law is fulfilled by "the obedience of faith."[51]

With regard to Galatians 3:10-12, Fuller opts for the possibility that he rejects in Romans 10:5-8. That is to say, he concludes that in Galatians 3:10-12 there is a contrast. The contrast is not between the law and the gospel, but between "the Jewish misinterpretation of the law" and the gospel.[52] Here is his assessment:

> Consequently, data from before Galatians 3:10, as well as from that verse itself, provide a strong basis for the conclusion that by "works of the law" Paul meant a usage of the law that destroyed its very foundations, and that all those guilty of such works were under the curse of the law of Deuteronomy 27:15-26. In light of this conclusion, Calvin can no longer say that Galatians 3:10-12 is, along with Romans 10:5-8, a passage which "most clearly" affirms an antithesis between the conditional promises of the law and the supposedly unconditional ones of the gospel. To the contrary, Galatians 3:10-12 affirms that the law and the gospel are one and the same, and the antithesis stated in Galatians represents the Jewish *mis*interpretation of the law. We also conclude that the two passages (Galatians 3:10-12 and Romans 10:5-8) indicate that all of God's soteric promises are fulfilled on the basis of satisfying the condition which the Scripture calls "the obedience of faith" (Rom. 1:5; 16:26.)[53]

We have seen that in the Reformation confessional tradition the contrast between law and gospel ultimately came to be rooted (at least in its Reformed wing) in a contrast between the covenant of works made with Adam and the covenant of grace made with Christ. As we shall see, this development proceeded (at least in part) from the realization

---
[51] Ibid., 66-88.
[52] Ibid., 88-105.
[53] Ibid., 103.

beginning with Calvin himself that there was a real continuum (to use Fuller's word) between the Old and New Covenants. Fuller prosecutes his attack on the contrast between law and grace even to its Reformed citadel, the contrast between the covenants of works and grace.

Fuller's specific attack on the covenant of works is quite brief in *Gospel & Law*. This is probably because he regards his attack on the contrast between the law and the gospel as implying or assuming the difficulty with the covenant of works. He does note, however, in the early pages of this book that part of the covenant theology (which along with Dispensationalism) he is rejecting is the doctrine of the covenant of works.

> . . . all my previous Christian teaching had been from the vantage point of what is, generally speaking, covenant theology. There the conditional promises of the Bible echo "the covenant of works" into which God *supposedly* entered with Adam and Eve when, according to Genesis 2:17, he made the enjoyment of eternal life conditional upon their refraining from eating of the tree of the knowledge of good and evil.[54]

Fuller's comments on this matter are lengthier in *The Unity of the Bible*. He argues that God required not meritorious works of Adam, but simply "the obedience of faith" and rejects the notion that the covenant of works was conditional, while the covenant of grace was unconditional.[55] Again, Calvin takes the brunt of Fuller's criticism. He remarks:

> In my opinion, this idea of Calvin's has introduced great confusion into the understanding of Scripture. Since his thinking is so widespread in Protestantism, I will keep stressing how all obedience to God is an "obedience that comes from faith," and never an obedience of works, for "God is not served by human hands, as if he needed anything" (Acts 17:25).[56]

It is clear that Fuller's opposition to the Reformation contrast between law and grace is absolute. It includes opposition not only to any such contrast between the Old and New Covenants, but even any such contrast between a covenant of works and a covenant of grace. In Fuller

---

[54]Fuller, *Gospel & Law*, ix-x. The emphasis is mine.
[55]Fuller, *The Unity of the Bible*, 180-182.
[56]Ibid., 182.

the contrast between law and grace has melted into the continuum of "the obedience of faith."

- **The Assessment of Fuller's Continuum**

This assessment will be organized in terms of *concessions* and *concerns*.

It must be admitted that Fuller is grappling with important and difficult issues raised by the Reformation contrast between law and gospel. In the first place, it may be admitted that the status of the Mosaic Covenant in the Reformation tradition is a difficulty. The almost proverbial saying that the Mosaic Covenant is a "legal administration of the covenant of grace" epitomizes the tension. Fuller provides a number of examples of problematic statements in which covenant theologians attempt to explain how the Mosaic Covenant both contains a legal element and yet is an administration of the covenant of grace.[57] Fuller, it seems to me, is correct when he remarks:

> It is extremely difficult to grasp covenant theology's explanations of how a line of thought, which has the structure of the covenant of works, nevertheless functions as part of the covenant of grace.[58]

It is interesting to note that here Fuller recognizes that there is a tension within Reformed theology with regard to the Mosaic Covenant. Frequently, however, he speaks as if Calvin simply said without qualification that the Mosaic Covenant was a covenant of works. Perhaps Fuller would, if permitted, qualify his presentation of Calvin in the same way that he has qualified his presentation of covenant theology. If the impression of Calvin one receives from Fuller in *Gospel & Law* is that he regards the Mosaic Covenant as straightforwardly a covenant of works, then Fuller is simply wrong. As we have seen in our treatment of Calvin's contrast of law and gospel, Calvin strongly stresses the gracious character of the Old Covenant and the "third use of the law." It might, in fact, be easier to miss the contrast between law and gospel than the continuity of the Old and New. The most cursory reading of Calvin's treatment of the law in Book Two of the *Institutes* is sufficient to undermine the impression left by Fuller.[59] Underscoring the continuity of Old and New in Calvin, Bandstra remarks:

---

[57] Fuller, *Gospel & Law*, 6, 51-54.
[58] Ibid., 51.
[59] *Inst.*, 2:7-9. [*Joannis Calvini Opera Selecta* (ed. P. Barth, G. Niesel) *OS* [1926-

Thus Calvin himself may have to shoulder some of the blame for the fact that his views on law and gospel have often been only partially presented. His position on law and gospel has been presented most frequently only under the two rubrics of unity of substance and difference of form. The rubric of antithesis of letter and Spirit has hardly received a hearing; no doubt this is in part due to the fact that this aspect is not so clearly represented in the *Institutes*.

On the other hand, the *Institutes*, no matter how important, do not represent Calvin's total view. Calvin the exegete is as important as Calvin the theologian. Surely the commentary materials need to be taken seriously in attempting to assess the whole of Calvin's view on the law-gospel motif. When this is done, it is clear that the antithesis of law and gospel, properly defined, is a necessary and important part of his total perspective.[60]

For Fuller to recognize a tension with regard to this matter in Reformed theology is, however, not to prove that its approach is misguided, or his is correct. It might be that there really is a tension on this matter within the Bible and Paul himself.

In the second place, Fuller must also be credited with pointing out the problematic character of using the antithesis between conditional and unconditional to describe the contrast between law and gospel. At a number of points Fuller makes clear that such a distinction is difficult to carry out.

> The conclusion, then, is that instead of two sets of promises in the Bible—conditional and unconditional—there is only one kind of promise throughout Scripture, and the realization of its promises is dependent upon compliance with conditions which are well characterized as "the obedience of faith."[61]

> ... Calvin (thought that) ... there are unconditional promises (in the gospel) in distinction from conditional ones (in the law). ... all biblical

---

1959] 3:326-403]. Footnote citations written as *Inst.* in this chapter are from John Calvin, *Institutes of the Christian Religion*, trans. Ford Lewis Battles, ed. John T. McNeill (London : S.C.M. Press, 1961). Footnote citations written as *Comm.* are from *Calvin's Commentaries*, 22 vols. (Grand Rapids: Baker Book House, 1981).

[60] Andrew J. Bandstra, "Law and Gospel," in *Exploring the Heritage of John Calvin*, ed. David E. Holwerda (Grand Rapids: Baker, 1976), 38. Bandstra remarks in a footnote that the dichotomy between law and gospel is, however, present in the *Institutes* in muted form in 2:11 and in more explicit fashion in 3:17:6.

[61] Fuller, *Gospel & Law*, 105.

> promises (except those in the Noahic and Davidic Covenants) are conditional promises . . .[62]

> But while mercy is undeserved favor, it is not unconditional favor, for it comes to people only if they believe (Eph. 1:19).[63]

> Calvin, of course, wanted to keep faith in Christ completely free from any of the commandments or conditions in the Mosaic law for receiving the promises.[64]

It cannot be denied, in my opinion, that *in some sense* according to the Bible initial justification is conditioned on saving faith, final salvation is conditioned on perseverance, and the blessings of the Mosaic Covenant were conditioned on the obedience of faith by the nation (and not perfect, perpetual obedience). So far Fuller is right, and he is right to make this point strongly, because much of the relevant discussion has obscured these biblical facts.

It must be remarked, however, that Calvin was not oblivious to these realities. He admitted at least that faith was the instrumental cause of justification. "For faith is said to justify because it receives and embraces the righteousness offered in the gospel."[65] Faith, then, as Calvin says is only the instrumental cause of justification—not its efficient, material, or meritorious cause.

> When therefore we are justified, the efficient cause is the mercy of God, the meritorious is Christ, the instrumental is the word in connection with faith. Hence faith is said to justify, because it is the instrument by which we receive Christ, in whom righteousness is conveyed to us.[66]

The same is true for the Reformation tradition. Buchanan notes that the term 'condition' was used in that tradition and was allowable as long as it was properly understood and defined. He remarks:

> In regard to the influence or efficacy which is ascribed to Faith in connection with our justification, the question, whether it may be best described as a means,—or as instrument,—or as a condition, is of little

---

[62]Ibid., 121.
[63]Fuller, *The Unity of the Bible*, 219.
[64]Ibid., 475.
[65]*Inst.* 3:11:17 [*OS* 4:200-201]. *Comm.* Gen. 15:6 [*CR* 51:211-214].
[66]*Comm.* Rom 3:22, 24 [*CR* 77:57-62].

importance, so far as it relates merely to the use of these terms,—for every one of them might be applied to it in a sound sense . . . . Protestant divines have generally held, that it is simply an instrumental means,—like the hand which a beggar stretches out to receive alms,—by which we apprehend Christ, and appropriate to ourselves the benefits of His salvation,—these benefits being at once the fruits of His purchase, and the free gifts of His grace; and while they have sometimes used the term 'condition,' as in the Larger Catechism of the Westminster divines,—they have been careful to explain the two senses in which it may be understood—as denoting either a legal condition, on the fulfillment of which eternal life becomes due, as wages are due for work done, in which sense it is rejected, or as denoting an indispensable means merely in the order of the divine appointment for the attainment of an end, just as breathing is necessary for the support of life, while it is the air which really sustains it; or as eating is necessary for the nourishment of the body, while it is the food which really ministers to its health and strength; in which sense the term may be admitted, although, from its ambiguity, it is more expedient to employ another, that will be less liable to be misunderstood or misapplied.[67]

It must also be noted that it is likely that the term 'unconditional' was suggested to Calvin and to others in the Reformed tradition because the entire redemptive arrangement flows from unconditional election. As Huckaby notes:

If Reformed leaders teach an "unconditional covenant of grace," it is likely they are using the word "unconditional" in reference to God's sovereign prerogatives and eternal purpose . . . rather than referring to the human responsibilities of the saints to both exercise faith and persevere in faith.[68]

It certainly was Calvin's view that faith rested in God's electing purpose as it had come to expression in the grace to be found in Christ. Faith, for Calvin, involved assurance of salvation as a result.[69]

---

[67] James Buchanan, *The Doctrine of Justification* (Grand Rapids: Baker Book House, 1977), 380.

[68] Huckaby, "A Modern Evangelical Dialogue with Martin Luther," 220.

[69] Other commendations might be offered to Fuller, but they would take us away from the central purpose of this dissertation. I only note here that Fuller's concerns about the terminology "covenant of works" cannot be completely dismissed. In the Pauline contexts "works" seems sometimes to attribute a mercenary and meritorious character to the deeds done. It connects the relationship the Judaizers thought they sustained to God

Two concerns need to be expressed here. The first concern is with Fuller's denial of the contrast between law and gospel. This seems inevitably to involve the denial of double imputation or, in other words, the positive imputation of Christ's righteousness to the believer in the sense of what has been called his "active obedience." This concern must not be misunderstood. We are not affirming that Fuller holds an unorthodox view of the atonement in the sense of denying either the penal, substitutionary character of the atonement or what has been called Christ's "passive obedience." Indeed, he affirms "limited atonement," a position that usually assumes such a penal, substitutionary view of the atonement.[70] Neither are we asserting that Fuller rejects a strictly forensic view of justification. He may hold that justification consists only in the forgiveness of sins and not include in justification the infused righteousness of sanctification.[71] We are affirming, however, that there is no evidence that Fuller holds an imputation of Christ's righteousness and good reason to think that he does not.

The evidence for this is as follows. *First*, Fuller nowhere affirms (that I can find) such a positive imputation of Christ's righteousness to the believer. *Second*, in his treatments of the atonement and justification in *The Unity of the Bible*—where he might naturally have affirmed such

---

with Adam. Such a connotation cannot be ascribed to the deeds required of Adam by God or to the original relationship of Adam to God as a whole. Fuller, however, is not alone in this assessment of the terminology, "covenant of works." John Murray accepts such terminological criticisms of the "covenant of works," while maintaining in substance its structural meaning for theology. See John Murray, "The Adamic Administration," in *Collected Writings* (Edinburgh: Banner of Truth Trust, 1977), 2:49. It also seems undeniable that Paul's use of the Old Testament and, in particular, language descriptive of the Old Covenant in Rom 10:5-8 and Gal 3:10-12 is problematic. Thus, Fuller is justified in reconsidering these passages. While, on the one hand, there is ample reason to conclude that the Mosaic Covenant was not a covenant of works, on the other hand, it certainly *prima facie* appears that Paul is using its language as if it were a covenant of works. This is, indeed, a problem! Part of the resolution to this problem may be, and probably is, to realize (as Fuller does in his exegesis of Gal 3) that Paul is engaged in a polemic against the Judaizers and is refuting their misuse of the law. John Murray, *The Epistle to the Romans* (Grand Rapids: Eerdmans, 1965), 2:51-54, 249-251, recognizes and grapples with this very difficulty—as do many other interpreters. One may, however, recognize the problem without being forced to Fuller's extreme resolution of it.

[70]Fuller, *The Unity of the Bible*, 205-221. In this chapter, Fuller clearly asserts propitiation, 218, and subscribes to the doctrine of limited atonement, 220-221.

[71]Ibid., 310-322, seems at a number of points to equate justification with forgiveness of sins. He notes, for instance, that Jonathan Edwards with whom he seems to agree, "insisted that a person is justified at his first act of believing" (316).

a view—it is glaringly absent.[72] *Third*, his critical reaction to Piper's defense of such a positive imputation, though it does not explicitly reject positive imputation, seems inexplicable except on this assumption.[73] This is the case especially because Piper suggests that Fuller sees justification as consisting merely in the forgiveness of sins in *Counted Righteous in Christ*.[74] *Fourth*, his rigorous denial of any contrast between law and gospel—including his rejection of a covenant of works—leads inevitably to the conclusion that Fuller denies a positive imputation of righteousness. The doctrine in question only makes sense on such a basis or within such a framework.[75]

The significance of this probable denial of imputed righteousness for this thesis is that Fuller has altered the objective character of the gospel as it comes to us in the Reformation tradition. Faith does not lay hold of an imputed righteousness, but at most the forgiveness of sins. Thus, the *possible* implication is that faith, that is, the obedience of faith, becomes in some way constitutive and not merely receptive of the believer's justifying righteousness. This means in turn that, since *sola fide*—the subjective response to the gospel—is necessarily shaped by the objective content of the gospel, *sola fide* has also been altered.

But this problem with the positive imputation of righteousness is simply an indication of a larger and more systemic difficulty with Fuller's affirmation of *sola fide*. This brings us to a second concern.

The affirmation that gospel and law exist on a continuum—and not in contrast—requires that faith be at one and the same time a response to this undistinguished *mass* of gospel and law. If the law is part of the gospel, as Fuller clearly says, then this must be so. For Calvin, Luther, and the Reformation Confessions, the very significance of justifying faith was that it was a response to gospel as contrasted with law. The act of faith which justified was its resting on and receiving Christ exclusive of the other and further acts of faith which obeyed the law's commands and trembled at its threatenings.[76]

We are not left simply to deduce Fuller's views on this matter. In his response, for instance, to Piper he explicitly denies any distinction

---

[72]Ibid., 205-221, 310-322.

[73]Fuller, "Another Reply to *Counted Righteous in Christ*," 115-120.

[74]John Piper, *Counted Righteous in Christ*, 116. Piper is commenting on Fuller's statements in *the Unity of the Bible*, 255-256.

[75]W. Robert Godfrey, "Back to Basics," 82, notes the same implication with regard to a positive imputation of righteousness.

[76]See *The Westminster Confession of Faith*, 14:2. *The Creeds of Christendom*, 3:630-631.

between justifying faith and sanctifying faith describing such a distinction as "dangerous" talk.[77] In his treatment of the relationship of God and Adam and the covenant of works, Fuller argues that the sin of Adam consisted in the sin of unbelief, that the words of Genesis 2:17 encouraged faith, and that *such* faith was the condition of the forgiveness of sins.[78] Once again Fuller clearly does not see justifying faith as distinct from that required of Adam or as even distinctively elicited by the provisions of redemption.

The contrast between law and grace was formative for the Reformation understanding of justification *sola fide*. The conclusion is inevitable that Fuller in denying this contrast *root and branch* cannot and does not hold the Reformation understanding of justification by faith alone. This conclusion may be displayed more fully by tracing the results of Fuller's rejection of the contrast between law and gospel in the two other dimensions of *sola fide*–the distinction between justifying faith and obedience and the definition of justifying faith.

The Distinction between Justifying Faith and Obedience

A whole complex of features from Fuller's writings present themselves as evidence that Fuller rejects this distinction. We will consider four– persevering faith as the condition of justification, the distinction between two senses of works, Paul and James harmonized, and evangelical "works" as the condition of justification.

- **Persevering Faith as the Condition of Justification**

Fuller clothes himself frequently in the orthodoxy of Jonathan Edwards in presenting his novel views.[79] Edwards argued that the condition of justification was not "the faith of a moment," but persevering faith. Fuller's assumption is apparently that works were an inextricable part of perseverance and consequently a condition of justification for Edwards.

---

[77]Fuller, "Another Reply to *Counted Righteous in Christ*," 119.

[78]Fuller, *The Unity of the Bible*, 180-182.

[79]Fuller in *Gospel & Law*, 5, 6, 9, refers to Edwards, but not explicitly to his views of justification. In both *The Unity of the Bible*, 315-316 and "Another Reply to *Counted Righteous in Christ*," 117-118, he cites Edwards' sermon on justification: *The Works of President Edwards* (New York: Leavitt & Allen, 1958), 3:515-516. Fuller, *The Unity of the Bible*, 315-316, notes that "for some reason certain key statements in this passage have been omitted from the Banner of Truth version."

The propriety of this assumption on Fuller's part is questionable. The Reformation position has always been that we are justified by a faith that works by love. It would be surprising, indeed, to learn that Edwards had departed from such a fundamental aspect of his own tradition.[80]

Calvin and the Reformation could have in a certain sense affirmed that we are justified by *a faith that works through love* (Gal 5:6), but they would have added that this does not mean that we are justified by *faith working through love*, but through faith resting on Christ. Similarly, this formula of Edwards *could* mean that we are justified only by a faith that perseveres, but not mean at all that we are justified through faith persevering. Whatever Edwards means, the fact is that Fuller is glossing over a crucial distinction when he assumes that justification by persevering faith means justification because faith perseveres. The Reformation understanding of justification *sola fide* carefully distinguishes two different questions. *What kind of faith justifies?* is strictly distinguished from the question, *Why does it justify?*[81]

- **The Distinction between Two Senses of "Works"**

But here we come to a distinction that is vital for Fuller—the distinction between two kinds of works. Vital to his understanding of justification is a distinction between works done to boast and for merit and works done in faith and by grace.

> But Luther (and Calvin) did not enjoy the benefits of the rather recent movement in biblical theology and so were apparently unaware that Paul used "works" in two very different senses. Thus Luther unfortunately repudiated James as subcanonical.[82]

---

[80]"Faith, thus receiving and resting on Christ and his righteousness, is the alone instrument of justification: yet is it not alone in the person justified, but is ever accompanied with all other saving graces, and is no dead faith, but worketh by love." *The Creeds of Christendom*, 3:626. *The Westminster Confession of Faith*, 11:2.

[81]The views of Jonathan Edwards deserve much more extended treatment than I have given them here. I suspect that Fuller is understanding Edwards in a way that is unnecessarily contrary to the Reformation tradition. Even if Edwards is somewhat astray from that tradition, my argument in this dissertation is not affected. As I said in Chapter Four, the Reformation tradition must be defined in terms of its public Confessions and not by the eccentricities of individual theologians—even theologians as important and popular as Edwards.

[82]Fuller, *The Unity of the Bible*, 311.

Had Calvin realized that Paul spoke of works in the two sharply different senses noted above (see n. 4), he would not have had to explain why he changed what Scripture calls a cause (e.g. Gen 22:18) into a "step," "as it were."[83]

Paul used it [works] pejoratively for works in which people thought they could boast before God (Rom 3:27-28, lit. trans.; 4:6; 9:32; Eph 2:9; Titus 3:4-5, lit. trans.). But he also spoke of works that were viewed as honoring God because they proceeded from faith (1 Thess 1:3; also Gal 5:6 and 2 Thess 1:11 in the Greek).[84]

The faith that is their essential characteristic is therefore never a faith separate from the works of love. . . . Thus works that stem from faith—that is, from confidence and joy in what God will do for us, enforced by the love he has already shown us—are often spoken of as the condition of salvation. . . . But as we saw in the preceding chapter, such works are very different from those done to boast in what we are in ourselves.[85]

Fuller illustrates this distinction repeatedly.[86] The works of faith are never to be understood as a *job description* but as a *doctor's prescription*.[87] This distinction is introduced in explanation of Romans 4:3-5.[88] Here is what he means by it:

In what sense, then, are works to be excluded from that attitude which is indispensable for receiving God's grace? Depending on the context, the word "works" in Paul's vocabulary means either (1) those actions such as a workman like the supermarket checker would perform, or (2) the things done by a client, customer, patient, or employer in order to benefit fully from the expertise of a workman. According to Paul, men should never think of themselves as doing the first kind of works for God. Neither in his decision to become a Christian nor in his subsequent walk as a follower of Christ should a man think of himself as working for God in the sense of supplying God with some need, so that God should be obligated and grateful to man.[89]

---

[83] Ibid., 314.
[84] Ibid., 323.
[85] Ibid., 335.
[86] Besides the quotations cited below, see Fuller, *The Unity of the Bible*, 55-56, 151-153, 315; idem, "A Response on the Subjects of Works and Grace," 75-76; idem, *Gospel & Law*, 117-120.
[87] Fuller, *The Unity of the Bible*, 53.
[88] Fuller in *Gospel & Law*, 105-106.
[89] Ibid., 109-110, see 105-108.

- **Paul and James Harmonized**

Fuller is convinced that it is in terms of this distinction between two kinds of works that Paul (in Romans 3-4) and James (in Jas. 2) are to be harmonized. He criticizes both Luther's rejection of James as subcanonical and Calvin's attributing to "justification" a different meaning in James.[90] In this context he introduces the distinction between two kinds of works as the proper resolution of the problem.

> But Luther (and Calvin) did not enjoy the benefits of the rather recent movement in biblical theology and so were apparently unaware that Paul used "works" in two very different senses.[91]

> Had Calvin realized that Paul spoke of works in the two sharply different senses noted above (see n. 4), he would not have had to explain why he changed what Scripture calls a cause (e.g. Gen. 22:18) into a "step," "as it were."[92]

- **Evangelical "Works" as the Condition of Justification**

We are now able to see clearly the conclusion that Fuller draws from his distinction between two kinds of works. It is that works in the sense of evangelical obedience, works in the sense of the faith that works through love (Gal 5:6), are also the condition of justification. To refer to such works and to refer to faith is to refer to the same, identical thing for Fuller. Persevering faith includes the works of which James is speaking, and persevering faith is the condition of justification.

> These two facts from Abraham's life thus lead to the thesis that *the condition for justification is persevering faith*.[93]

> These several inconsistencies in his attempt to harmonize James and Paul regarding Abraham's justification therefore confirm our thesis that justification does depend on persevering faith. . . .[94]

---

[90]Fuller, *The Unity of the Bible*, 311.
[91]Ibid., 311.
[92]Ibid., 314.
[93]Ibid., 310.
[94]Ibid., 315.

This conclusion must also follow from the way in which Fuller insists on harmonizing James and Paul. If James is speaking of the very justification of which Paul is speaking, and James insists that works are the condition of such justification, then the conclusion inevitably follows that men are justified by works and works are the instrumental cause of justification in the same way that faith is.

Thus, Fuller has no problem straightforwardly affirming that works are the condition of salvation. The implications of this astonishing assertion might be mitigated if Fuller somehow distinguished between salvation more generally and justification, but no such distinction is made. He seems to regard the statements that (1) works are the condition of justification and that (2) works are the condition of salvation as equivalent.

> Thus works that stem from faith—that is, confidence and joy in what God will do for us, enforced by the love he has already shown us—are often spoken of as the condition for salvation . . . .[95]
>
> They are anxious to avoid anything that seems to make salvation conditional on works. But it just may be that the Bible teaches that God's forgiveness is conditioned not only on Christ's dying for our sins, but also on our repentance, which would include forgiving those who have wronged us.[96]
>
> Since the connection is *inseparable*, and genuine faith cannot but produce works, the Bible sometimes speaks of faith and sometimes of works when it speaks of the condition to be met in receiving the forgiveness of sins or subsequent blessings from God. So there is no need for establishing an elaborate division in Scripture as is done in covenant theology and dispensationalism.[97]
>
> If Robertson were to agree with this, then he could handle the many passages in Scripture in which good works are made the instrumental cause of justification.[98]

Notwithstanding Fuller's distinction between two kinds of works, he has drastically deviated from the entire Reformation tradition of justification *sola fide*. Justification *sola fide* did not mean simply

---

[95]Ibid., 335.
[96]Fuller in *Gospel & Law*, 61-62.
[97]Ibid., 113.
[98]Fuller, "A Response on the Subjects of Works and Grace," 79.

justification by faith as opposed to boasting works. As we have seen in our treatments of Calvin, Luther, and the Reformation Confessions, it meant justification by faith as opposed to any works whatsoever—including faith itself considered as a work. Justification *sola fide* meant a distinction between justifying faith and evangelical obedience that Fuller does not and cannot (within the orbit of his views) hold. Justification by faith alone meant justification by faith resting and not by faith working. It means no such thing for Fuller. Godfrey is only summarizing the necessary application of what we have proven at length previously, when he remarks:

> Fuller's revision affects the basic understanding of the application of redemption. Historic Protestantism insisted that justification was by faith alone because faith alone looked outside of itself to rely on the perfect work of Christ. Faith justifies not because it is a virtue that pleases God, but because faith abandons all self-confidence and rests in Christ and his finished work. Faith trusts that Christ has fulfilled all righteousness and borne God's wrath for sin. Fuller, by contrast, changes faith's whole relation to justification. He defines faith in terms of obedience. Faith is work. Justifying faith then is not an exclusively extraspective resting in the work of another.[99]

Fuller and the Definition of Faith

Godfrey's concluding statement brings us directly to the last dimension of *sola fide* in light of which Fuller must be weighed–the definition of faith. Here, of course, our special concern is with what is called justifying faith.

- **Sanctification by Faith Alone?**

At first glance, it seems a little audacious even to question Fuller's commitment to justification by faith alone. For Fuller not only affirms justification by faith alone, he even affirms *sanctification* by faith alone.

> ... But perhaps my most radical conclusion is that in Pauline and other biblical theology, true faith is not merely accompanied by good works as something coordinate with it, but that faith itself is the mainspring for producing good works. I have had to regard as Galatianism any teaching that sees faith as merely giving one the assurance of salvation,

---

[99] W. Robert Godfrey, "Back to Basics," 81.

and the Holy Spirit and the law as impelling good works. Sanctification, like justification, must be by faith *alone*.[100]

This passage leaves no doubt that the problem at Galatia was sanctification, rather than justification. Galatianism, therefore, is a faulty view of sanctification. . . . Galatians 5:6 provides another argument to support the conclusion that sanctification, like justification, is by faith alone.[101]

Yet more, according to Fuller, anyone who denies sanctification by faith alone or distinguishes between justifying and sanctifying faith trends dangerously close to the Galatian heresy.[102] It might seem like audacity to challenge such claims to *sola fide*. Fuller's affirmation of sanctification by faith alone reveals, however, either that he does not understand or does not hold justification *sola fide* in the Reformation sense.

Though Fuller's readings of Church History are often suspect, as we have seen, in this case this author agrees with Fuller with regard to the issue of sanctification by faith alone.[103] That is, Calvin neither believed nor taught sanctification by faith alone nor is sanctification by faith alone part of the Reformation tradition.

Here is why. Justification *sola fide* means in the Reformation tradition justification by faith resting. The definition of justifying faith is, in other words, passive. It is not because faith works through love that it justifies. The meaning of sanctification in the context of this discussion is *ongoing sanctification*. We are speaking, in other words, of *the process of sanctification*. The Bible and the Reformation following its teaching assert that ongoing sanctification involves many other acts of faith than merely faith resting.[104] It involves, in other words, faith working through love. It is clear from all this, then, that we are not, in the Reformation sense of *sola fide*, sanctified *by faith alone*. Justification *sola fide* meant justification solely by faith resting in Christ. Since we are not sanctified in the sense under discussion solely by faith resting on Christ, but also by

---

[100]Ibid., ix.

[101]Ibid., 115. See also Fuller's comments in "A Response on the Subjects of Works and Grace," 77.

[102]Fuller, "Another Reply to *Counted Righteous in Christ*," 119.

[103]I do not, however, agree with Fuller that the Galatian heresy was the denial of sanctification by faith alone.

[104]*The Creeds of Christendom*, 3:630-631. *The Westminster Confession of Faith*, 14:2.

faith working through love, then for the Reformation tradition, we are not sanctified by faith alone.

This is also clear from the Reformation tradition's distinction between justification and sanctification. Justification is a once-for-all definitive act. Sanctification is an ongoing process (as Fuller intends it in this discussion.) Thus, faith resting on Christ completes justification, but it does not complete sanctification. Unless one wishes to affirm the unlikely proposition that none of the other actings of faith (mentioned in *The Westminster Confession*[105]) are involved in our sanctification, it cannot possibly be maintained that we are sanctified by faith alone, that is, faith resting.

No doubt, it is true that faith resting commences sanctification. No doubt, it is true that faith resting continues in sanctification. It is simply not true, however, that faith working is excluded as an instrumental means from our sanctification. Both faith resting and faith working are involved in sanctification. Calvin affirmed a place for the threatenings of the law in sanctification.[106] It is part of the obedience of faith to tremble at such threatenings. Works—including faith working—is, however, by the Reformation tradition excluded as the instrumental means of our justification.

The point of all this is that it is only by importing his activistic view of faith into the meaning of *sola fide* that Fuller can assert that sanctification is by faith alone. Sanctification is by faith alone for Fuller, in other words, because by faith alone he means the obedience of faith. It is only by redefining *sola fide* that Fuller can affirm sanctification *sola fide*. The fact that he does so is the best proof possible that he has departed from the passive (or merely instrumental) definition of justifying faith taught in the Reformation tradition.[107]

---

[105]*The Creeds of Christendom*, 3:630-631. *The Westminster Confession of Faith*, 14:2: "By this faith, a Christian believeth to be true whatsoever is revealed in the Word, for the authority of God himself speaking therein; and acteth differently upon that which each particular passage thereof containeth; yielding obedience to the commands, trembling at the threatenings, and embracing the promises of God for this life, and that which is to come. But the principal acts of saving faith are accepting, receiving, and resting upon Christ alone for justification, sanctification, and eternal life, by virtue of the covenant of grace."

[106]Fuller, "A Response on the Subjects of Works and Grace," 78, cites some of the statements of Calvin that he finds offensive.

[107]Fuller is, however, wrong when he asserts that Calvin denied that good works proceed from faith: *Gospel & Law*, xi: ". . . But perhaps my most radical conclusion is that in Pauline and other biblical theology, true faith is not merely accompanied by good works as something coordinate with it, but that faith itself is the mainspring for producing

- **Assurance of Salvation?**

When he asserts that the condition of justification is persevering faith, Fuller is confronted with a problem when it comes to assurance of salvation. Thus, in his chapter on "Abraham's Persevering Faith" in *The Unity of the Bible* he is forced to take up the question: *Can believers have the assurance of sins forgiven when they first believe?*[108] The difficulty in which Fuller has entangled himself becomes evident in the way in which he grapples with this problem.[109] "If perseverance in faith is the test of its genuineness, how can we have the assurance of sins forgiven when we first believe?"[110] The only satisfactory answer is the one given by the Reformation tradition. It teaches that we are justified by a true faith that perseveres, but which may be known as a true faith *prior to its persevering.*[111] This is not, however, what Fuller says. Instead, he concludes by pointing his readers to John Wesley![112] Wesley believed that genuine believers could fall away permanently and be lost. Whatever Wesley may have believed personally about assurance of salvation, he could not teach consistently anything that the Reformation tradition could recognize as assurance of salvation. He certainly could not consistently teach that we may be assured of our eternal salvation prior to enduring to the end.

The point of relevance for this discussion of the definition of justifying faith is just this. If faith is inseparable and indistinguishable from works, prior to and in the absence of such works there can be no assurance of salvation. Thus, Fuller's struggles here point to a definition of faith that is far different than the justifying faith that for both Luther

---

good works. I have had to regard as Galatianism any teaching that sees faith as merely giving one the assurance of salvation, and the Holy Spirit and the law as impelling good works. Sanctification, like justification, must be by faith *alone.*" Fuller, *The Unity of the Bible*, 313, asserts, "Paul would also have agreed with James that Abraham's work of preparing to sacrifice Isaac was an obedience of faith because it demonstrated his confidence in God's promises. But he would have disagreed strongly with Calvin, who saw obedience and works as only accompanying, and not stemming from, genuine faith." As the chapter on Calvin has shown, such an assessment is simply nonsense. Calvin believed that the Christian was joined to Christ by faith alone and that as a result he was both sanctified and justified. How is this teaching that works only accompany, but do not stem from genuine faith?

[108]Fuller, *The Unity of the Bible*, 319.
[109]Ibid., 319-322.
[110]Ibid., 319.
[111]*The Creeds of Christendom*, 3:638. *The Westminster Confession of Faith*, 14:3.
[112]Fuller, *The Unity of the Bible*, 321-322.

and Calvin immediately involved assurance of salvation. Fuller actually affirms such a definition of faith when he remarks:

> But somehow he [Robertson] wants this faith to be abstracted from good works so that the remaining faith would be the instrumental cause of justification. But what is left when good works are abstracted from the good works which Christ enables? So I have difficulty defining faith as nothing more than Christ's enablement.[113]

It is exactly what Fuller calls *abstracting faith from good works* that the Reformation tradition meant by distinguishing faith and obedience in their understanding of justification by faith alone. Again Fuller clearly has a definition of justifying faith that includes human good works and that is not exclusively passive. This is a patent departure from the meaning of *sola fide* in the Reformation tradition.

- **Justifying Faith Defined**

Fuller actually provides for us a definition of justifying faith in a couple of ways. He denies any distinction between justifying and sanctifying faith as tending toward the Galatian heresy. Thus, we need not concern ourselves with whether in any given place Fuller is defining sanctifying faith or justifying faith. They are one and the same for him. Thus also clearly, works done as response to the *doctor's prescription* are necessarily included in the definition of justifying faith.

Fuller also provides what appears to be a rather straightforward definition of saving faith in *The Unity of the Bible*.

> Reminding them that it was through faith alone that the great blessings they had received had come, he admonished them to "consider Abraham . . ." This faith that we are to exercise comprises three essential elements. . . . These elements are (1) faith's futuristic orientation, (2) its power to motivate obedience to God, and (3) its demand for perseverance.[114]

This definition of faith is odd from a number of perspectives. The point of importance for us, however, is that it drastically diverges from

---

[113]Fuller, "A Response on the Subjects of Works and Grace," 79.
[114]Fuller, *The Unity of the Bible*, 270.

the definition of justifying faith taught by Luther, Calvin, and the Reformation tradition.

Fuller versus the Reformation

At every single point and with reference to every single one of the key perspectives on justifying faith we have uncovered, Fuller's understanding diverges from the Reformation tradition. He may affirm justification *sola fide*, but with reference to each of its characteristic features, he denies it. He rejects the contrast between law and gospel, the distinction between justifying faith and obedience, and the (passive) definition of justifying faith. His view clearly represents a departure from the classical meaning of *sola fide*.

CHAPTER 6

SOLA FIDE IN NORMAN SHEPHERD

Introduction

Norman Shepherd's ministry and career must be located near the center of American Evangelicalism. He was trained at the premier Reformed and evangelical seminary in the United States. Westminster Theological Seminary in Philadelphia was founded to be the successor seminary of Old Princeton by J. Gresham Machen. Shepherd joined the faculty in 1963 and later succeeded John Murray in the chair of systematic theology. He was a minister of the Orthodox Presbyterian Church until 1982 when he was formally transferred to a classis of the Christian Reformed Church. Before retiring in 1998, he served two pastorates in that denomination.[1] Shepherd's Reformed and evangelical credentials are undeniable. This is why his views of justification *sola fide* are so relevant for this study.

Shepherd's views are also important for two further reasons. *First*, because his views became controversial prior to the popularity of the so-called "new perspective on Paul," they cannot be simply viewed (or dismissed) as a variant of the "new perspective."[2] *Second*, Shepherd's views have had a considerable influence, especially in Presbyterian circles.[3]

Peculiar problems confront the study of Shepherd's views of faith, obedience, and justification. One problem is that Shepherd has not been a prolific writer. Another is that many of his relevant statements are dated

---

[1]This biographical data is gleaned from a number of sources: O. Palmer Robertson, *The Current Justification Controversy* (Unicoi, TN: The Trinity Foundation, 2003), 82-84; Norman Shepherd, "Justification by Faith Alone," *Reformation and Revival Journal* 2, no. 2 (Spring 2002), 89; Norman Shepherd, *The Call of Grace: How the Covenant Illuminates Salvation and Evangelism* (Phillipsburg, NJ: P&R Publishing, 2000), back cover.

[2]David Van Drunen, "When the Covenant Obscures Justification," *Modern Reformation* (March/April 2002), 40, remarks, "Perhaps Shepherd taught a precursor to the New Perspective before the New Perspective as such was unveiled, but failed to receive proper credit for it."

[3]*The Auburn Avenue Theology Pros & Cons: Debating the Federal Vision–The Knox Theological Seminary Colloquium on the Federal Vision*, ed. E. Calvin Beisner (Fort Lauderdale, FL: Knox Theological Seminary, 2004), 101, 102, 144, 145, 146, 212, 265, 313, 315, shows that those defending the "new perspective"-influenced "Federal Vision" are also pervasively indebted to Norman Shepherd's views.

and not, perhaps, representative of his present views. The primary basis of the present treatment must, therefore, be distinguished from its secondary basis.

The primary basis for the critique offered here of Shepherd's views of justification *sola fide* is composed of his two recent writings on the subject. The first is his book entitled *The Call of Grace*, published in the year 2000. The second is an article entitled "Justification by Faith Alone," published in 2002.

Shepherd has made his views of these subjects known in a number of other ways. For a variety of reasons these "ways" can be of only secondary consideration in the present study. Much of the relevant material—as noted previously—is dated. Of this sort are his taped lectures given in the early 1970s at Westminster and a paper entitled "The Relation of Good Works to Justification in the Westminster Standards," presented to the Westminster faculty in 1976. Shepherd later refined the views presented in these materials. Thus, they must be handled carefully when used as a basis for understanding his views.

Among what I am calling the secondary materials there are, however, two of more interest and relevance to the present study. If used cautiously, they may prove helpful in the clarification of his views. The first is a paper written by Shepherd in 1979. Entitled "The Grace of Justification," it is a refinement of his earlier statements which sets out his views in a relatively careful and moderate form.[4] Also relevant are

---

[4]Norman Shepherd, "The Grace of Justification," (unpublished paper written in 1979), 22 pp. This paper is available from the PCA Historical Center: The Archive and Manuscript Repository for the Continuing Presbyterian Church, 12330 Conway Road, St. Louis, MO 63141 (314-469-9077). The PCA Historical Center publishes an extensive collection of documents related to the Shepherd controversy on the Internet. It is available at //www.pcanet.org/history/documents/shepherd/justification.html. The previously mentioned paper, "The Relation of Good Works to Justification in the Westminster Standards," is also available from this source. Robertson, *The Current Justification Controversy*, 48-50, implies that "The Grace of Justification," is a more careful and moderate statement of Shepherd's views. "Report of the Special Committee to Study Justification in Light of the Current Justification Controversy," Presented to the 258th Synod of the Reformed Church of the United States (accessed 5 January 2005), www.trinityrcus.com/Articles/reportshepherd1.htm, remarks, "After the May 23, 1978 Board meeting, Shepherd was given a leave of absence in order to revise his position and then report back to the Board. On February 8, 1979, the Board received Shepherd's paper, 'The Grace of Justification,' [41] and discussed it, along with Shepherd's 'Thirty-four Theses,' which currently was being evaluated by the Presbytery of Philadelphia of the OPC. The Faculty concluded that Mr. Shepherd held essentially to the substance of his formulations as developed in the October 1976 paper. The modification of certain phrases as requested by the Board had not changed the substance of his position. Good

two recent lectures delivered by Shepherd. Given in August of 2003 at a conference entitled Contemporary Perspectives on Covenant Theology, which was sponsored by the Southern California Center for Christian Studies, the lectures were titled "Justification by Faith in Pauline Theology" and "Justification by works in Reformed Theology."[5] Both these sources are relevant to the present study, but with certain limitations. "The Grace of Justification" was written over twenty-five years ago in a context of debate in which Shepherd's statements of his views were changing and evolving. The taped lectures are not available in written form currently and, thus, must also be used cautiously.

Indispensable in approaching and assessing Shepherd's views of justification is some understanding of the lengthy and difficult controversy over them at Westminster Seminary. This controversy spanned the years 1976-1982 and was in certain respects even longer. It involved many of the most prominent names in evangelical and Reformed circles.[6] It was a contributing cause to the failure of the OPC's merger with the PCA.[7] It was confusing and divisive. Major deciding votes related to the controversy in the seminary, presbyteries, and denominations involved were again and again split so evenly that a decisive response to Shepherd's views was never given. He was finally dismissed from the faculty of Westminster not precisely because he had been found guilty of substantial doctrinal error by seminary or presbytery, but because his views were enormously controversial.[8]

---

works were necessary as the way of justification, and not simply as its fruit. Walking in the way of justification was necessary to maintain justification. The sinner seeking justification might just as well be told to follow Jesus as to believe in Jesus." According to Robertson, *The Current Justification Controversy*, 29-30, this paper was intended as a modification of Shepherd's views. Robertson notes that the Board of the Seminary by a vote of 11 to 8 subsequently found no sufficient cause to continue discussing Shepherd's views and, thus, cleared him of any potential charges.

[5]These tapes are available from the Southern California Center for Christian Studies at (714) 572-8358.

[6]Robertson, *The Current Justification Controversy*, 48-50, mentions those called in as outside advisors to the seminary.

[7]Ibid., 61-66, records how central this issue was in the failure of the merger of the OPC and PCA.

[8]Robertson, *The Current Justification Controversy*, is a contemporary and in many cases even an eyewitness account of the controversy that maintains a high degree of objectivity. Mark Karlberg, *The Changing of the Guard: Westminster Theological Seminary in Philadelphia* (Unicoi, TN: The Trinity Foundation, 2001), offers an assessment that is more severe, finds error concerning the doctrine of justification in Richard Gaffin, and traces the roots of this error to John Murray's teaching at Westminster Seminary on the covenants. Shepherd's firing is also detailed in an article

This historical background should caution us against any "rush to judgment" and drive us to look more deeply into why Shepherd's views were so difficult to assess. It should not, however, cause doubt over the possibility of coming to any clear assessment of Shepherd's views in this critique. Time (over 25 years now since this controversy emerged at Westminster) does serve to give perspective. Much of importance has transpired theologically over the last three decades with regard to the doctrine of justification that may serve to put Shepherd's views into sharper perspective. Some of what has transpired has been detailed in previous chapters. Shepherd's recent writings may also serve this end.

It will also be helpful to ask about the motivations of Shepherd in asserting and maintaining a view that led to such controversy among brethren and, no doubt, caused him no little grief personally. What were and are Shepherd's motivations in his teaching on this subject? His motivations can be summarized by saying that he sees a big problem to which he believes he has a crucial answer. The big problem is "easy-believism." The crucial answer is the covenant.

That "easy-believism" is the big problem is clear from his writings. This is the note on which he chooses to begin his article entitled "Justification by Faith Alone." He remarks:

> There is an expression we commonly hear that goes something like this: "Jesus accepts you just the way you are." The idea seems to be that we are sinners and not worthy of God's attention. In fact, we even deserve to be punished for our sin. But not to worry! Jesus accepts you just the way you are. We are justified by faith and not by works. There is nothing we can do or need to do to escape from sin and its consequences. Only Jesus can save us and he saves us when we put our faith in him. That's all it takes, a simple act of faith. Jesus accepts us just the way we are! Is that what we mean when we say that we are justified by faith alone?[9]

In the pages that follow, Shepherd makes abundantly clear that this is (in his opinion) a one-sided distortion of justification by faith alone. Towards the end of his article, he asserts:

---

entitled "Westminster Seminary Fires Theologian," *Christianity Today* 26 (January 1, 1982): 49.

[9]Shepherd, "Justification by Faith Alone," 75-76.

> To return to a question asked at the beginning, does Jesus accept us just the way we are? The answer is "no" if we mean that coming to Jesus in faith does not require repentance and a change of lifestyle. . . .
>
> Can those be saved who do not turn from their ungrateful and impenitent ways? By no means. Scripture tells us that no unchaste person, no idolater, no adulterer, thief, no covetous person, no drunkard, slanderer, robber, or the like is going to inherit the kingdom of God.
>
> Sinners must turn from their ungrateful and impenitent ways. Our preaching and teaching are seriously defective and misleading if we do not make that fact known up front in the preaching of the gospel.[10]

This seems to be something of Shepherd's original concern in the views that caused the eruption of the controversy at Westminster. Toward the end of "The Grace of Justification," we hear these sharp remarks:

> Faith which does not issue in obedience to Christ is a mockery of the grace of the New Covenant. This is what the inquirer must understand if he is to believe unto the salvation of his soul.
>
> Similarly, the exhortations and warnings of the apostles given to believers are not intended to lead those who have begun in the Spirit back to the flesh (Gal. 3:3). They are designed to encourage the people of God to persevere in a living and active faith.[11]

The crucial answer offered by Shepherd to this big problem is the biblical idea of the relation between God and man as covenantal. The covenant is the answer to the problem of easy-believism or, as he calls it in *The Call of Grace*, antinomianism. The difficulty, as Shepherd sees it, is how to correct this problem without falling into the opposite evil of legalism. Shepherd believes that the answer is the covenant. He says:

> The issue can be formulated by posing these questions: How do you preach *grace* without suggesting that it makes no difference what your lifestyle is like? In other words, how do you preach grace without being antinomian? On the other hand, how do you preach *repentance* without

---

[10] Ibid., 89. Notice also the references to easy-believism in Shepherd, *The Call of Grace*, 68, 96.

[11] Shepherd, "The Grace of Justification," 21-22. The present writer cannot disagree with Shepherd's assessment that such "easy-believism" was and is a major problem in evangelicalism. The question is whether he has reacted properly to the problem or *over-reacted*.

calling into question salvation by grace apart from works? How do you insist on obedience without being legalistic? We can find the answers to these questions in the light of the biblical doctrine of the covenant. We will begin by looking at the covenant that the Lord God made with Abraham. Then we will look successively at the Mosaic and the new covenants, before seeking to draw some conclusions. The Bible does not leave us caught on the horns of a dilemma. Divine grace and human responsibility are not antithetical to each other. They are the two sides, or the two parts, of the covenant that God has made with us and with our children.[12]

Shepherd's view seems to be that in the biblical doctrine of the covenant we have a structure that reconciles law and grace, the spiritual tendencies that result in antinomianism and legalism.

> The covenant is initiated and imposed by God. It is a gracious structure. The relationship it creates is, however, one of mutual fellowship and communion. Thus, there is within the gracious context of the covenant a necessary requirement for a response of faithfulness to the obligations God lays out in the covenant.
> We can describe a covenant as a divinely established relationship of union and communion between God and his people in the bonds of mutual love and faithfulness.[13]

One might allow that this approach could prove helpful, but the first glimpse of difficulty is found in connection with this offered solution. For Shepherd offers this solution not to the problems merely of contemporary evangelicalism, but to an "old problem" stemming from the Reformation itself. He remarks:

> It is not my purpose to discuss the details of these documents or to explore the nuances of this debate. We simply note the significance of this discussion. It is another indication of some unresolved questions that are really the legacy of the Protestant Reformation. . . . . We are profoundly grateful for the progress that was made by the Reformation. We were led into a more biblical understanding of the way of salvation. Nonetheless, unresolved issues remain.[14]

---

[12] Shepherd, *The Call of Grace*, 8-9.
[13] Ibid., 12.
[14] Ibid., 4-5.

These remarks correspond to a remarkable implication left hanging by Shepherd later in his book.

> For its part, evangelical Protestantism has always insisted that salvation is wholly by God's grace. We have rightly rejected the idea that a human being can do anything to achieve his own salvation. We have rightly rejected the idea that a person can work to merit the reward of eternal life. However, we have not always rejected the very idea of merit itself. . . . if we do not reject the idea of merit, we are not really able to challenge the Romanist doctrine of salvation at its very root.[15]

It is clear, as Shepherd implies, that the Reformation did not reject *per se* the concept of merit with regard, for instance, to the death of Christ. Thus, the Reformation did not challenge Rome at its very root. It is, thus, Shepherd's view that contemporary problems with antinomianism and legalism stem from problems with the Protestant Reformation itself.[16] The very problems that the Reformation claimed to solve *for Shepherd* are unresolved. The Reformation offers inadequate solutions to the central issues it addressed—the issues of grace and merit, faith and works, justification and sanctification. This is an extraordinary claim!

It should not surprise us, therefore, that Shepherd offers his answer to these questions as a way of rapprochement between Rome and the Reformation. Here are his words:

> Is there any hope for a common understanding between Roman Catholicism and evangelical Protestantism regarding the way of salvation? May I suggest that there is at least a glimmer of hope if both sides are willing to embrace a covenantal understanding of the way of salvation.[17]

Does Shepherd claim to believe in justification by faith alone? It is not easy to summarize his views here. In his early paper from 1979, "The

---

[15] Ibid., 61-62. See also Shepherd's statements on this issue in "Justification by Faith Alone," 85-87.

[16] Shepherd, *The Call of Grace*, 8-9, remarks, "The strength of antinomianism is its appeal to what is at the heart of the Reformation: salvation by grace through faith, not by merit through works."

[17] Shepherd, *The Call of Grace*, 59. *Call of Grace*, 3-4, begins with a reference to the efforts for rapprochement between Rome and evangelicals and notes that they have "met with a broad measure of support in the evangelical community."

Grace of Justification," Shepherd distinctly and unqualifiedly affirms *sola fide*. He remarks:

> Fidelity to the attainments of the Protestant Reformation requires fidelity to the principle of Scripture alone as well as to the principle of justification by faith alone, and Scripture alone (<u>sola</u> <u>scriptura</u>) requires obedience to the whole of Scripture (<u>tota</u> <u>scriptura</u>).[18]

Later in the same paper, he provides a very clear and traditional distinction between justification and sanctification. In the process, he affirms *sola fide*.

> There is a radical distinction between justification and sanctification. Justification is an act of God's free grace with respect to his people whereby he pardons their sin and accepts them as righteous on the ground of the righteousness of Jesus Christ imputed to them and received by faith alone. Sanctification is a work of God's free grace in them whereby He transforms them progressively into the image of his Son.[19]

These statements are in themselves clear affirmations of *faith alone*. They also make clear that Shepherd accepts a traditional distinction between justification and sanctification. He sees no place for faith as the ground of justification. It is only the instrument of justification. The insistence that faith is no part of the ground of justification seems to continue unabated in his writings.[20] While the traditional distinction between justification and sanctification seems to endure, problems arise with regard to *sola fide* as the instrument of justification.

The assertions of "faith alone" in *Call of Grace*, while at first appearing clear, on closer examination are somewhat ambiguous. In the first such assertion Shepherd affirms that "Luther came to see that salvation was by grace alone through faith alone." He immediately puts his own interpretation on this, however, by explaining:

---

[18]Shepherd, "The Grace of Justification," 1.
[19]Ibid., 14.
[20]Shepherd, "Justification by Faith Alone," 76-77, affirms, "We are not justified because we believe. Faith serves rather only as an instrument to receive the righteousness of Jesus Christ. There is no ground in ourselves on the basis of which God can declare us righteous. God imputes the righteousness of Jesus Christ to us and on that ground we are justified."

Because of what Jesus had done during his life and in his death on the cross, sinners could be saved by receiving him in faith. We are saved by grace through faith. We are not saved by good works through merit.[21]

In Shepherd's second reference, the fact that faith alone is problematic becomes clear. The words, "Salvation is by grace alone through faith alone," appear, but careful scrutiny shows that they are put in the mouth of the antinomian who says, "You receive Jesus as your Savior, but whether you receive him as Lord of your life is another matter."[22]

Shepherd's problems with justification by faith alone are fully and remarkably revealed in his article, "Justification by Faith Alone." Here he makes a number of assertions that challenge the value of the formula, *justification by faith alone*. Among his revealing and surprising assertions here are the following:

> Although "justification by faith alone" is commonly used among us. The interesting thing is that the Westminster Standards do not use that formula.
>
> When the Catechisms say that imputed righteousness is received by faith alone they are describing the instrumental function of faith. They do not use the formula, "justified by faith alone."
>
> . . . there is also a difference between the classic Lutheran and Reformed doctrines of justification.
>
> By not using the formula, justification by faith alone, the Westminster Standards avoid a serious misunderstanding of the gospel.
>
> Either we suppress this emphasis in our preaching and teaching altogether, or we resort to the idea that repentance and obedience automatically follow upon justification as evidence of salvation that is granted by faith alone apart from repentance and obedience. Recourse to this idea is a dogmatic necessary [*sic*] but textually unwarranted.

---

[21]Shepherd, *The Call of Grace*, 5. As we shall see, Shepherd wants to contrast faith not with all good works, but only with meritorious works (Ibid., 59-63).
[22]Ibid., 6.

> Luther inserted the word "alone" into his translation of Romans 3:28 . . . . this is the origin of the dogmatic formula, justification by faith alone. However, his insertion actually distorts Paul's meaning.
>
> We can use the formula, "justification by faith alone," . . . . Use of that particular formula, however, cannot be made a litmus test for orthodoxy. If it were both Scripture and the Westminster Confession would fail the test.
> We can use the formula, "justification by faith alone," as long as we understand and avoid the ambiguities and liabilities involved in it.[23]

At the end of the day, Shepherd seems willing to use the formula, *justified by faith alone*, but only after much struggle, explanation, and qualification. The last paragraph of "Justification by Faith Alone" contains this sentence: "We are justified and saved only by faith in Jesus Christ, his blood and righteousness."[24] Thus, Shepherd affirms justification by faith alone in what he thinks is its confessional sense. The question is whether he is right in what he thinks is its confessional sense and means by it what the Protestant Reformation meant.

This introduction has already intimated that the heart of Shepherd's agenda has to do with the meaning of "faith alone" as the instrument of justification. He specifically disavows any interest in somehow inserting faith into the ground of justification.[25] This once again vindicates the focus of this study on the meaning of *sola fide* for evangelicals like Shepherd. We return then to three windows into the meaning of faith alone that we have isolated earlier–the definition of justifying faith, the distinction between justifying faith and obedience, and the dichotomy between law and gospel. The first of the three windows through which

---

[23]Shepherd, "Justification by Faith Alone," 76, 78, 81, 85, 87, 88. The assertion that the Westminster Standards do not use the formula "justification by faith alone" is astonishing. Shepherd by this assertion asks us to believe that its authors distinguished between *faith as the alone instrument of justification* and *justification by faith alone*. Of course, they qualify this statement, but that is the point. The assertion that *faith is the alone instrument of justification* needs to be qualified just as much as the statement that *we are justified by faith alone*. Shepherd also asks us to believe that somehow *the righteousness of Christ being received by faith alone* is somehow significantly different than *being justified by faith alone*. Such contortions only serve to reveal that there is something very un-confessional in Shepherd's view of justification by faith alone.
[24]Shepherd, "Justification by Faith Alone," 89.
[25]This does not necessarily mean that there are no results for Shepherd's understanding of the ground of justification, but simply that this is not his starting-point.

Sola Fide in Norman Shepherd

we will consider Shepherd's view of faith alone is the traditional distinction between justifying faith and obedience.

The Distinction between Justifying Faith and Obedience

- **Alleged Difference between Classic Lutheran and Reformed Views**

Both in "Justification by Faith Alone" and *The Call of Grace* Shepherd asserts a difference between Lutheran and Reformed views of *sola fide*. In *The Call of Grace* he notes the differences between Lutheran and Reformed with regard to the uses of the law.[26] He does not prove, however, that such differences lead to diverse views of *sola fide*.

In "Justification by Faith Alone" he argues that the Lutheran and the Reformed posit different views of the relation of faith and good works. Here is what he says:

> At this point there is also a difference between the classic Lutheran and Reformed doctrines of justification. Lutheran doctrine holds that the Holy Spirit kindles faith in us by the hearing of the gospel. Faith then lays hold of Christ and Christ's righteousness is imputed to the believer for justification. After the believer has been justified, he is renewed and sanctified by the Holy Spirit and good works follow. Lutheranism can also maintain that "faith is never alone," but means by this that saving faith is always *followed* by works and is productive of works. The sequence is of fundamental importance. This is not what the Westminster Confession means when it says that justifying faith is never alone and cites James 2:17, 26 together with Galatians 5:6 to support that affirmation.[27]

The first problem with the distinction Shepherd posits here is that the description he provides of Lutheranism very neatly summarizes the view of *John Calvin*. This study has shown that Calvin also "holds that the Holy Spirit kindles faith in us by the hearing of the gospel. Faith then

---

[26]It is true that differences have emerged between the two traditions on this issue. It is not easy to sort out the relation between Luther and Lutheranism and Melanchthon and Lutheranism on such issues. Luther's views in particular are subject to some debate. Some believe that Luther held a third use. Others deny this. See Paul Althaus, *The Theology of Martin Luther* (Philadelphia: Fortress Press, 1966), 266-273; Philip Melanchthon, *Melanchthon on Christian Doctrine: Loci Communes 1555*, trans. and ed. Clyde L. Manschreck, intro. Hans Engelland (Grand Rapids: Baker, 1965), x-xii.

[27]Shepherd, "Justification by Faith Alone," 81.

lays hold of Christ and Christ's righteousness is imputed to the believer for justification. After the believer has been justified, he is renewed and sanctified by the Holy Spirit and good works follow."[28] Thus, Shepherd's distinction posits Lutheranism of Calvin! This brings us to the second problem with his distinction.

This problem is that the Reformed confessional tradition also and persistently makes good works the fruit or results of faith.[29] To give just one of the many examples cited in an earlier chapter, *The Belgic Confession* affirms:

> For it is by faith in Christ that we are justified, even before we do good works; otherwise they could not be good works, any more than the fruit of a tree can be good, before the tree itself is good.[30]

Even worse for his cause, a little later in his article Shepherd is forced to deal with the statement of *The Westminster Confession* that good works are the fruit of faith. His own statement reveals the problems this statement raises for the distinction he posits:

> Chapter 16, section 2, speaks of the good works done in obedience to God's commandments as "the fruits and evidences of a true and lively faith," and they certainly are that. But we have to avoid misunderstanding the metaphor used at this point. It is not as though faith could exist without its fruits and evidences the way an apple tree can exist without apples hanging from its branches."[31]

The problems with this statement of Shepherd are manifold. *First*, one wonders on what basis Shepherd justifies treating this passage as a metaphor? He provides no proof for this assertion. Why not take the statement in 11:2 that faith is never alone metaphorically?

The problem here is that Shepherd's own confusion and his own problems with *sola fide* are creating mirages for him in the Reformation tradition. That tradition persistently taught that justifying faith was a faith that worked through love, but that actual good works and moral renewal followed justifying faith. As the confessional tradition shows, Lutheran and Reformed theology cannot be turned against each other

---

[28]*Inst.* 3:1-11[*OS* 4:55-67]. See chapter three of this study.
[29]See chapter three of this study.
[30]*The Creeds of Christendom*, 3:411. [*CC* 2:417]. The Belgic Confession, Article XXIV.
[31]Shepherd, "Justification by Faith Alone," 82.

here.[32] Ultimately, the difficulty Shepherd feels arises not from a tension in the Reformation tradition, but from Shepherd's skewed view of *sola fide*. He fails to distinguish the nature of justifying faith (as a faith that works through love) from the power of faith that justifies (resting on and receiving Christ).

- **"Isolation" of Faith and Obedience**

The above discussion begins to reveal that Shepherd has deviated from the key distinction of Calvin between justifying faith and obedience. This is made even clearer when Shepherd complains about the isolation of the call to faith from the call of obedience.

> When the call to faith is isolated from the call to obedience, as it frequently is, the effect is to make good works a supplement to salvation or simply the evidence of salvation. Some would even make them an optional supplement.[33]

A good construction might conceivably be put on Shepherd's complaint. The problem is, however, that his complaint is ambiguous with regard to a key Reformation distinction regarding *sola fide*. Such ambiguity is not helpful when it is precisely *sola fide* that Shepherd is discussing.

As we have seen multiple times, Protestantism with one voice argued that, while justifying faith and evangelical obedience were *distinguishable*, they were nevertheless *inseparable*. This is the whole point of the statement of *The Westminster Confession* that "faith . . . the alone instrument of justification is never alone." The question is whether by complaining about the isolation of the call to faith from the call to obedience Shepherd is rejecting the distinction between faith and obedience or the idea that they are separable. Are we to take the idea of isolation as designating separation or distinction? Shepherd's ambiguity here is not helpful, if he wishes to make clear his meaning within the Reformation tradition. The trend revealed in Shepherd's ambiguity becomes even more visible as he rejects the isolation of faith from regeneration, repentance, and good works.

---

[32] Again, see chapters two and three of this study where these assertions are proven in detail.

[33] Shepherd, *The Call of Grace*, 104.

- **Faith Not to Be Isolated From Regeneration**

Shepherd argues that regeneration is confessionally the inception of sanctification. Since regeneration is also the source of faith, this situates saving faith firmly within the orbit of sanctification. This distinguishes the Reformed view from the Lutheran view that sanctification in every respect follows upon justification.

> Regeneration is the link between calling and sanctification. . . . Chapter 13 says that "They, who are once effectually called, and regenerated . . . are further sanctified," as already noted. It is after chapter 13 on sanctification that the Confession goes on to deal with saving faith, repentance, and good works in chapters 14, 15, and 16. The point is, of course, that saving faith does not precede the new birth, but follows upon regeneration. Regeneration initiates the process of sanctification, and saving faith, or justifying faith, emerges in the believer in the process of sanctification. This process brings to life not only faith but repentance and obedience. Just this priority of regeneration to faith explains why faith can never be alone . . . .
>
> Faith is logically prior to justification. We believe with a view to being justified. Because regeneration is prior to faith and is the initiation of sanctification, we have to say that the process of sanctification is prior to justification. This does not mean that justification is sanctification, or that sanctification is the ground of justification. This was the erroneous teaching of the Council of Trent. Justification is forensic, not transformative. But it does mean that the Reformed view differs from the Lutheran view that sanctification in every respect follows upon justification.[34]

A number of statements in this somewhat lengthy quotation from Shepherd exhibit profound confusion. *First,* his deduction from the order of the Confession that sanctification precedes saving faith is simply wrong. If he were right, we would also have to conclude that justification precedes saving faith, a position the Confession explicitly rejects. By the same logic, the fact that the chapter on justification precedes saving faith would mean that in the order of salvation justification precedes saving faith. The Confession rather deals topically in chapters 10 to 18. In chapters 10 to 13 the *divine activities* of effectual calling, justification, adoption, and sanctification are discussed in order. In chapters 14 to 18 the *human activities* (graces) of saving faith, repentance, good works,

---

[34] Shepherd, "Justification by Faith Alone," 83.

perseverance, and assurance are treated in order. Within these two subdivisions there is, of course, logical order, and this is where Shepherd's weakness is exposed. The order of the Confession suggests (when properly understood) that justification precedes sanctification and that faith precedes repentance and good works. The order of the Confession actually suggests, in other words, the very view that Shepherd rejects.

Shepherd assumes without qualification or discussion that regeneration precedes faith. Actually, the Confession never clearly, actually, or verbally asserts this. It chooses the category of effectual calling within which to assert the divine and monergistic origin of faith. In the chapter on effectual calling (10:2) it speaks of their being quickened and renewed by the Holy Spirit so that they embrace the grace offered, but does not explicitly call this regeneration. It may or may not have been the view of the authors of *The Westminster* that regeneration precedes faith. As we have seen, however, in Calvin the relation of regeneration to faith is not straightforward. In the sense of faith being a gift of God, Calvin could occasionally speak of regeneration as logically preceding faith. It was more usual for Calvin to use regeneration in the sense of moral renewal, sanctification, and repentance and to insist that regeneration followed the faith that united the sinner to Christ. This structure maintains itself throughout the Reformation Confessions—whatever terminology is used to express it. It is fundamental to *The Westminster Confession* as well.

Shepherd urges that faith emerges within "the process of sanctification." This is an astonishing overstatement. Even if one grants that regeneration is to be understood as the inception of sanctification and the origin of faith, this does not mean that faith emerges within the *process* of sanctification. At most it means that faith originates with the inception of sanctification. Actually, and here we come to a consideration that establishes as well the previous points, the Confession teaches that faith precedes sanctification. The words of 14:2 are explicit: "the principal acts of saving faith are accepting, receiving, and resting upon Christ alone for justification, sanctification, and eternal life."[35] If sanctification is by means of faith, even its *inception* cannot logically precede faith. The *process* of sanctification certainly cannot precede saving faith.

Of more concern and importance than these confessional problems, but their clear implication, is the way in which Shepherd embeds faith in

---

[35] *The Creeds of Christendom*, 3:630-31. *The Westminster Confession of Faith*, 14:2.

the process of sanctification. This has the direct tendency of subsuming faith under the category of sanctification and erasing any distinction between faith and moral renewal. It tends to the view that identifies faith indistinguishably with repentance and obedience as the "way" or means of justification. It, thus, obscures the distinction between justifying faith and evangelical obedience essential to the meaning of *sola fide* in the Reformation. This becomes even clearer in Shepherd's argument that faith must not be *isolated* from either repentance or a certain kind of works.

- **Faith Not to Be Isolated from Repentance**

Shepherd observes:

> Faith and repentance are inseparable twins. As John Murray correctly observes, it is impossible to disentangle faith and repentance. Repentance is not the same thing as faith.[36]

In itself this statement is unobjectionable. The statements that faith and repentance are inseparable, but distinct ("not the same thing") is, indeed, a carefully balanced and important expression of the teaching of Scripture. Trouble arises, however, on two fronts for Shepherd's teaching on the relation of faith and repentance.

The first is that Shepherd equates repentance with or includes in repentance new obedience.

> Repentance, as defined in chapter 15, is not only a sorrow for and hatred of sin but also a turning from sin with a purpose and endeavor to walk with the Lord in all the ways of his commandments.[37]

> Repentance as defined by the Confession in chapter 15 includes not only a sorrow for sin, but also a turning away from sin. Justification means that God forgives sinners; but he does not forgive impenitent sinners. He forgives penitent sinners, sinners who turn away from their sin and who in faith cry out for mercy.[38]

> The New Testament, as well as the Old, clearly teaches that repentance entails more that [sic] just sorrow for sin. Repentance

---

[36]Shepherd, "Justification by Faith Alone," 84.
[37]Ibid.
[38]Ibid., 85.

includes turning away from sin and making a new beginning. . . . You cannot turn to Christ in faith without turning away from what is opposed to Christ in repentance.

Third, faith produces repentance, and repentance is evident in the lifestyle of the believer. Thus, the obligations of the new covenant include not only faith and repentance, but also *obedience*.[39]

The second front on which Shepherd's doctrine of repentance runs into trouble is that he equates repentance so defined with faith as necessary for the forgiveness of sins or justification, or a condition of justification.

This means that without repentance the sinner will not be pardoned. Repentance is like faith. It is neither the cause nor the ground of pardon. Yet it is absolutely necessary for the forgiveness of sins. Repentance is presented in the Confession not simply as the fruit and evidence of pardon, but also as necessary *for* the remission of sin. . . .

Now justification either is or includes the forgiveness of sins. Chapter 11, section 1, says that God justifies sinners by pardoning their sins. If justification includes forgiveness, and if repentance is necessary for forgiveness, then repentance is necessary for justification.[40]

When the preceding two assertions are combined, the combination of them leads directly to the conclusion that repentance in the sense of new obedience is necessary unto justification. That is to say, new obedience (or evangelical good works) is a condition of justification. This is certainly not a conclusion drawn by the Reformation tradition. Where has Shepherd gone astray from his own tradition?

First, he has equivocated on a distinction crucial to Calvin's presentation of *sola fide*. In his *Institutes*, Calvin clearly asserted that repentance in the sense of new obedience or sanctification was a consequence both of union with Christ and of the faith that was unto such union with Christ. When Calvin allowed and recognized in other places that justifying faith was preceded or accompanied by repentance, he carefully qualified the meaning of repentance. In the sense that repentance preceded and accompanied justifying faith, it was not new obedience, but shame, fear, humiliation, and displeasure with ourselves.[41] Calvin made these distinctions to protect the meaning of *sola fide*.[42]

---

[39]Shepherd, *The Call of Grace*, 47.
[40]Shepherd, "Justification by Faith Alone," 84-85.
[41]*Comm*. Acts 20:21[*CR* 76:462-64] and Ps 130:4 [*CR* 60:334-36]. Footnote

Shepherd has also equivocated the distinction instituted by *The Westminster Confession* between faith and repentance with regard to the instrumental cause of justification. He says, "Repentance is like faith. It is neither the cause nor the ground of pardon." This, however, misses an important distinction made by the Confession and the Reformation tradition. *Faith is not like repentance for the Confession.* For faith *is* in an important sense the *cause* of justification—its instrumental cause. When the Confession calls faith "the alone instrument of justification" in 11:2, this statement means that faith is the instrumental cause of justification. It reflects a long tradition beginning with Calvin that designated faith as such a case.[43] Thus, when in 15:3 the Confession denies that repentance is "any cause of the pardon thereof," it is denying that repentance has the place of faith in justification. Faith is the instrumental cause of justification. Repentance is not.

By (first) equating repentance with new obedience and (second) equating the place of repentance with the place of faith in justification, Shepherd deviates from the Reformation tradition and teaches a justification that is conditioned on new obedience. This is a subtle undermining and denial of the Reformation doctrine that faith alone is the instrumental cause of justification.

- **Faith Not to Be Isolated from Works**

It is no surprise, then, that Shepherd is perfectly willing to assert that a kind of works is necessary unto (or a condition of) being justified.

> Eternal life is promised as an undeserved gift from the Lord. He forgives our sins and receives us as righteous because of Jesus Christ and his redemptive accomplishments on our behalf. At the same time, faith, repentance, obedience, and perseverance are indispensable to the enjoyment of these blessings. They are conditions, but they are not meritorious. Faith is required, but faith looks away from personal merit to the promises of God. Repentance and obedience flow from faith as the fullness of faith. This is faithfulness, and faithfulness is

---

citations written as *Comm.* are from *Calvin's Commentaries*, 22 vols. (Grand Rapids: Baker Book House, 1981).

[42]Biblically speaking, repentance is, first of all, *metanoia*, a change of mind. New obedience and an altered lifestyle are strictly speaking the external results of this inner turning.

[43]*Comm.* Rom 3:22 and 24.

perseverance in faith. A living, active, and abiding faith is the way in which the believer enters into eternal life.[44]

This assertion that we are justified by believing works is made repeatedly in connection with James 2. Shepherd, in fact, proceeds to cite James 2 immediately after this quotation.[45] Elsewhere in *Call of Grace* Shepherd remarks:

> James 2 is even more explicit. Verse 21 says that Abraham was considered righteous for what he did when he offered his son Isaac on the altar. His faith and his actions were working together, and his faith was made complete by what he did. . . .
> James goes on to say that faith without deeds is dead. For that reason, he can also say in verse 24 that "a person is justified by what he does and not by faith alone." The faith credited to Abraham as righteousness was a living and active faith.[46]

Assumed in such references to James 2 is Shepherd's conviction that James is using "justify" in the same sense as Paul. Shepherd argues in some detail against the idea of justification having a "demonstrative sense" in James 2. He opts instead for the view that "justify" is used in a forensic sense as in Paul. James is saying that a man is saved or justified by works and not by faith alone. James expressly relates good works to justification and it is this fact that appears to bring James into conflict with Paul.[47]

Shepherd resolves this conflict by arguing that not all works, but only a certain kind of works are opposed to faith. Later in "The Grace of Justification" he remarks:

> Faith is opposed to all doing of the "works of the law." It is opposed to all doing that is self-affirming and self-congratulatory. It is opposed to all doing that find the cause or ground of acceptance with God in that doing. It is opposed to all merit. But faith is not opposed to doing the will of God. It is consonant with doing the will of God. As Paul says, faith works through love (Gal. 5:6).[48]

---

[44]Shepherd, *The Call of Grace*, 50.
[45]Ibid.
[46]Shepherd, *The Call of Grace*, 16. Shepherd, "Justification by Faith Alone," 79, 81, 88, repeatedly cites Jas. 2.
[47]Shepherd, "The Grace of Justification," 2.
[48]Ibid., 7. See also for similar statements pp. 5 and 8 of the same document. The language used here by Shepherd is ambiguous in terms of the Reformation doctrine of

In both *The Call of Grace* and "Justification by Faith Alone" Shepherd affirms this same distinction between works of merit and works of faith. In *Call of Grace* we read:

> But on a deeper level, what must be challenged in the Roman Catholic doctrine is the very idea of merit itself. God does not, and never did, relate to his people on the basis of a works/merit principle. The biblical texts to which Rome appeals must be read in light of the covenant. Then the biblical demands for repentance and obedience, together with the warnings against disobedience, can be seen for what they are. They are not an invitation to achieve salvation by human merit. They are a call to find salvation wholly and exclusively in Jesus Christ through faith in him.[49]

The conclusion is inevitable that, though we are not justified by the works of merit, we are justified by the works of faith. This, however, raises a question. How can the works of faith be a condition for something that has already occurred in the first moment of believing? In other words, how can the works of faith be a condition for the justification that the Bible asserts believers have prior to doing the works of faith? Here we confront a peculiar phenomenon in Shepherd. Though he never attacks the idea that believers are justified immediately upon believing, yet in a number of places he seems to assume that justification is yet future. This is not only the implication of his making obedience and perseverance a condition of justification; it is the constant implication in passages where he speaks of justification and eternal life as still future for the believer.

This tendency to speak of justification in "not yet" terms is already visible in "The Grace of Justification."[50] It continues to be evident in his more current writings. In *The Call of Grace* Shepherd speaks of justification and eternal life in "not yet" terms. The most striking evidence of this is found in a statement already quoted.

---

justification by faith alone. "But faith is not opposed to doing the will of God" is, of course, true—in the sense that faith is *inseparable* from doing the will of God. It is not true, however, if Shepherd means that faith is *indistinguishable* from doing the will of God. The power or quality by which faith justifies is not "doing the will of God," but resting on and receiving Christ. Some *opposition* in this latter sense between faith and obedience is, as chapter two to four have shown, necessary to the Reformation doctrine.

[49]Shepherd, *Call of Grace*, 60-61. See also idem, "Justification by Faith Alone," 88.
[50]Shepherd, "The Grace of Justification," 13.

Eternal life is promised as an undeserved gift from the Lord. He forgives our sins and receives us as righteous because of Jesus Christ and his redemptive accomplishments on our behalf. At the same time, faith, repentance, obedience, and perseverance are indispensable to the enjoyment of these blessings. They are conditions, but they are not meritorious. Faith is required, but faith looks away from personal merit to the promises of God. Repentance and obedience flow from faith as the fullness of faith. This is faithfulness, and faithfulness is perseverance in faith. A living, active, and abiding faith is the way in which the believer enters into eternal life.[51]

Not just eternal life, but also being received as righteous is made contingent on obedience and perseverance.[52]

The Definition of Justifying Faith

Chapters Two to Four have argued that justifying faith is *passive* in the Reformation tradition. That is to say, the justifying quality or power of faith and its principal acting is resting on and receiving Christ for salvation. Justification is by *this* acting of faith alone. Within the orbit of Shepherd's thought, such a view of justifying faith is nonsensical. We are not and cannot be justified alone by faith resting on Christ. We are also justified by faith working for Christ in the new life of repentance, obedience, and perseverance.

This seemingly straightforward and even necessary conclusion from Shepherd's views is, however, confronted with what appears to be a more traditional understanding of the matter in Shepherd's earlier writing, "The Grace of Justification." There he straightforwardly affirms

---

[51]Shepherd, *The Call of Grace*, 50. See also 44, 45, 100.

[52]It is true, of course, that the Bible speaks of future dimensions of both justification and eternal life, but surely one must carefully distinguish those future dimensions from the present blessings of eternal life and justification already possessed. Shepherd does not seem anywhere to do so. Illustrating Shepherd's imbalance toward the "not yet" is his use of the phrase 'eternal life'. Eternal life is always a future blessing for Shepherd, even though the Gospel of John makes clear that believers have in one sense already received eternal life (John 3:36; 5:24; 6:47, 54; 17:3). Shepherd, *Call of Grace*, 44, cites two passages from John's writings (John 10:10 and 1 John 2:25) that are likely present in force and gives them a future reference. Thus, he remarks, "On the Day of Judgment, those who belong to Jesus by faith will enter into eternal life. 'Believe in the Lord Jesus Christ, and you will be saved' (Acts 16:31). . . . The gospel promises pardon for sin and acceptance by God. It promises eternal life after the final judgment." Shepherd seems to give eternal life an *exclusively* future reference. Shepherd, as a result, cannot make the classical, Reformation distinction between justifying faith and evangelical obedience.

the orthodox, Reformation view of the function of faith in justification. Yet more, he surrounds his own statement with a litany of quotations from stalwarts of the Reformed faith strikingly affirming the same thing.[53] Here are Shepherd's own words:

> But if Paul says that the faith which avails for justification is faith working through love, does he mean that faith derives its power to justify from love so that it is after all love or works that justify and not faith? Not at all! This is the Roman Catholic interpretation of Gal. 5:6 which transforms the working of faith into "works of the law." This interpretation affirms precisely what Paul denies in the very same verse as well as in the Epistle as a whole. Faith alone justifies—that is Paul's doctrine. Faith does not look either to itself or to its own working for justification. Faith lays hold of Jesus Christ and his righteousness and the righteousness of Jesus Christ is imputed to the one who believes. This is the distinctive function of faith in justification which it shares with no other grace or virtue. The righteousness of Jesus Christ is imputed to the sinner the moment he believes. He believes and is justified.[54]

There is no question that in these words taken by themselves we have the orthodox Reformation doctrine of justification *sola fide*. This is an admirable statement of the ground of justification, *the righteousness of Jesus Christ*, the instrument of justification, *faith alone*, and the time of justification, *the moment he believes*. Most relevant to our present concern, Shepherd seems clearly to affirm a *passive* definition of justifying faith. No wonder that, when this statement was placed side by side with Shepherd's other statements (even those in "The Grace of Justification"), there was such confusion and division over Shepherd's views in the controversy at Westminster!

How shall we explain the above statement in conjunction especially with Shepherd's current statements in *The Call of Grace* and "Justification by Faith Alone"? Theoretically, a number of explanations are possible. One solution might be that Shepherd is simply incoherent. That is to say, his statements cannot be logically reconciled then or now. He is and always has been inconsistent. A second explanation could be that Shepherd's position has changed and developed in the 25 years since he wrote "The Grace of Justification." Thus, we might conclude that he

---

[53]Ibid., 2-5, cites the "golden" names and statements of J. Gresham Machen, John Calvin, John Murray, Robert Shaw, A. A. Hodge, and Francis Turretin.
[54]Ibid., 3.

no longer holds the views he states here. A third solution might incorporate elements of both the previous explanations. The present author is inclined to adopt the third solution for the following reasons.

First, it is difficult to doubt that Shepherd must have felt a great deal of pressure in the midst of the protracted controversy surrounding him at Westminster. This would have led him to restate his views (as he was doing in "The Grace of Justification") in the most moderate and acceptable fashion possible. One illustration of this is his quotation of Calvin in the "The Grace of Justification" with regard to the meaning of James 2. He even cites Calvin as explaining "he is justified by works, that is, his righteousness is known and proved by its fruits."[55] This is exactly the "demonstrative" explanation of James 2 that Shepherd has been at pains to refute in the opening pages of "The Grace of Justification"![56] The problem for Shepherd is that Calvin's defense of *sola fide* in James 2 is squarely built on his view that the justification in view there is not forensic.[57] Shepherd refutes this, but still wants to keep Calvin's view of *sola fide*.

Second, there is nothing like the clear statement of justification by faith alone in his current writings that Shepherd gave in "The Grace of Justification". There are rather statements that seem to challenge the sole instrumentality of faith he earlier affirmed. For instance, rather than maintaining the unique function of faith in justification, he remarks:

> Repentance is like faith. It is neither the cause nor the ground of pardon. Yet it is absolutely necessary for the forgiveness of sins. Repentance is presented in the Confession not simply as the fruit and evidence of pardon, but also as necessary *for* the remission of sin. . . .
>
> Now justification either is or includes the forgiveness of sins. Chapter 11, section 1, says that God justifies sinners by pardoning their sins. If justification includes forgiveness, and if repentance is necessary for forgiveness, then repentance is necessary for justification.[58]

---

[55]Ibid. See Calvin, *Comm.*, Jas. 2:24-25.

[56]Ibid., 1-2.

[57]Calvin, *Comm.*, Jas. 2:21, remarks, "That we may not fall into that false reasoning which has deceived the Sophists, we must take notice of the two-fold meaning of the word *justified*. Paul means by it the gratuitous imputation of righteousness before the tribunal of God; and James, the manifestation of righteousness by the conduct, and that before men."

[58]Shepherd, "Justification by Faith Alone," 84-85.

Shepherd asserted in "The Grace of Justification" that there is a "distinctive function of faith in justification which it shares with no other grace or virtue."[59] What has now become of that? If "repentance is like faith . . . neither the cause nor ground of pardon," what has become of the unique instrumental function of faith in justification as opposed to the other graces of the Christian life?

Shepherd does, of course, refer to 11:2 of *The Westminster Confession* where faith is called "the alone instrument of justification,"[60] but, as we have seen, his purpose is to distinguish this statement from the idea that we are justified by faith alone. This suggests that Shepherd's views may have developed and changed over the years since he wrote "The Grace of Justification."

There seems to be evidence that his views of the ground of justification have changed. While the statement in "The Grace of Justification" clearly asserts that the ground is "the righteousness of Jesus Christ," Shepherd now seems to reject the positive imputation of Christ's righteousness. He opts instead for a forensic justification that is equivalent to the forgiveness of sins.[61]

The explanation for the contrast between Shepherd's more traditional assertion of *sola fide* in "The Grace of Justification" and his current views may be rooted in his developing understanding of the implications of his distinction between works of merit and works of faith. This distinction is found in "The Grace of Justification," as we have seen, but it seems that its implications have gradually become clearer to Shepherd.

In "Justification by Faith Alone," he reflects on this distinction in a way that is quite relevant to the question at hand. He asserts that "our evangelical tradition" "shares with Roman Catholic theology the basic idea that good works are meritorious." He then remarks:

> From this perspective, "justification by faith alone" is not only a useful formula but also necessary if we are to avoid any suggestion that justification and salvation are by the merit of good works. The integrity of the gospel hangs on this formula. And again, this is true as long as we subscribe to the basic notion that good works are meritorious.

---

[59] Shepherd, "The Grace of Justification," 3.

[60] Shepherd, "Justification by Faith Alone," 76-79.

[61] Ibid., 84, remarks that "justification either is or includes the forgiveness of sins." In his recent tapes "Justification by Faith in Pauline Theology" and "Justification by works in Reformed Theology" Shepherd reduces justification to the forgiveness of sins. Cf. "RCUS Report," 18.

The problem is that this perspective offers no way of accounting for the gospel demand for both faith and repentance as necessary for the forgiveness of sins and no way of accounting for obedience as necessary for entering eternal life.[62]

Yes, but what if we now reject the whole notion of merit, root and branch? What then becomes of "justification by faith alone?" Well, in that case, Shepherd remarks that we solve the problems that arise from justification by faith alone. Then we see that good works are simply the answer to His love and the faithfulness required by His gracious covenant.

From a biblical perspective we need to reject the Roman Catholic doctrine that good works are meritorious. God never required his image bearers to earn eternal life by the merit of their good works. What he asks of us is to answer his love and faithfulness in the covenant bond of union and communion that he establishes with his people.[63]

Though Shepherd does not say so in so many words, the direct implication of the above statements appears to be that, once we reject the idea that good works are meritorious, we no longer need justification by faith alone to safeguard the gracious character of salvation. Furthermore, we solve the problem this doctrine raises with the biblical emphasis on repentance and obedience. When, therefore, Shepherd goes on to allow that we may still use the phrase, justification by faith alone, he means that it may be used provided that we understand it in a way that does not assume the merit of works. Since justification by faith alone *did* assume the merit of works in the Reformation tradition, Shepherd's words amount to the idea that we may say *justification by faith alone* only if we understand something different by this phrase than what it originally meant.

What we confront here is a transition in Shepherd himself from the original view to a different view of justification. Originally, justification by faith alone meant justification by faith opposed to all works whatever—even the works of faith. Now, Shepherd tells us we must take into account the idea that good works are not meritorious and the distinction between works of merit and works of faith. Taking this into account we come to a different view of justification by faith alone. So

---

[62]Shepherd, "Justification by Faith Alone," 86.
[63]Ibid., 88.

reconstructed, justification by faith alone means justification by the works of faith as opposed to the works of merit. This is, of course, not justification by faith alone and not a passive definition of justifying faith.

Shepherd's teachings with regard to both the distinction between justifying faith and obedience and the definition of justifying faith are his most obvious deviations from the Reformation doctrine of justification *sola fide*. As we have seen, however, these deviations result from a fundamental and formative distinction between the works of merit and the works of faith. The rejection of the very concept of merit that we have noticed in Shepherd leads directly to problems with the third, crucial perspective on the Reformation doctrine of *sola fide*—the dichotomy between law and gospel.

The Dichotomy of Law and Gospel

In coming to an accurate assessment of Shepherd's view of law and gospel, a number of factors must be understood.

- **Merit as a Theological Concept Rejected**

We have seen already that Shepherd rejects what he calls "the basic notion that works are meritorious."[64] A rejection of the very concept ("basic notion") of human works, however, as ever meritorious leads directly to the conclusion that Christ's works were not meritorious. No distinction can be made, then, between Christ's obedience to the law as meritorious and our obedience as non-meritorious. This immediately raises questions about whether there is any room in Shepherd for a contrast between law and gospel. This question becomes even more pressing when Christ is set forth as the model of the obedience of faith.

- **Christ as the Paradigm of Faith**

Shepherd describes the redemptive work of Christ in terms of obedient faith and even remarks that Christ's faith was credited to Him as righteousness.

> All of this is made possible through the covenantal righteousness of Jesus Christ. His was a living, active, and obedient faith that took him

---
[64]Ibid., 86.

all the way to the cross. This faith was credited to him as righteousness.
. . .

    Nothing demonstrates the conditional character of the Abrahamic covenant more clearly than the way in which the promises of that covenant are ultimately fulfilled. They are fulfilled through the covenant loyalty and obedience of Jesus Christ.

    But just as Jesus was faithful in order to *guarantee* the blessing, so his followers must be faithful in order to *inherit* the blessing.[65]

We will not be surprised at this presentation of the redemptive work of Christ if we remember Shepherd's complete rejection of the notion of merit. If there are no works of merit, then Christ's work can only be a work of faith.

This presentation bristles, however, with difficulties. Evidently, Shepherd wants to somehow distinguish between the faithfulness of Jesus *guaranteeing* the blessing and the faithfulness of believers *inheriting* the blessing. But what can this distinction be? Shepherd makes clear that the Abrahamic Covenant (like the Mosaic and New Covenants) is not a covenant of works. That is to say, it does not require perfect, perpetual obedience to the law, but only the works of faith.

    The Abrahamic covenant cannot give comfort to the antinomians, but neither can it give comfort to the legalists. The Abrahamic covenant was not unconditional, but neither were its conditions meritorious. This is the light that is shed on the way of salvation by the biblical teaching on covenant.

    In the Abrahamic covenant, there are promises and obligations. The blessings of the covenant are the gifts of God's free grace, and they are received by way of a living and active faith. Salvation is by grace through faith. By *grace* and through *faith!* Those are the two parts of the covenant. Now we want to see how this theme carries through into the Mosaic covenant, and from there into the new covenant.[66]

The problem for Shepherd is he wants to distinguish Christ's work of faith from our work of faith, but in denying the very concept of merit, and without affirming some form of the covenant of works with Adam,[67] he has no category by which to make such distinction. All he can say is

---

[65] Shepherd, *The Call of Grace*, 19.
[66] Ibid., 22.
[67] As we shall see, Shepherd studiously avoids affirming such a covenant. Indeed, I do not believe that he could consistently affirm it given his rejection of the very concept of works of merit. See Shepherd, *Call of Grace*, 26-27.

that both Christ and the believer keep the covenant by works of faith. He cannot explain why the work of Christ *guarantees* it, while the work of the believer only *inherits* it. If all the Abrahamic Covenant required was faith and its non-meritorious works, why did it need to be guaranteed by some work of Christ uniquely different from that of the ordinary believer?

Shepherd's reviewers have taken special notice of his characterization of the work of Christ as the obedience of faith. Cornelis P. Venema argues:

> By this language Shepherd treats Christ as though he were little more than a model believer whose obedient faith constituted the ground for his acceptance with God in the same way that Abraham's (and any believer's) obedient faith constituted the basis for his acceptance with God. In his zeal to identify the covenant relationship between God and man in its pre- and post-fall administrations, Shepherd leaves little room to describe Christ's work as Mediator of the covenant in a way that honors the uniqueness, perfection, and sufficiency of Christ's accomplishment for the salvation of his people.[68]

- **The Obedience of Faith as the Righteousness of Faith**

In the statement of Shepherd quoted above, he makes the surprising remark that Christ's *faith was credited to him as righteousness.*[69] Within the boundaries of the Reformation doctrine of justification, this statement can only be applied to sinners who through the instrumentality of their faith have the righteousness of Christ imputed to them. Shepherd's remark, however, can only mean that Christ's believing obedience was equivalent to His righteousness. Thus, he seems to think that Genesis 15:6 asserts that the obedience of faith is the righteousness of faith. One might regard this implication as unintended, but in two other places (at least) Shepherd asserts that the obedience of faith is the righteousness of faith. These statements follow:

---

[68]Cornelis P. Venema, "*The Call of Grace: How the Covenant Illuminates Salvation and Evangelism*: A Review Article," *Mid-America Journal of Theology* 13 (2002), 234-235. David Van Drunen, "Justification by Faith in the Theology of Norman Shepherd," *Banner of Truth*, 4, accessed 7 January 2005, available from www.banneroftruth.org/pages/articles/article_detail.php?186. Van Drunen incisively argues that by this parallel between Christ's faith and ours Shepherd raises serious questions about what he means by *sola fide*. See also David Van Drunen, "When the Covenant Obscures Justification," 39.

[69]Shepherd, *The Call of Grace*, 19.

The obedience required of Israel is not the obedience of merit, but the obedience of faith. It is the fullness of faith. Obedience is simply faithfulness to the Lord; it is the righteousness of faith (compare Rom. 9:32).[70]

For Abraham, the sign of both covenant privilege and covenant responsibility was circumcision. Paul calls circumcision "a seal of the righteousness that he had by faith" (Rom. 4:11). The righteousness of faith is the obedience of faith (Rom. 1:5; 16:26), and is therefore simultaneously covenant privilege and responsibility.[71]

Classic Protestantism contrasted the righteousness of the law and the righteousness of the gospel. The righteousness of the gospel was the righteousness of God conceived of as the obedience of Christ imputed to us and received by the instrumentality of faith. Shepherd, by speaking of believing obedience as the righteousness of faith, has annihilated this distinction. He has departed from the idea of faith as receiving an alien righteousness and come to the idea of faith as working out a personal righteousness through the believer's own obedience. By annihilating the classic contrast between the righteousness of the law and the righteousness of the gospel, Shepherd has, of course, also annihilated the classic dichotomy between law and gospel.

- **Shepherd, the Law, and the Gospel**

In *The Call of Grace*, Shepherd avoids the question of a covenant of works with Adam. He takes the less controversial, but more ambiguous, position that the Mosaic Covenant was not a covenant of works.[72] Nevertheless, the assertions of Shepherd reviewed in the previous

---

[70] Ibid., 39.
[71] Ibid., 76.
[72] Ibid., 23-27. Some of his critics assert that Shepherd denies a covenant of works *per se*. Though I will argue that this is the implication of his statements, it is not accurate to say that he directly denies a covenant of works in *Call of Grace*. Venema, "A Review Article," 233-34, for instance, asserts that "Shepherd makes clear that he rejects the traditional Reformed doctrine of a pre-lapsarian "covenant of works" that promised Adam life "upon condition of perfect obedience."" What Shepherd actually says in *Call of Grace,* 27, is "We must leave aside for the moment the question whether the relationship into which God entered with Adam ought to be described as a covenant of works." Of course, I agree with Venema that the clear implication of Shepherd's position is that no such covenant of works exists. I simply want to make clear that Shepherd does not explicitly deny such a covenant in *Call of Grace*.

paragraphs make perfectly clear that there is no place in Shepherd's theology for anything like the dichotomy between law and gospel that lays at the foundation of justification *sola fide* for the Reformation. If there is no such thing as meritorious works, if Christ's work was believing obedience, if the obedience of faith is the righteousness of faith, then we are clearly dealing with a system of doctrine that has no way to express the Reformation's contrast between law and gospel. Such a system cannot consistently affirm the justification *sola fide* squarely built on this contrast.

Allegiance to *The Westminster Confession* is often understood as subscription to its "system of doctrine." *The Westminster Confession* accurately represents the Reformation system of doctrine when it grounds its soteriology on a contrast between the law ("the covenant of works") and the gospel ("the covenant of grace"). Shepherd has no place for such a structure in his theology and cannot, therefore, affirm consistently the "system of doctrine" taught in the Confession he cites so often in his writings.

CHAPTER 7

SOLA FIDE IN DON GARLINGTON

Introduction

Don B. Garlington is one of the major conduits of "the new perspective on Paul" into Reformed and evangelical circles. While embracing its critique of the traditional, Reformation approach to Paul, he has also attempted (as we shall see) to present his own position in a fashion which seems designed to allay evangelical concerns about the influence which "the new perspective" has had upon him. This study focuses attention on his claim to hold justification by faith alone. This claim is an overt attempt to place himself in the Reformed and evangelical tradition. We will examine the legitimacy of this attempt to assure his readers of his orthodoxy in the following study.

Though other writings and reviews of his work have been consulted, our study is based primarily on four of Garlington's writings. What follows provides a brief introduction to each of these publications.

The purpose of Garlington's *The Obedience of Faith*[1] is at least twofold. At one level its purpose is to extend E.P. Sanders' thesis that "the working principle of ancient Judaism" was "'covenantal nomism'"[2] by an examination of the Old Testament apocryphal literature—a literature not examined by Sanders' in his now celebrated *Paul and Palestinian Judaism*. At another level, and here Garlington pursues an agenda akin to James D.G. Dunn and not Sanders, it is to show that Paul's phrase in Romans 1:5, ὑπακοὴν πίστεως (*"the* obedience of faith"), should be understood by means of and in interaction with the covenantal nomism of ancient Judaism. This is related to yet a third purpose of Garlington's dissertation—to shed light on the much disputed question of Paul and the law.

We will examine what happens specifically to the Reformation doctrine of *sola fide* in his dissertation (and Garlington's other publications). Garlington himself raises this question by noting "the dissatisfaction which many have now come to feel with the Lutheran/Reformation approach to Judaism."[3] It is clear that Garlington shares this dissatisfaction.

---

[1] Don B. Garlington, *The Obedience of Faith* (Tubingen: J.C.B. Mohr, 1991).
[2] Ibid., *The Obedience of Faith*, 4.
[3] Ibid., 5.

In *Faith, Obedience, and Perseverance*, Garlington collects a series of essays on the Epistle to the Romans that seek to develop the theme of "the obedience of faith" he first addressed in his doctoral dissertation.[4] He makes clear that in addressing this subject he proceeds along "the Sanders-Dunn trajectory."[5] He means that, though Sanders is known for identifying the religion of inter-testamental Judaism as "covenantal nomism," he agrees with Dunn where he differs from Sanders. Specifically, Dunn differs from Sanders in saying that Paul does not distort or misrepresent Judaism in his writings.[6] *Faith, Obedience, and Perseverance* contains five chapters on various portions of Romans. These chapters are preceded by an introduction and concluded with a final chapter entitled, "Reflections." Each of the five chapters was previously published, three of them (chaps. 1, 3, and 4) in the *Westminster Theological Journal*. The five chapters deal respectively with the meaning of the obedience of faith mentioned in Romans 1:5,[7] the disobedience of Israel mentioned in Romans 2:22, the doers of the law mentioned in Romans 2:13, the obedience of Christ in Romans 5:12-19, and the conflicted obedience of the Christian in Romans 7:14-25.

The treatment of Romans 7:14-25 makes a good case for the traditional Reformed view that it is a Christian's inner conflict in view there (and not the experience of a non-Christian). Garlington titles the chapter, "The Obedience of Faith as Life Between Two Worlds." This title intimates that Garlington sees the inner conflict of the Christian as the product of the eschatological "overlapping of the ages."

The treatment of Romans 2:22 argues that the accusation of sacrilege or robbing temples (ἱεροσυλεῖς) in that verse refers to the Torah idolatry of which the Judaizers were guilty.[8] It is, however, in chapters 1, 3, and 4

---

[4] Don B. Garlington, *Faith, Obedience, and Perseverance* (Tubingen: J.C.B. Mohr, 1994).

[5] Ibid., 8.

[6] Ibid.

[7] The identical phrase, "obedience of faith," may also be mentioned in Romans 16:26, but a textual variant raises questions about its occurrence there.

[8] A number of reviewers beside myself have found this treatment unconvincing. David A. deSilva, "*Faith, Obedience, and Perseverance: Aspects of Paul's Letter to the Romans*: A Review Article," *Critical Review of Books in Religion* 9 (1996), 208; Brendan Byrne, "*Faith, Obedience, and Perseverance: Aspects of Paul's Letter to the Romans*: A Review Article," *Catholic Biblical Quarterly* 58 (1996), 787; Judith M. Gundry-Volf, "*Faith, Obedience, and Perseverance: Aspects of Paul's Letter to the Romans*: A Review Article," *The Evangelical Quarterly* 69, no. 1 (1997), 84; Thomas R. Schreiner, "*Faith, Obedience, and Perseverance: Aspects of Paul's Letter to the Romans*: A Review Article," *JETS* 41, no. 4 (December 1998), 654-655.

that Garlington's thesis finds its most important outworking. The examination of his statements in those chapters will be central in this study.

Garlington addresses the doctrine of justification specifically in "A Study of Justification by Faith."[9] In his study of the biblical terminology related to justification, Garlington argues that justification is not merely forensic, but involves God's making His people covenant-keepers by giving them the virtue of *faith-faithfulness*.

Garlington's *Imputation or Union with Christ? A Response to John Piper*[10] first appeared as an internet paper but was subsequently published in a slightly revised form in the *Reformation and Revival Journal*. Garlington responds to Piper's *Counted Righteous in Christ* and sets forth his own take on the major passages Piper cites in favor of justification as the imputation of Christ's righteousness to us.

While voicing his differences from Reformation orthodoxy openly, Garlington also attempts to mitigate those differences with the Reformation doctrine of justification by citing esteemed Reformation voices in his favor wherever he can.[11] At different points, he cites Martin Luther, *The Augsburg Confession*, Geerhardus Vos, John Murray, and even John Calvin.[12] Of most interest for this study is Garlington's

---

[9]Don B. Garlington, "A Study of Justification by Faith," *Reformation and Revival Journal* 2, no. 2 (Spring 2002), 54-91.

[10]Don B. Garlington, "Imputation or Union with Christ," *Reformation and Revival Journal* 2, no. 4 (Fall 2003), 45-113. This essay may also be found on the Internet under the same title in a slightly different form—at least as I have it. I accessed it 13 October 2004. Available from www.thepaulpage.com/Piper_Rejoinder.pdf. In this essay I will cite the version found in the *Reformation and Revival Journal*. Garlington has added a couple further paragraphs in the *Reformation and Revival Journal* that do not appear to significantly alter his argument.

[11]Garlington's attempts to strike a kind of balance in this regard are clear. As noted already, Garlington in *The Obedience of Faith*, 5, speaks of "the dissatisfaction which many have now come to feel with the Lutheran/Reformation approach to Judaism." In *Faith, Obedience, and Perseverance* (4), he adds, "It has appeared to me that adjustments to the customary Protestant/Reformed scheme are in order." He adds, however, a few lines later, "I would add that the positions herein espoused are not without precedent among Protestants—including the Reformers—as will become evident enough."

[12]For Luther see Don B. Garlington, "A Study of Justification by Faith," *Reformation and Revival* 2, no. 2 (Spring, 2002), 69. For *The Augsburg Confession* see Don B. Garlington, "Imputation," 96. For Geerhardus Vos see "Imputation," 101. For John Murray see "Imputation," 69, 70, 75, 98. For John Calvin see "Imputation," 33. Garlington's attempts to clothe his views in the citations of such men is misleading. Vos, for instance, while a leading advocate of an orthodox form of biblical theology, did not see it as an alternative to or competitor with systematic theology. Neither did he support any deviations from the Reformation doctrine of justification. See the articles of

repeated and emphatic affirmation of the doctrine of justification *sola fide*. Here are a number of those affirmations.

> To be sure, in Jewish literature there is a place for believing Gentiles; but faith according to these documents, was invariably complemented by the particulars of the Jewish religion. The Judaism represented by such writings could never have limited its demand to *faith alone* for 'getting in' (in Sanders' phrase).[13]

> Taken, then, in connection with the broader spectrum of Paul's thought on Jew/Gentile relations in Christ, 'the obedience of faith among all the nations for his name's sake' is seen to be a Pauline manifesto that to be acceptable to God as a faithful covenant-keeper, it is no longer necessary to become and then remain Jewish; the privileges entailed in Israel's identity as the people of God can be had by virtue of faith alone in the risen Christ, the Seed of David and the powerful Son of God. As Dunn states it so well . . .[14]

> Whereas "the obedience of faith" in Paul's day was commensurate with devotion to the law ("covenantal nomism"), for him a reversal has taken place. The phrase is his declaration that to be acceptable to God as a faithful covenant-keeper it is no longer necessary to become and then remain Jewish: the privileges entailed in Israel's identity as the people of God can be had by virtue of faith alone in the risen Christ, the Seed of David and the powerful Son of God.[15]

> Achior the Gentile believed in God with all his heart, was circumcised and joined the house of Israel, remaining steadfast for the entirety of his life. . . . By contrast, for Paul the obedience of faith was no longer contingent on individuals becoming Achiors; rather, the way into God's (new) covenant was by faith alone.[16]

Geerhardus Vos, "The Idea of Biblical Theology," and "The Doctrine of the Covenant in Reformed Theology," in *Redemptive History and Biblical Interpretation* (Phillipsburg, NJ: Presbyterian and Reformed Publishing Co., 1980), 3-24, 234-267, in which he affirms both systematic theology and the covenant of works in traditional terms. Garlington clearly does turn biblical theology against systematizing at the place cited in this footnote and also differs from Vos on justification. Similar points could be made with regard to each of the other citations.

[13]Ibid., 29.
[14]Ibid., 247.
[15]Garlington, *Faith, Obedience, and Perseverance*, 5.
[16]Ibid., 42.

While Paul is adamant that it is faith alone which justifies here and now, he is equally insistent that it is the "doers of the law," Rom. 2:13, who will be justified in eschatological judgment. As Cosgrove rightly stresses, *justification*, not simply judgment, belongs not only at the beginning of life in Christ but also at its final consummation: there are in fact two moments of justification. In addressing the problem, we shall argue that it is none other than "faith's obedience" which bridges the gap between these seemingly polar opposites.[17]

From the entire foregoing discussion we may conclude that the passage from present justification by faith alone to future justification by the obedience of faith is natural enough, given the broader purview—and most notably the creation character—of Paul's theology of faith and obedience. However, practically speaking, this conclusion is sufficiently important (and controversial) that something more must be said.[18]

In declaring that the obedience of faith is a possibility for all races by faith alone, Paul has effectively rewritten the ground rules of covenant fidelity...[19]

We proceed, however, with an awareness that the underlying motivation of the *ordo salutis* is entirely laudable, viz., the maintenance of the sovereignty of God's grace and the preservation of *sola fide*.[20]

So, it is well to go on record that justification by faith as such is not in contention, only the mechanics of how justification "works." Likewise, that the righteousness of Christ becomes our possession by faith alone is taken for granted, and indeed defended, in the following pages.[21]

These passages make abundantly evident that Garlington regards himself as holding the distinctive Reformation teaching of justification *sola fide*. The purpose of the rest of this study is not to challenge Garlington's veracity. It is rather to ask if this assertion means by *sola fide* what its classic articulation during and following the Reformation meant.

In the classic articulation of *sola fide* the justifying power of faith lay precisely in its passive character. In the classic articulation of *faith alone*

---

[17]Ibid., 44.
[18]Ibid., 69.
[19]Ibid., 114.
[20]Ibid., 158.
[21]Garlington, "Imputation," 46.

justifying faith is distinguished from the internal renewal of the sinner. Faith does inevitably, of course, renew the life of the sinner unto godliness, but its justifying power and effect does not reside in this. The classic articulation of the *sola fide* is found in the framework of a contrast between law and gospel (grace). The relevance for justification *sola fide* is that the primary and justifying act of faith was seen as a response to grace—gratuitous promises in distinction from a response to the law of God. While Protestantism affirmed that faith did also offer an obedient response to God's law, it was emphatically not in this that its justifying power resided.[22] It will be argued that with regard to each of these features of the classic articulation of justification by *faith alone* Garlington's approach is substantially different. Simplicity of treatment will be achieved by examining in order Garlington's views of the definition of faith, the distinction of faith, and the dichotomy assumed in the *sola fide*.

The Definition of Justifying Faith

The classic articulation of justifying faith in the Reformation tradition maintained that justifying faith "receiving and resting on Christ and His righteousness is the alone instrument of justification."[23] It maintained that justification took place by "receiving and resting on Him and His righteousness by faith."[24] It contended that "the principal acts of saving faith are accepting, receiving, and resting upon Christ alone for justification, sanctification, and eternal life."[25] These definitions echo Calvin's definition of faith in terms of a knowledge of, assurance of, and rest in God's gracious promises in Christ.[26] The essence of justifying faith was thus defined as passive—receiving from another a gift and resting on another for grace. While Calvin and the Reformation tradition could acknowledge that faith also worked by love and produced obedience, and indeed was itself an act of obedience, this was emphatically not its justifying essence.

This view of justifying faith does not appear to be Garlington's. Fairness to him demands that we note that he is aware that trust is the

---

[22]Ibid.
[23]*The Creeds of Christendom*, 3:626. [*CC* 2:621]. *The Westminster Confession of Faith*, 11:2.
[24]Ibid., 3:626. [*CC* 2:620]. *The Westminster Confession of Faith*, 11:1.
[25]Ibid., 3:630-631. [*CC* 2:623]. *The Westminster Confession of Faith*, 14:2.
[26]*Inst.* 3:2:7 [*OS* 4:15-16].

first part of faith. He is also aware that obedience is the product of faith—a sentiment that seems to distinguish faith from obedience. At several places, however, he argues that both trust and obedience are constituent elements of faith. These statements seem to provide for some distinction between initial trust, faith, or hope and the obedience, faithfulness, or perseverance that flow from it. As we will see, however, they seem to run counter to the thrust of the statements of Garlington to be cited below that equate faith and obedience. Whatever we make of Garlington's affirmation of a "two-sided" character of faith, one thing is clear: a definition of justifying faith in simply passive terms is alien to Garlington's thought. Such a definition is, however, exactly what the Reformation tradition contends for when it affirms justification by faith alone. Garlington defines it as both trust and obedience—both faith and faithfulness. The following extracts confirm this.

> Faith in the OT is not merely belief in or assent to a given set of propositions. As articulated especially . . . 'faith' is both active and passive at the same time. According to E. Perry, "The import of the active sense of *emuna* is "trust" and "obedience" while the passive sense signifies the condition of sustained trust and obedience which is "trustworthiness." On this basis, then, it is artificial to distinguish between faith and obedience.[27]

> In sum, according to 32.24-33:3: "trust in the law is tantamount to trust in God, and *vice versa*; (2) faith in the law entails obedience to it; (3) the fear of God, which is wisdom, is trust in the law."[28]

> . . . the two sides of the term are inseparable.[29]

> Thus, the strength of Israel is to be had by the simultaneous and inseparable acts of reliance on Yahweh and remaining within the realm of law.[30]

---

[27] Garlington, *The Obedience of Faith*, 10. This paragraph requires a little comment. In it Garlington seems to distinguish between an active and passive sense of faith in the Old Testament. Yet as one reads on it becomes clear that he does not mean at all to lend support to the Reformation distinction. The passive sense he refers to is the meaning of the Hebrew *emuna* where it refers to trustworthiness. Notice, then, how his conclusion neglects any such thing as the Reformation distinction: "On this basis, then, it is artificial to distinguish between faith and obedience."
[28] Ibid., 34.
[29] Ibid., 72. In context "the two sides of the term" are faith and faithfulness.
[30] Ibid., 122.

However, even the most scrupulous obedience is founded on a prior faith and hope in God . . .[31]

Our investigation of the sources examined compels the conclusion that although the actual phrase ὑπακοὴ πίστεως does not occur before Paul, the idea embodied in it is clearly present. The obedience of God's people, consisting in their fidelity to his covenant with them, is the product of a prior belief in his person and trust in his word. Far from being a quest for meritorious self-justification, faith's obedience is the appropriate response of Israel, the covenant partner, to the election, grace and mercy of God. Hence, the notion resident in ὑπακοὴ πίστεως is not in any sense original with or unique to Paul. Indeed, because of the prominence of the motif in the Jewish materials, there is reason to believe that when he formulates the phrase in Rom. 1:5, he does so cognizant of its roots in these traditions.[32]

The Jewish position may be summarized in the sentence: fulfillment of the divine commandment is valid when it takes place in conformity with the full capacity of the person and from the whole intention of faith.[33]

In the OT and Second Temple Judaism, faith and obedience are virtually synonymous . . . . "faith" in the Hebrew Bible is two-sided: trust *and* a commitment (to the covenant) resultant from trust. Without going into any real detail, we note, with Edmund Perry: The Old Testament does not set trust and obedience in contrast to each other as separate ways of satisfying the demand of God . . . .[34]

Nevertheless, in a certain qualified sense, one may say that righteousness does consist of faith. But a formulation of the matter must be carefully nuanced. Strictly speaking, righteousness is, by definition, conformity to the covenant relationship; it *consists of* a faithful obedience to the Lord whose will is enshrined in the covenant. Yet the beginning of "faithfulness" is "faith." In keeping with the Hebrew term *'emunah*, the Greek noun translated "faith," *pistis*, is two-sided: faith and faithfulness. Given this set of data, righteousness does consist of *pistis* in the expansive sense of *'emunah*, that is, covenant conformity. At the same time, however, as Piper correctly observes from Rom. 10:10, *pistis* as initial trust in Christ has righteousness as its

---

[31] Ibid., 162.
[32] Ibid., 233.
[33] Ibid.
[34] Garlington, *Faith, Obedience, and Perseverance*, 17.

goal, that is, righteousness as covenant standing. In one sense, faith leads to righteousness; and in another, faith consists in righteousness.[35]

It is true, as previously intimated, that the Reformation tradition also allows that faith is productive of obedience and that there are other actings of faith beside its principal act of resting on Christ.[36] Thus, troubling as the difference is between Garlington's definition of justifying faith and that of the Reformation, one might be inclined to judge his views of this matter (in isolation from the rest of his thought) as merely ill-stated. His views regarding what we have called the distinction and dichotomy of faith require, however, a darker judgment.

The Distinction of Faith

Garlington's view of the relation of justifying faith and evangelical obedience goes right to the heart of his approach to faith. We will attempt both to do it justice and to offer a critique of it under two headings that describe his viewpoint. We will examine, *first*, his assertions that faith and obedience are inseparable and, *second*, his assertions that faith and obedience are indistinguishable.

- **Faith and Obedience Inseparable**

The least acquaintance with Garlington's major works (*Obedience of Faith* and *Faith, Obedience, and Perseverance*) is sufficient to inform the reader that one has in them a major polemic against any separation of faith and obedience. Again and again, Garlington reiterates that any separation of faith from obedience in the Jewish tradition or in Paul's writings is unthinkable. The very title of *Obedience of Faith* sufficiently informs the reader of this theme. Garlington argues that in the apocryphal literature of the Old Testament it is clear that the religion of Israel was a "covenantal nomism" in which the very idea of separating faith and obedience is nonsensical. Several statements illustrative of this aspect of Garlington's thesis follow.

---

[35] Garlington, "Imputation," 52.

[36] It also acts, for instance, by way of "yielding obedience to the commands." *The Westminster Confession of Faith*, 14:2. *The Creeds of Christendom*, 3:630-631.

... 'the faithful' ... receive their basic identity from their allegiance to the law and covenant of Israel. Below it will be seen that the faithful are particularly those who obey wisdom (=the Torah)."[37]

Thus, πίστις, which accompanies πραότης, ... is best taken as faithful endurance, i. e., faithfulness.[38]

In sum, according to 32.24-33:3: "trust in the law is tantamount to trust in God, and *vice versa*; (2) faith in the law entails obedience to it; (3) the fear of God, which is wisdom, is trust in the law.[39]

... the two sides of the term are inseparable.[40]

Thus, the strength of Israel is to be had by the simultaneous and inseparable acts of reliance on Yahweh and remaining within the realm of law.[41]

While it is true that he and they differed as to requirements for getting in and staying in, and while it is also true that one is disinclined to speak of Paul's theology in terms of a 'nomism', the basic pattern is the same.[42]

Similarly in *Faith, Obedience, and Perseverance* there is the constant refrain that faith and obedience in Paul are inseparable. Garlington builds on the thesis of *Obedience of Faith* that faith and obedience to the law were inseparable for the Jews.

In the OT and Second Temple Judaism, faith and obedience are virtually synonymous . . . . "faith" in the Hebrew Bible is two-sided: trust *and* a commitment (to the covenant) resultant from trust. Without going into any real detail, we note, with Edmund Perry:
. . . . the Old Testament does not set trust and obedience in contrast to each other as separate ways of satisfying the demand of God . . .[43]

---

[37]Garlington, *The Obedience of Faith*, 20.
[38]Ibid., 22.
[39]Ibid., 34.
[40]Ibid., 72. The "two sides" are faith and faithfulness.
[41]Ibid., 122.
[42]Garlington, *The Obedience of Faith*, 265. The "he" is Paul, and "they" are the Jews.
[43]Garlington, *Faith, Obedience, and Perseverance*, 17.

He goes on to insist that Paul's view of faith and obedience cannot differ substantially from that of inter-testamental Judaism.

> Of course, it is possible to argue that Paul's ideology of faith represents a radical break with his Jewish heritage. Nevertheless, one of the most striking phenomena of the extant letters is that he nowhere debates the meaning of faith with his opponents. Faith as such was never a point of controversy; Paul simply assumes the OT conception as the common ground between him and those with whom he disagrees.[44]

It is, thus, not surprising that Garlington reaches the following conclusion towards the end of *Faith, Obedience, and Perseverance*

> ... *faith, obedience, and perseverance*, in other words, are not separate entities but three aspects of the same entity. The faith with which the Christian walk commences is unreserved trust in Jesus the Son of God. This faith, however, does not exist in the abstract; its quality as trust is put to the test in the trials and exigencies which attend "this present evil age." Thus tested, "faith" becomes the "obedience" which is "perseverance." In short, *faith, obedience, and perseverance are one and the same*.[45]

Garlington must not be misrepresented. It is necessary to say, in the *first* place, that he does not regard the *believing obedience* summarized in the phrase, "the obedience of faith," as having to be perfect or perpetual obedience. The opposite of this obedience is not sin, but apostasy.[46]

It is also important to note, in the *second* place, that Garlington makes clear that for Paul believing obedience is offered to Christ not the Torah and its boundary-markers.

> Whereas "the obedience of faith" in Paul's day was commensurate with devotion to the law ("covenantal nomism"), for him a reversal has

---

[44]Ibid.,18-19.

[45]Ibid., 163.

[46]Ibid., 3, 89, 93. See also Garlington, *Obedience of Faith*, 81. He remarks there: "... the apostasy of his compatriots is unbelief, and their unbelief is apostasy." Note also p. 161: "... disobedience is apostasy ... *the disobedient Jew is one who has ceased to be a Jew*." Of course, Garlington's tendency to take statements that have traditionally been thought to refer to sin and make them refer only to the sin of apostasy creates other problems. What, for instance, shall we make of his assertion in *Faith, Obedience, and Perseverance*, 93, that 1 Pet. 2:22's assertion that Christ committed no sin means that He did not apostatize like Adam? Garlington surely believes in the absolute sinlessness of Christ, but how will he prove it with a hermeneutic like this?

taken place. The phrase is his declaration that to be acceptable to God as a faithful covenant-keeper it is no longer necessary to become and then remain Jewish: the privileges entailed in Israel's identity as the people of God can be had by virtue of faith alone in the risen Christ, the Seed of David and the powerful Son of God.[47]

It is also true to say, in the *third* and last place, by way of clarification that Garlington's contention that faith and obedience are inseparable is not yet contrary to the classic articulation of *sola fide*. Contemporary, evangelical "easy-believism" has divorced faith and obedience in the name of grace alone and faith alone. As we have seen, Luther, Calvin, and the Reformed tradition did not. Faith, the alone instrument of justification, was never alone in the justified person, but always accompanied by the other Christian graces—including obedience. Yet the assertion cited above that "*faith, obedience, and perseverance are one and the same*"[48] alerts us to a tendency in Garlington to identify faith and obedience. Such identification is alien to the meaning of *sola fide* for the Reformation.

- **Faith and Obedience Indistinguishable**

Very relevant here is a class of passages in which Garlington appears to commit himself to the position that faith is not only inseparable from obedience, but *indistinguishable*. We will examine two species of passages that appear to make faith and obedience indistinguishable: *first*, passages that seem to identify faith and obedience will be noted and, *second*, passages that contrast faith—not with the works of the law in general, but only—with those works that were badges of Jewish identity.

1. Passages that seem to identify faith and obedience. The following examples seem to identify faith and obedience. In contrast to the Reformation understanding of justification by faith alone, they permit no distinction between justifying faith and evangelical obedience.

---

[47]Garlington, *Faith, Obedience, and Perseverance*, 5. It seems accurate to say that Garlington holds a kind of Christological nomism.
[48]Ibid., 163.

Thus, the strength of Israel is to be had by the simultaneous and inseparable acts of reliance on Yahweh and remaining within the realm of law.[49]

V.P. Furnish, however, has seen the connection between this and the obedience of faith. . . . 'It is precisely the obedience character of faith which makes it the means of the believer's participation in Christ's death and resurrection and which discloses how this is at the same time a "walking in newness of life"'.[50]

In the OT and Second Temple Judaism, faith and obedience are virtually synonymous . . . . "faith" in the Hebrew Bible is two-sided: trust *and* a commitment (to the covenant) resultant from trust. Without going into any real detail, we note, with Edmund Perry: "The Old Testament does not set trust and obedience in contrast to each other as separate ways of satisfying the demand of God . . ."[51]

The evidence previously pointed out makes clear, however, that the Reformation tradition did distinguish faith and obedience as having different roles in satisfying the demands of God.

Of course, it is possible to argue that Paul's ideology of faith represents a radical break with his Jewish heritage. Nevertheless, one of the most striking phenomena of the extant letters is that he nowhere debates the meaning of faith with his opponents. Faith as such was never a point of controversy; Paul simply assumes the OT conception as the common ground between him and those with whom he disagrees. Furnish, therefore, is justified in speaking of *faith as obedience* in Paul. What is radical about Paul, however, is *faith's object*—Christ.[52]

It is true, as we have seen, that the Reformation tradition could speak of *faith as obedience*. What it meant was, however, that faith had the character of obedience. Faith was an act of obedience to the gospel. At the same time, it went on to point out that the crucial core and essential nature of justifying faith was passive. It was faith's passivity as trust and reception that was the key to its role in justification. It is extremely doubtful that either Garlington or Furnish (whom he quotes) have any such qualification in mind.

---

[49]Garlington, *The Obedience of Faith*, 122.
[50]Ibid., 252.
[51]Garlington, *Faith, Obedience, and Perseverance*, 17.
[52]Ibid., 18-19.

In short, any idea of faith as obedience and obedience as faith must reckon with the broader eschatological/ethical dimensions of Paul's thought, in particular transfer of lordship, which lies at the heart of the Pauline "obedience of faith."[53]

This statement is interesting in the way that it identifies what is at the heart of the Pauline conception of the obedience of faith. Garlington identifies this in light of the eschatological judgment according to works. He identifies the heart of the obedience of faith as the transfer of lordship. Since it certainly agrees that faith is and produces obedience, such a transfer is certainly part of the Reformation concept of faith. What is starkly missing, however, is the Reformation emphasis on the passivity of faith as trust in and reception of Christ as priest and savior. This is at the heart of justifying faith for the Reformation tradition.

Garlington also remarks, "Thus, faith and obedience should not be compartmentalized or turned into separate stages of Christian experience."[54] It is to be granted that in one sense the Reformation view of *sola fide* assumes that faith takes the form of obedience from its very inception. It is also to be granted that faith resting and faith working characterize the entire life of the believer. Still a distinction is maintained between faith itself, on the one hand, and its fruits, on the other hand. Faith resting and faith working are clearly distinguished by the Reformation tradition throughout the life of the believer. Perhaps this distinction is not what Garlington is attacking when he attacks compartmentalization and separate stages of experience. However this may be, the crucial distinction between faith and obedience is absent.

Perhaps the statement most alien to the Reformation ethos in this matter is this affirmation of Garlington, "In other words, *faith and works are two ways of saying the same thing.*"[55] In the context in which Garlington makes this telling assertion he is discussing the statement of Romans 2:13 that "the doers of the law" will be justified and affirming that this statement is not hypothetical.[56] Garlington so closely identifies

---

[53] Ibid., 19.
[54] Ibid., 144.
[55] Ibid., 146.
[56] Ibid., 60. Here is what he says: "Along similar lines are those interpretations which effectively, if not formally, make the verse hypothetical, i.e. Paul formulates the principle of justification according to strict justice for the purpose of demonstrating that no one can be justified by the law (assuming the factor of sin)." Garlington cites John Calvin, Charles Hodge, and Doug Moo as commentators who do this. With Garlington I reject the hypothetical interpretation of this text. I agree that Paul is speaking of an event that

initial justification by faith and final justification according to works that he can say that *faith and works are two ways of saying the same thing*.[57] When he does this, he is forced to utter a sentiment that is strangely alien to the Reformation tradition. Garlington at this point makes a claim that runs directly contrary to the Reformation tradition *exactly with regard* to *sola fide* itself! Whatever that tradition meant by justification by faith alone, it did not mean *justification by works alone. Justification by works alone* is, however, the direct implication of Garlington's statement.

2. Passages that contrast faith only with those works which were badges of Jewish identity. Here we must turn to the second class of passages mentioned above. Garlington, when he speaks of *sola fide*, has a quite different contrast in mind than the Reformation tradition. As we have seen, justification by faith alone in the Reformation tradition is contrasted with justification by the works of the law. By *the works of the law* the Reformation tradition meant any works done in obedience to the law of God—ceremonial or moral—in order to be justified. Faith, in other words, was not contrasted only with obedience to the ceremonial law (the claim of Tridentine Catholicism.) The fact is that Garlington's position at this point is much closer to that of Tridentine Catholicism than that of the Reformation.

To apprehend rightly Garlington's views on this matter, it is necessary to remember that he identifies himself with what he calls the "the Sanders-Dunn trajectory." The point of importance for us in this is that Dunn in unison with other exponents of the "new perspective on Paul" argues that the "works of the law" with which Paul contrast faith in Romans 3 and 4 and Galatians 2 and 3 do not refer to the works required by the moral law, but to those points of the law that distinguished Jews from Gentiles. Thus, the gist of Paul's assertion of justification by faith without the works of the law (Rom 3:28) is that Gentiles do not need to adopt those aspects or works of the law in order to become part of the people that God will justify or vindicate. They only have to believe in

---

will really happen. At the last judgment it is only the doers of the law that will be justified. It is—and this is also my own interpretation of this text—only those whose faith has demonstrated itself in doing the law, who will be vindicated as truly God's people in the last day.

[57] Though it is not the intention of this study to solve the difficulty, I pause to point out that a right understanding of the relation of initial and final justification is an acute problem today. The clear understanding of "the already and the not yet" provided by biblical theology has related initial and final justification that cannot be ignored and calls for a solution consistent with the doctrine of justification *sola fide*.

Jesus as Lord. Embodied, of course, in this faith would be a commitment of obedience to any number of ordinances and commandments given by the Lord. Faith alone then was not to be contrasted with obedience to the moral law of God, but only with those ceremonial laws that were associated with the self-identity of the Jews and marked them off from other nations.

Justification by faith in Jesus Christ and justification by the works of the law (understood as described above) are antithetical for Dunn and Garlington. Either faith in Jesus as Messiah is sufficient or it is not. The faith of justification is, however, neither passive nor the opposite of good works in general, but only of the idea that the distinctively Jewish markers were necessary. Justification by faith is also not the opposite of ritual in general.[58]

Garlington's indebtedness to Dunn and "the new perspective" is evident at a number of places. In the quotations to follow Garlington states his novel definition of *faith alone*. It is contrasted not with any and all obedience to the law or works of the law, but with "the particulars of the Jewish religion."

> To be sure, in Jewish literature there is a place for believing Gentiles; but faith according to these documents, was invariably complemented by the particulars of the Jewish religion. The Judaism represented by such writings could never have limited its demand to *faith alone* for 'getting in' (in Sanders' phrase).[59]

> Faith, therefore, assumes a nationalistic bias.[60]

> Believing obedience, therefore, was inconceivable apart from the totality of the Torah's requirements, and especially those 'badges' of Jewish identity which had come under such unmitigated attack by the Hellenizers.[61]

> Taken, then, in connection with the broader spectrum of Paul's thought on Jew/Gentile relations in Christ, 'the obedience of faith among all the nations for his name's sake' is seen to be a Pauline manifesto that to be acceptable to God as a faithful covenant-keeper, it is no longer necessary to become and then remain Jewish; the privileges entailed in

---

[58]See James D.G. Dunn's treatment of Gal 2:16 in *Jesus, Paul, and the Law: Studies in Mark and Galatians* (Louisville: Westminster/John Knox Press, 1990).
[59]Garlington, *The Obedience of Faith,* 29.
[60]Ibid., 65.
[61]Ibid., 124. This statement is made with specific reference to 1 Maccabees.

Israel's identity as the people of God can be had by virtue of faith alone in the risen Christ, the Seed of David and the powerful Son of God. As Dunn states it so well . . . .[62]

For Paul it was possible for people of every race to be regarded as faithful and obedient apart from the distinctive marks of the Jewish identity; no longer was commitment to circumcision, food laws, sabbath and feast days the test of loyalty to God and the enduring ideals of Judaism. All of the privileges of Israel, and more especially her standing as the special possession of God, were available to the nations simply by faith in Jesus the risen Christ, in whom God's eschatological design for his ancient people had been fulfilled."[63]

Whereas "the obedience of faith" in Paul's day was commensurate with devotion to the law ("covenantal nomism"), for him a reversal has taken place. The phrase is his declaration that to be acceptable to God as a faithful covenant-keeper it is no longer necessary to become and then remain Jewish: the privileges entailed in Israel's identity as the people of God can be had by virtue of faith alone in the risen Christ, the Seed of David and the powerful Son of God.[64]

The foregoing quotations make clear that what Garlington means by faith alone is faith alone without the further requirement of obedience to "the distinctive marks of the Jewish identity . . . to circumcision, food laws, sabbath and feast days." Faith alone is emphatically not to be contrasted with or distinguished from "the obedience of faith" to the moral law and to Christian ordinances.[65]

In the next quotation Garlington adopts the idea often found in "new perspective" literature that Paul's teaching of justification by faith and his repudiation of works is subordinate (only a tool) to obliterate distinctions between Jew and Gentile and not the center of his thought.

The relation of faith and works in Paul is illuminated to be no small degree by the way in which "the obedience of faith" serves in Paul's hands as a tool for obliterating distinctions between Jew and Gentile.[66]

---

[62]Ibid., 247.
[63]Ibid., 253.
[64]Garlington, *Faith, Obedience, and Perseverance*, 5.
[65]See Garlington's rebuttal of D. Moo, D. Fuller, and S. Westerholm who see the works as meritorious rather than as Jewish identity markers in *The Obedience of Faith*, 265.
[66]Ibid., 11.

When one understands that faith alone in Garlington does not mean faith as opposed to any and every work of the law, but only to the badges of Jewish identity, the following quotations make perfect sense. Garlington does not contrast faith alone with obedience to the moral law, but only with obedience to the ceremonial laws that became badges of Jewish identity. Thus, he has no difficulty saying something that is incomprehensible in Reformation parlance. In the last quotation cited below, Garlington actually remarks: *Faith and works are two ways of saying the same thing.* He can make this incredible statement because within his framework of thought faith is only to be contrasted with adherence to Jewish identity markers and not to works in general.

> Achior the Gentile believed in God with all his heart, was circumcised and joined the house of Israel, remaining steadfast for the entirety of his life. . . . By contrast, for Paul the obedience of faith was no longer contingent on individuals becoming Achiors; rather, the way into God's (new) covenant was by faith alone.[67]

> Hence, the only distinction to survive the resurrection is that of faith and unbelief as respects him, God's Christ. In this light, Israel's preference for the law to the exclusion of Christ could for Paul be nothing less than ἱεροσυλειν, an act of sacrilege.[68]

> I must add my voice to that of Stendahl, Fitzmyer, and others: Paul employs justification as a tool for bringing down the "dividing wall of hostility" between Jew and Gentiles (Eph. 2:14). Throughout Romans particularly, justification, along with other arguments, serves to buttress the proposition that "there is no distinction" between Jew and Gentiles.[69]

> In declaring that the obedience of faith is a possibility for all races by faith alone, Paul has effectively rewritten the ground rules of covenant fidelity.[70]
> In other words, faith and works are two ways of saying the same thing.[71]

---

[67] Ibid., 42.
[68] Ibid., 43.
[69] Ibid., 47-48.
[70] Ibid., 114.
[71] Ibid., 146.

Clearly, Garlington has deviated drastically from the Reformation conception of both the definition of justifying faith and the distinction of justifying faith assumed in the doctrine of justification by *faith alone*. He holds in this matter what is substantially the ground taken by Roman Catholic theologians against Luther and Calvin. When Garlington professes to believe in justification *sola fide*, it is not the doctrine articulated by the Reformation. This will become even clearer as we examine next the dichotomy assumed in *sola fide*.

The Dichotomy of Faith

Garlington also deviates from the dichotomy between law and gospel assumed in the Reformation's view of justification by faith alone. Three features of Garlington's thought in which he departs from this dichotomy held in the Reformation tradition require notice here–his equation of faith and works, his equation of faith and righteousness, and his denial of imputed righteousness.

- **Garlington's Equation of Faith and Works**

We have already seen that Garlington does not hold the distinction implicit in the Reformation articulation of *sola fide* between faith, on the one hand, and works as obedience to the moral law, on the other. This distinction was maintained, however, against the broader backdrop of a distinction between law and gospel/grace. The distinction between faith and works/obedience is for the Reformation tradition simply the subjective reflection of the objective distinction between law and gospel/grace.

We have already noted in this study that the objective distinction between law and gospel/grace was articulated in different ways by Luther, Calvin, and *The Westminster Confession*. These articulations of the law and gospel/grace distinction, however, were unified in understanding that Paul and the New Testament articulated their view of gospel/grace as over against a legalistic form of Judaism. This legalistic Judaism was viewed against various backdrops by the different articulations of the Reformation contrast between law and gospel/grace. It was variously seen against the backdrop of an old covenant viewed as a covenant of works or against the backdrop of the covenant of works made with Adam. The Judaism of Paul's opponents was, however, always viewed as legalistic in the sense that man's salvation was ultimately conditioned on his own "meritorious" efforts to keep God's law and so "earn" salvation.

This study has shown that Garlington has adopted a drastically different paradigm within which to understand the Judaism of Paul's opponents. He has adopted the view of Sanders, Dunn, and the so-called "new perspective on Paul." This view embodies "the dissatisfaction which many have now come to feel with the Lutheran/Reformation approach to Judaism."[72] Garlington shares this dissatisfaction and so quotes approvingly the following statement. "D. Hill likewise remarks that Judaism has really no place for a rigid distinction between faith and works: faith can only fully exist when it is embodied in works."[73] Garlington describes the result of this view for *the works of the law*:

> The phrase, in other words, is intended to express not the compilation of good deeds for the purpose of earning the favour of God but the requirements of the covenant as these particularly come to focus in the 'identity markers' and 'badges' of Jewish ethnic identity.[74]

Paul's quarrel with the Judaizers, according to Garlington, is not with their legalism, but with their nationalism. It is not with their attempts to earn God's favor, but with their biased ethnocentricity. Indeed, for the new perspective on Paul it seems clear that the Jewish religion was a "covenantal nomism" which resting on God's election of Israel was a religion of grace.[75]

It is not the purpose of this study to examine the biblical or historical legitimacy of this view of the Judaism of Paul's day. The purpose here is simply to inquire whether the adoption of such a view is consistent with Garlington's affirmation of the Reformation's *sola fide*. In other words, can *sola fide* as articulated by the Reformation be maintained when it is set over against, not legalism, but covenantal nomism? It seems clear from the evidence that we have reviewed already that it cannot. When faith alone is opposed, not to all works of obedience to the law in general, but simply to "the 'identity markers' and 'badges' of Jewish ethnic identity," the distinction between faith and obedience crucial to the Reformation articulation of *sola fide* disappears.

---

[72] Garlington, *The Obedience of Faith*, 5.
[73] Ibid., 10.
[74] Ibid., 5-6. See also 72 of the same work where in a footnote Garlington disputes D. Moo and D. Fuller in their claim to find the idea of merit in Rabbinic Judaism.
[75] Ibid., 195-196, 233. See also Garlington, *Faith, Obedience, and Perseverance*, 46-47.

- **Garlington's Equation of Faith and Righteousness**

Closely related to the Reformation's articulation of *sola fide* is its insistence that a perfect and perpetual obedience is necessary in order to be justified before God. It is such a righteousness that the sinner receives and rests upon in Christ by faith alone. As argued above, justification *sola fide* was part of a scheme that looked to a forensic justification and imputed righteousness as the means of becoming right with God.

Garlington's approach to this aspect of *sola fide* considerably obscures these components of justification. This problem commences with his tendency to obscure the need of a perfect and perpetual righteousness by emphasizing that only apostasy separates the person from God and incurs His wrath. This problem consummates with Garlington's rejection of what he calls a "strict doctrine of imputation."[76]

Garlington's tendency to speak of apostasy as the only sin which separates men from God has already been noted. Here it is necessary to document it more fully. He strongly equates sin with apostasy and obedience with covenant-keeping. Of course, the problem is not that Garlington asserts that the Bible contains doctrines of apostasy and covenant-keeping. In this he is certainly correct. The problem is that there is little place in his theology for a perfect, perpetual, and universal obedience being demanded by the law. Consider the following extracts from his writings.

> Disobedience is apostasy . . . . the disobedient Jew is one who has ceased to be a Jew . . .[77]

> The foundational principle of the writing is best described as covenantal nomism: although she has sinned grievously, Israel can rest assured of God's mercy and be received back into his favour by repentance. Probably due to the distress of the times, actual sacrifice was out of the question. Nevertheless, the Lord is willing to receive the sacrifices of a broken heart, the effective means of reinstatement into covenant relationship.[78]

> The obedience of God's people, consisting in their fidelity to his covenant with them, is the product of a prior belief in his person and trust in his word. Far from being a quest for meritorious self-

---

[76] Garlington, "Imputation," 101.
[77] Garlington, *The Obedience of Faith*, 161.
[78] Ibid., 195-196.

> justification, faith's obedience is the appropriate response of Israel, the covenant partner, to the election, grace and mercy of God. Hence, the notion resident in ὑπακοὴ πίστεως is not in any sense original with or unique to Paul. Indeed, because of the prominence of the motif in the Jewish materials, there is reason to believe that when he formulates the phrase in Rom. 1:5, he does so cognizant of its roots in these traditions.[79]
>
> As modern research has demonstrated δικαιοσύνη is essentially a relational concept. As predicated of God, it is his fidelity to the covenant with Israel.[80]
>
> Hence, for Paul the renewal of the creation mandate is embodied in the obedience of faith, i. e., the work of endurance upon entrance into Christ. . . . The difference between faith and unbelief is exactly the theme of the story of Eden. Men align themselves with Adam, the type of the Man of wickedness [2 Thess 2:3] . . . or with God.[81]
>
> By way of contrast, the obedience of Christ, as we shall argue, can be defined as his perseverance in faith and in his consequent realization of what humanity was intended to be in the first Adam.[82]
>
> Thus far it has been intimated that within the cadre of the present passage the terms "sin" and "disobedience" are to be regarded specifically as "apostasy."[83]

The "present passage" mentioned in the last quotation above is Romans 5:12-19. This is significant because it implies that the obedience of Christ that Paul contrasts with the sin and disobedience of Adam is covenant faithfulness. This seems to be the point of the preceding quotation as well. The issue in justification is not, then, perfect righteousness, but covenant faithfulness.

This seems to be the point in the astounding assertion that Garlington makes about 1 Peter 2:22. According to Garlington 1 Peter 2:22 does not teach the sinlessness of Jesus, but only His faithful perseverance through trial.

---

[79] Ibid., 233.
[80] Garlington, *Faith, Obedience, and Perseverance*, 45.
[81] Ibid., 67.
[82] Ibid., 83.
[83] Ibid., 89.

In light of these data, the assertion of 1 Pet. 2:22 is not a generalized or abstract statement of the sinlessness of Jesus: it is an assurance that the believer can endure in the midst of persecution, because his Lord, the one who refused to repeat the infidelity of Adam, "did not sin."[84]

The issue for Garlington is not perfect righteousness, but covenant faithfulness. This is the case in his surprising assertion that Eve did not apostatize from God in the Garden of Eden: "Eve, like Paul later, gave in momentarily to idolatry, but she did not in principle renounce Yahweh the Creator."[85] Thus, Adam's sin is disobedience/apostasy.

> Hence, as we shall argue presently, just as Adam, by his disobedience/apostasy, was responsible for the disobedience/apostasy of his race, Christ, by his obedience/perseverance, has restored to his community the image of God and enables it to persevere in that capacity where the first Adam and the old humanity failed. The question is how Christ's obedience does this, just as the question is how Adam's disobedience did the reverse.[86]

Garlington intimates this understanding of righteousness in his comments on Romans 5:12-19. The righteousness under discussion, he says, includes a commitment to a relationship and the holiness and perseverance appropriate to such a commitment. This is consistent with his previous assertion that "righteousness is essentially a relational concept."

> What is in view in [Romans 5] v. 16 is not merely a declaration and a resultant status, but a commitment to a relationship, evidenced by the holiness of the covenant and a determination to persevere in it.[87]

Garlington makes clear in a surprising parallel between the believer and Adam that the issue is covenant faithfulness—not perfect righteousness. This is clear because in the following quotation the believer is enabled to persevere in the faith-commitment incumbent *on the first Adam*. This implies—if it does not assert—that what was required of Adam was only perseverance in a faith-commitment and not perfect, perpetual obedience.

---

[84]Ibid., 93.
[85]Ibid., 118.
[86]Ibid., 100.
[87]Ibid., 32.

In short, the believer has been delivered from the slavery of his former existence (Romans 6:15-23; 8:2; Ephesians 2:1-3) and enabled to persevere in the faith-commitment incumbent originally on the first Adam."[88]

In the preceding litany of quotations from Garlington the concept of a strictly perfect righteousness disappears and is replaced by a relational view of righteousness. This relational view of righteousness does not seem to require perfect obedience, but only covenant-keeping.[89] This is the view of righteousness that informs Garlington's approach to the subject of imputation. To Garlington's views of imputation we must now turn.

- **Garlington's Denial of Imputed Righteousness**

There is no shortage of material from which to explicate Garlington's views on imputation.[90] The difficulty is that he qualifies himself at points and in ways that are not very clear.[91] Assuming that Garlington's

---

[88] Ibid., 33.

[89] Though the purpose of this study is not to offer a biblical critique of Garlington's views, it seems necessary to say several things about his views by way of my personal, biblical response to them. I do not deny that the Bible does often speak of righteousness and mean not perfect righteousness, but simply covenant fidelity or the obedience of faith. But it seems clear to me that a covenant fidelity or righteousness that is marred (but not broken) by sin is the product or manifestation of redemptive foundations that must perfectly correspond to the justice of God. Our marred covenant fidelity does not by itself or in and of itself satisfy God's justice or righteousness. It pleases God only because it is the manifestation of the work of Christ that did fully satisfy God's justice. Our imperfect covenant fidelity pleases God only because it participates in Christ's perfect covenant fidelity. Further, though every sin does not constitute apostasy (There is a sin not unto death according to 1 John 5:16), every sin is incipient apostasy and calls for repentance lest it become apostasy. Sin, when it is finished, brings forth death (Jas. 1:15). Garlington's emphasis deeply obscures these important realities.

[90] See the lengthy discussions in three of Garlington's works that are under discussion here: *Faith, Obedience, and Perseverance*; "Imputation"; and *Study*.

[91] Garlington, "Imputation," 101. The following statement is a good case in point of how opaque Garlington's qualifications can be: "In closing, it must be placed beyond all doubt that imputation as a concept is hardly objectionable: what evangelical could, at least with any degree of consistency, protest the notion that Christ has become our righteousness in the gospel? But as pertains to a strict doctrine of imputation, exegesis of texts must be the deciding factor. It has been the conviction of this paper that exegesis will steer us away from imputation to union with Christ." Perhaps Garlington understands the difference between "imputation as a concept" and "a strict doctrine of imputation," but it is not self-evident to me. To complicate matters, Garlington ends by saying "that

treatment of this subject is coherent, his rejection of imputed righteousness can be made clear by a number of statements about it that can be plainly derived from his writing. In what follows, it will be argued that Garlington holds a participationist view of justification in which we are justified on the ground of the righteousness or believing obedience ("the obedience of faith") that Christ imparts to us. At this point Garlington's participationist view of justification is indistinguishable from the doctrine of justification through infused or imparted righteousness.[92] In prosecuting this argument we will first consider the evidence in favor of the assertion that Garlington holds a participationist view of the ground tantamount to that of Tridentine Catholicism. Then we will consider possible evidence against it. We will conclude with a summation of the inference to be drawn from the evidence. The following arguments favor the thesis that Garlington rejects imputation.

The first line of argument is this: Garlington's view of Romans 5:12-19 erases the concept of imputation from the passage. In the following quotations we have an indication of what Garlington means by setting union with Christ over against imputation. He means to assert that we must understand the ground of justification in participationist terms rather than strictly forensic terms. Imputation is not the mechanism of justification. He says this, in fact, in so many words: "It is the contention of this paper that the free gift of righteousness comes our way by virtue of *union with Christ*, not imputation as classically defined."[93] This first becomes evident in his opening statement with regard to this passage.

> Romans 5:12: To begin, there can hardly be any disagreement as to the basic analogical nature of Paul's argument: just as the work of Adam resulted in condemnation and death, so also the work of Christ has resulted in righteousness and life. The question, of course, pertains to whether these divergent effects are due to imputation or some other factor.[94]

---

exegesis will steer us away from imputation to union with Christ." But what does Garlington mean here by imputation? Apparently, he means "a strict doctrine of imputation," because he tells us earlier "that imputation as a concept is hardly objectionable." Yet, if imputation as a concept is hardly objectionable, how can he say "that exegesis will steer us away from imputation (not a 'strict doctrine of imputation') to union with Christ?"

[92]I am not implying that Garlington shares the semi-Pelagianism of many who hold this view of justification.
[93]Garlington, "Imputation," 46.
[94]Ibid., 86. What Garlington notes here is fair enough by itself. One unavoidable datum of the passage about which there can be no dispute is that the analogy between

> Hence, as we shall argue presently, just as Adam, by his disobedience/apostasy, was responsible for the disobedience/apostasy of his race, Christ, by his obedience/perseverance, has restored to his community the image of God and enables it to persevere in that capacity where the first Adam and the old humanity failed. The question is how Christ's obedience does this, just as the question is how Adam's disobedience did the reverse.[95]
>
> So, it is well to go on record that justification by faith as such is not in contention, only the mechanics of how justification "works."[96]
>
> The problem is that Piper thinks it necessary to resort to imputation to explain the "mechanics" of how we have become the righteousness of God. . . . I would submit otherwise: *union with Christ is the modality of our becoming "the righteousness of God."*[97]

Perfectly in line with this is Garlington's insistence that the "all sinned" of Romans 5:12 is a reference to the personal sinning of individuals. By means of the identical terminology of Romans 3:23 he argues the case that each individual's personal sinning is in view and not the representative sin of Adam. Orthodox exegetes take the position Garlington here defends. Garlington cites Calvin and Cranfield. In the setting of Garlington's theology this exegesis is part of a trajectory in which the imputation of both Adam's sin and Christ's obedience is denied.

> Πάντες ἥμαρτον, therefore, in both cases is to be taken in the same sense, i. e., death has spread to all because *all have sinned*, i. e. have apostatized because of their union with Adam. Thus interpreted, the aorist in each instance is constative and is to be translated by the English present perfect tense.[98]

Adam and Christ consists first of all in the fact that their actions exercise a controlling causality on their respective races. Adam's act resulted in condemnation and death. Even so Christ's work resulted in righteousness and life. There is analogical causality, but note that Garlington also raises the issue of modality. That is to say, for Garlington the question is not whether Adam and Christ exercise causality over their respective races, but how they do so. Is it by "imputation or some other factor?" This is a constant refrain in Garlington's approach to this issue.

[95] Garlington, *Faith, Obedience, and Perseverance*, 100.
[96] Garlington, "Imputation," 46.
[97] Ibid., 78.
[98] Garlington, *Faith, Obedience, and Perseverance*, 89-90. See also "Imputation," 29, where "all sinned" is again interpreted in light of Rom. 3:23.

It is not surprising that Garlington proceeds to interpret the rest of Romans 5:12-19 and especially the righteousness given to believers from Christ in participationist terms, that is to say, as righteousness imparted or infused (not imputed) from Christ and by means of our union with Him.

> What is in view in [Romans 5] v. 16 is not merely a declaration and a resultant status, but a commitment to a relationship, evidenced by the holiness of the covenant and a determination to persevere in it.[99]

> People, in other words, were really *made* sinners or righteous through the disobedience and obedience of the two men respectively.[100]
> *The restoration is not merely to a standing, but to an existence in the relationship.*[101]

> In brief, we have been reconciled to God through the death of his son (Rom. 5:1-11), making us "righteous" in the pointedly Hebrew sense of a renewed devotion to the Lord and his covenant.[102]

> My plea would be that instead of "counted righteous in Christ," we are "made righteous in Christ.[103]

A second line of argument that supports the assertion that Garlington denies imputed righteousness has to do with the (what is for Garlington problematic) issue of "the justification of the ungodly." That it is a problem for Garlington is clear enough in his approach to the issue. "If it is the righteous who are vindicated because of their fidelity, then how can Paul maintain that God justifies the *ungodly?*"[104] Garlington's solution to this issue provides a startling glimpse of his view of the grounds of justification.

> Indeed, we do not get righteousness directly from the judge, but we do get it from Christ. In his fidelity to his covenant (his righteousness), God the judge provides the means whereby he is able to

---

[99] Garlington, "Imputation," 92.
[100] Garlington, *Faith, Obedience, and Perseverance*, 105.
[101] Ibid., 106.
[102] Ibid.
[103] Garlington, "Imputation," 100.
[104] Garlington, "Study," 65.

vindicate/justify/exonerate his own. He writes his law on their hearts, gives them a new heart and raises them from the dead.[105]

Words really could not be plainer. God justifies the ungodly by writing His law on their hearts. He justifies the ungodly by making them godly and then pronouncing that they are so. As he prosecutes his answer to this question, this solution to Garlington's difficulty becomes evident again.

> We are now in a position to answer our question, "How can God justify the ungodly while being consistent with the practice of the Hebrew courtroom to acquit only the righteous?" The answer quite simply is that those who were formerly ungodly in Adam have been made righteous in Christ. Here the perspective of Philippians 3:9 is much to the point. Paul speaks of a "righteousness from God" (*dikaiosune ek theou*). It is God's own righteousness, defined as "covenant fidelity," that entails *the gift of righteousness* to the apostle. In his own righteousness, God enables us to become what he is—righteous (2 Corinthians 5:21). His loyalty to his people consists in his conforming them to himself, so that he and they may live in uninterrupted covenant fellowship. God's righteousness has provided Christ as the propitiation for sins (Rom. 3:21-26). In Adam all are guilty, but God has removed their guilt by means of Christ and thus can vindicate them as his faithful people. In these actions are embodied God's covenant faithfulness.... After all is said and done, Luther was right that the righteousness God requires is the righteousness he provides in Christ.[106]

Crucial to understanding Garlington here is paying close attention to his definition of righteousness. It is "covenant fidelity," and it is covenant fidelity for both God and man: "It is God's own righteousness, defined as "covenant fidelity," that entails *the gift of righteousness* to the apostle. In his own righteousness, God enables us to become what he is—righteous." Here we note the connection to what we have seen previously about the way in which Garlington tends to define sin and righteousness. Sin tends to be understood as apostasy. Righteousness for Garlington is not perfect and perpetual righteousness. It is covenant fidelity. Its opposite is not sin, but apostasy. Our righteousness is our covenant fidelity—"the obedience of faith."

---

[105]Ibid., 65-67.
[106]Ibid.

It is true that Garlington refers to Luther at the end of the above quotation. We shall deal with this later. It is interesting to note, however, that Garlington himself distances himself from Luther in a way that confirms the understanding given above.

> Given this specificity of 'αμαρτωλοί and δίκαιοι, the important consequence is that the Christian does not remain "a sinner." Rather than being *simul iustus et peccator*, the believer says of himself, *tunc peccator—nunc iustus* ("once a sinner, now righteous").[107]

> Without depreciating what Luther intended by his famous phrase, we are not, again in strictly Pauline terms, *simul iustus et peccator* but rather *tunc peccator – nunc iustus ("once a sinner, now righteous")*. The believer has died to "sin," i. e. [sic] age of apostasy as dominated by the flesh, and has been raised in newness of life that he might "live to God" (Rom. 6:1-11).[108]

It is quite clear that Garlington does not affirm that the Christian is at one and the same time a righteous man and a sinner. The reason is clear. In order to affirm this in Luther's sense one must hold that one is justified in view of a righteousness that is extrinsic to our moral natures. This is what Luther means by an alien righteousness.[109] Garlington, however, holds that the righteousness which is the ground of our justification is (at least in part) our believing obedience or covenant-keeping.

As a third line of argument for the assertion that Garlington does not hold imputed righteousness as the ground of our justification, a number of statements will be brought forward in which he clearly indicates that justification is not confined to forensic categories. If this is true, then clearly the mechanism of justification cannot be imputation alone. Consider these statements:

---

[107]Garlington, *Faith, Obedience, and Perseverance*, 104.

[108]Ibid., 156.

[109]Luther uses this phrase in more than one way according to Paul Althaus, *The Theology of Martin Luther* (Philadelphia: Fortress Press, 1966), 242-245. Sometimes it is used of the contradiction involved in justification (guilty, but forgiven). Sometimes it is used of the contradiction involved in sanctification and the internal warfare the Christian experiences. It is interesting that Garlington holds a view of Rom. 7:14-25 that would allow him to affirm Luther's phrase in the second of these uses. Of course, as Althaus points out, the second contradiction is an implication or result of the first. It may be for this reason Garlington simply rejects the *simul iustus*. Garlington, "Imputation," 45, affirms "alien righteousness." This affirmation will be considered below.

> The very notion of righteousness entails a comprehensive assessment of one's place in God's covenant: neither the OT nor Paul know of a righteousness which is merely forensic.[110]

> As is well-known, in the Psalms and the Prophets God's righteousness is synonymous with his salvation, i. e., his deliverance of Israel from bondage and his vindication of it in the presence of its enemies.[111]

In the pages following the last quotation above Garlington goes on to argue that God's righteousness means more than a heavenly decree. It indicates His saving intervention on behalf of his people. "The restoration is not merely to a standing, but to an existence in the relationship." "It is not just a vindicated status, but a vindicated life."[112] The following statement is similar in effect. *"The restoration is not merely to a standing, but to an existence in the relationship."*[113] Not surprisingly, as a result Garlington clearly refuses to distinguish justification and sanctification.

> To return, finally, to the original question, all of the above has a decided bearing on the justification/sanctification question. To put it forthrightly, I agree with Kasemann that no support can be found for distinguishing between the righteousness of the beginning and the righteousness of the end, between the righteousness of faith and the righteousness of life. . . . Among other things, any rigid distinction between "justification" and "sanctification" is actually the extension of "justification," or, better, "rightwising." Among other things, any rigid distinction between usage of "sanctification" seems to be ruled out of court by the actual usage of "sanctification" in the NT, which normally has reference to the inception of the believing life."[114]

> Yet I want to press further and suggest that the precise reason why "sanctification" does not receive separate mention by Paul is because it is comprehended within "justification."[115]

> Several comments are in order. For one, "righteousness" and "salvation" are synonymous.[116]

---

[110] Garlington, *The Obedience of Faith*, 251.
[111] Garlington, *Faith, Obedience, and Perseverance*, 45-46.
[112] Ibid., 48-49.
[113] Ibid., 106. Emphasis is Garlington's.
[114] Ibid., 155.
[115] Ibid., 160.
[116] Garlington, "Study," 61.

Thus, a formal definition of the Greek phrase *dikaiosune theou* could be stated as, "God's faithfulness to his covenant with Israel, as a result of which he saves her from her exile in Babylon."[117]

Justification in the apostle's thought is essentially the vindication of the righteous, i. e., the faithful people of God. Believers in Christ, so to speak, have been exonerated in the law court and have been readmitted into the privileges, responsibilities, and fellowship of the covenant.[118]

Garlington's view of justification is also made clear by the way in which he relates the justification of Romans 5 and the liberation of Romans 6. One attractive way of translating the use of justify in Romans 6:7 is with some synonym of liberate. Garlington regards this as including sanctification within the definition of justification. Here are his own words: "Justification entails liberation from mastery of sin."[119] This is ambiguous. To say that justification is forensic and to say that justification entails transformation are not contraries. There may be a difference between the essence and the entailments (in the sense of results) of something. The definition and results of anything are distinct categories of thought. This distinction seems to be lost on Garlington when he speaks of "justification in its liberating effects."[120] More confusion on Romans 6:7 and the essence and entailments of justification is found in the pages that follow this statement. One instance is found in the statement: "*Dikaioo* is thus seen to be flexible enough to overlap with *eleutheroo*."[121] Causation and identification are, however, not equivalent. Justification may entail sanctification in the sense of the internal moral renewal of the sinner without necessarily being as to its essence internal moral renewal. Furthermore, Garlington seems to assume that liberation cannot be understood in forensic categories. In fact, however, many cases of liberation are forensic. They begin with and even in one sense consist in a legal act in which the sinner is formally freed from his slavemaster.[122]

---

[117] Ibid.

[118] Ibid., 62.

[119] Ibid., 63. Two synonym finders I consulted suggested that an "entailment" may indicate something actually included in something else or something inevitably resulting from something else.

[120] Ibid., 67.

[121] Ibid., 70.

[122] Garlington's problem in much of the above appears to be his inability to make straightforward logical distinctions. This impression is confirmed when he makes the following remark in "Imputation," 96: "The attempt to fine tune the relationship of the

The three lines of argument recounted at some length above are unambiguous evidence that Garlington does not ground justification in the imputed righteousness of Christ, but grounds it rather in a participationist righteousness. That is to say, it is really grounded in the impartation—not the imputation—of Christ's righteousness. Now, however, we must consider the somewhat difficult issue of the qualifications that Garlington presents as ostensible evidence for his orthodoxy in this matter. These various and somewhat abstruse qualifications compose the evidence that might be supposed to contradict the thesis defended in the preceding pages. In the process of considering this evidence we will also shed light on the difficult question of whether justification for Garlington is "not forensic at all" or "not *merely* forensic." In the following treatment of the supposed evidence to the contrary, we will take up Garlington's various qualifications one by one.

Notice how Garlington appears to affirm the heart of Luther's doctrine of imputed righteousness by affirming "alien righteousness."

> That is to say, the *intention* of the doctrine of imputation is not to be disputed: *our righteousness comes from Christ and is for that reason an "alien righteousness."* However, it is a question of modality.[123]

Garlington's affirmation is, however, misleading. The phrase, "alien righteousness," for Luther and the entire Reformation tradition affirms imputed righteousness. That is to say, it affirms that we are justified on the grounds of a righteousness that is outside of us—not inside of us.[124] *Alien righteousness* does not merely affirm that our righteousness comes from Christ. Medieval Catholicism with Augustine could and did affirm this. It affirms that the righteousness by which we are justified is alien to and outside of us. *Alien righteousness* affirms, in other words, not only that our righteousness comes from Christ, but it also affirms the *mechanics* and *modality* by which that righteousness comes. For

---

various soteriological categories, such as making forgiveness of sin 'the constitutive element' of justification, so as to distance the former from the latter, reprises the old analytical, systematizing approach that attributes to Paul a methodology and set of assumptions conspicuously absent from his text. To a biblical theologian anyway, such over-refinement is practically pointless." I must insist that there is a logical, real, and important distinction between the essence and entailments of justification or to put this differently between its identity and its results. At this point, it seems the logical systematician has a lot to offer the biblical theologian.

[123] Ibid., 45.
[124] Althaus, *The Theology of Martin Luther*, 227-229.

Garlington to affirm *alien righteousness* and then say that "it is a question of modality," is—in terms of the classical meaning of this phrase—nonsensical.

> So, it is well to go on record that justification by faith as such is not in contention, only the mechanics of how justification "works." Likewise, that the righteousness of Christ becomes our possession by faith alone is taken for granted, and indeed defended, in the following pages.[125]

Again Garlington's protest is misleading. He says that justification by faith is not in contention, only its "mechanics." But in the classic Reformation tradition justification by faith assumed and was molded by a certain understanding of its "mechanics." Furthermore, Garlington may assert that the righteousness of Christ becomes our possession by faith alone, but what this means or can mean within his theology is subject to serious question. He does not mean that we embrace an imputed righteousness by faith. He does not hold that such an imputed righteousness is the ground of justification. Furthermore, faith itself—our believing obedience—is our righteousness or covenant fidelity. What can it mean to say that faith becomes our possession *by faith*? If the "obedience of faith" is our righteousness, how can it become ours by means of the "obedience of faith?" Note, however, the following statement of Garlington on this subject.

> Nevertheless, in a certain qualified sense, one may say that righteousness does consist of faith. But a formulation of the matter must be carefully nuanced. Strictly speaking, righteousness is, by definition, conformity to the covenant relationship; it *consists of* a faithful obedience to the Lord whose will is enshrined in the covenant. Yet the beginning of "faithfulness" is "faith." In keeping with the Hebrew term *'emunah*, the Greek noun translated "faith," *pistis*, is two-sided: faith and faithfulness. Given this set of data, righteousness does consist of *pistis* in the expansive sense of *'emunah*, that is, covenant conformity. At the same time, however, as Piper correctly observes from Rom. 10:10, *pistis* as initial trust in Christ has righteousness as its goal, that is, righteousness as covenant standing. In one sense, faith leads to righteousness; and in another, faith consists in righteousness.[126]

---

[125] Garlington, "Imputation," 46.
[126] Garlington, "Imputation," 52.

This is a difficult statement to understand. Garlington admits that righteousness consists of faith. Yet he proceeds to argue that, since faith is two-sided (faith and faithfulness) that it makes sense to say that we believe (the first side of faith) in order to achieve faithfulness (the second side of faith). If faith is, however, really two-sided in Garlington's sense, then faith is already faithfulness in its first acting. Remember the statement he cites with approval from Furnish:

> V.P. Furnish, however, has seen the connection between this and the obedience of faith.... "It is precisely the obedience character of faith which makes it the means of the believer's participation in Christ's death and resurrection and which discloses how this is at the same time a 'walking in newness of life'".[127]

It appears that in the same paragraph cited above Garlington attempts another explanation of his conundrum: "*pistis* as initial trust in Christ has righteousness as its goal, that is, righteousness as covenant standing." Here he takes righteousness not as our covenant-keeping, but as our covenant-standing. He appears to mean that we believe in order that God may both recognize us as having and pronounce us to have covenant-standing. The meaning would be, then, that we believe in the sense of commencing to keep the covenant in order that God may recognize and declare us to be covenant-keepers. This, indeed, makes better sense, but it is no closer to the Reformation tradition. For clearly on this view our justification is grounded on our believing obedience to the covenant—not an imputed righteousness.

It is possible that from the above we gain some insight into Garlington's unwillingness to say straightforwardly that justification is not forensic and his preference to say that it is not *merely* or *simply* forensic.[128] It may be that he is perfectly willing to admit that

---

[127] Ibid., 252.

[128] See Garlington, *Faith, Obedience, and Perseverance*, 45: "What is in view in [Romans 5] v. 16 is not *merely* a declaration and a resultant status, but a commitment to a relationship, evidenced by the holiness of the covenant and a determination to persevere in it." See also in the same work, pp. 48-49: "The restoration is not *merely* to a standing, but to an existence in the relationship.... It is not *just* a vindicated status, but a vindicated life." See also idem, "Imputation," 99: "Third, all of the above brings me to say that my main disagreement with Piper has to do with his insistence that justification has nothing to do with liberation from sin. To reiterate from above, justification and righteousness pertain to our conformity to God's covenant, not *simply* a forensic status." (The emphasis is mine in each of these quotations.)

justification involves a pronouncement or declaration on the basis of our believing obedience that we are faithful covenant-keepers.

> In sum, the evidence educed from these passages by Piper clearly confirms that the righteousness of God is none other than the righteousness of Christ. Nevertheless, it has not been established that *imputation* is the means by which Christ's righteousness becomes ours. As throughout, my contention is that Christ has become our righteousness by virtue of union with himself, plain and simple.[129]

The righteousness of God is none other than the righteousness of Christ appears to be an impressive statement of the traditional view of justification. That Garlington does not mean these words in that way should by this point be obvious. He means by the righteousness of Christ the righteousness that is imparted to us and infused into us by our participation in or union with Christ.

The following quotation is brought forward in order to illustrate Garlington's misrepresentation of the Reformation tradition. He knows or should know that neither Piper nor the Reformation tradition believe "that justification has nothing to do with liberation from sin." Again, Garlington is involved in a logical fallacy. Justification may inevitably result in moral liberation from sin. It may even be liberation from sin, if that liberation is understood forensically. Neither of these things require that justification be (even in part) essentially a matter of internal, moral renewal. Essence and entailment, identity and result are distinct things, as pointed out previously. What Garlington means to say is, however, quite clear by now. He means that it is not possible to distinguish between the moral and forensic aspects of salvation. To become righteous means to become believingly obedient to the covenant as a consequence of which God declares you to be what you really and personally are—a faithful covenant-keeper.

> Third, all of the above brings me to say that my main disagreement with Piper has to do with his insistence that justification has nothing to do with liberation from sin. To reiterate from above, justification and righteousness pertain to our conformity to God's covenant, not simply a forensic status.[130]

---

[129] Garlington, "Imputation," 81.
[130] Ibid., 99.

Garlington closes his response to Piper with a final qualification that surpasses all the others in its opacity.

> In closing, it must be placed beyond all doubt that imputation as a concept is hardly objectionable: what evangelical could, at least with any degree of consistency, protest the notion that Christ has become our righteousness in the gospel? But as pertains to a strict doctrine of imputation, exegesis of texts must be the deciding factor. It has been the conviction of this paper that exegesis will steer us away from imputation to union with Christ.[131]

Perhaps Garlington understands the difference between "imputation as a concept" and "a strict doctrine of imputation," but this author does not. To make matters worse, Garlington ends by saying "that exegesis will steer us away from imputation to union with Christ." But what does he mean here by imputation? Apparently, he means "a strict doctrine of imputation," because he tells us earlier "that imputation as a concept is hardly objectionable." Yet, if imputation as a concept is hardly objectionable, how can he say "that exegesis will steer us away from imputation (not a 'strict doctrine of imputation') to union with Christ?"

In light of our examination of his other such statements, Garlington may mean by "imputation as a concept" the general idea of forensic justification. If this is what he means, then his statement would make sense. Garlington does not believe that the ground of our justification is the imputed righteousness of Christ. That is what he refers to by a "strict doctrine of imputation." He does believe that part of justification is God's pronouncing believers to be what they really and personally are, faithful covenant-keepers. *Perhaps* this is what he means by "imputation as a concept."

This entire discussion of Garlington's views of imputation serves the major thesis of this study. That thesis is that, though Garlington frequently affirms *sola fide*, he does not mean by it what it was defined to mean in its classic articulation in the Reformation. Justification by faith alone in the Reformation meant justification by a faith that received and rested upon the imputed righteousness of Christ. To put this in somewhat broader terms, *sola fide* was defined in terms of a distinction between a righteousness of the law consisting in our own obedience and a righteousness of the gospel consisting of Christ's obedience. Justification by faith alone was understood and defined in this context.

---

[131]Ibid., 101.

Faith is the subjective response of the sinner to the objective gospel of imputed righteousness. Faith cannot remain the same if the gospel does not remain the same. The objective gospel controls and shapes the subjective response. When our faith becomes our believing obedience on the ground of which we are justified, it fulfills a role that it did not fulfill in the Reformation tradition. It is shaped by forces alien to the Reformation tradition. It looks in a direction it did not look in the Reformation. It becomes necessarily introspective and not extraspective. It is, in other words, distorted into a different shape than it possessed in the Reformation tradition. As such, Garlington misleads his readers when he affirms justification *sola fide*, because of his deviation from the Reformation doctrine of justification by imputed righteousness.

Conclusion

The Reformation's *sola fide* had a certain definition which emphasized its passive character. The Reformation's *sola fide* distinguished justifying from evangelical obedience. The Reformation's *sola fide* assumed a dichotomy between the law and the gospel. The foregoing investigation has shown that Garlington's view of faith underscores its active character, does not distinguish faith and works (obedience to the moral law), and rejects the dichotomy between law and gospel and the doctrine of the imputed righteousness of Christ central to (and enabled by) that dichotomy. As such Garlington's affirmation of justification by faith alone is misleading.

CHAPTER 8
CONCLUDING OBSERVATIONS
Introduction

An examination of the Reformation tradition in this study has uncovered several key perspectives on the meaning of justification *sola fide*. A passive definition of justifying faith, a distinction between justifying faith and evangelical obedience, and a dichotomy between the law and gospel are essential to the Reformation's *sola fide*. These three perspectives also reveal and embody the substantial doctrinal unity of the Reformation with regard to justification *sola fide*. They have provided this study with a useful balance upon which to weigh the claims of several, important, contemporary evangelical theologians that they believe justification by faith alone. It is now appropriate, therefore, to ask what we may learn of practical significance from this study. I will arrange the concluding observations by speaking first of secondary and then principal observations.

Secondary Observations

- **The Danger of an Overly Analytical Approach to the Reformation Doctrine of Justification by Faith Alone**

It is in the very nature of the scholarly enterprise to be severely analytical. Such precision of thought is a very good thing in itself. It is not to be dismissed as unnecessarily careful, cautious, or scrupulous. Nevertheless, scholars must beware that this virtue may become a vice. The analytic spectacles through which they view their disciplines may permit them to see only diversity and miss unifying perspectives. When diversity is seen everywhere, real and important distinctions may be missed! To enlarge on the old proverb–they may miss the forest for the trees, and they may (for this very reason) not realize when they have entered a whole new forest.

It seems to be that such dangers lurk in the contemporary discussion of justification. There is a danger of seeing such diversity in the Reformation tradition that minor variations are emphasized and its great unifying perspectives are lost. This may in turn make evangelical scholars insensitive to real and important changes taking place among evangelicals today.

There is no shortage of issues in which a certain diversity may be found in the Reformation tradition with regard to justification by faith alone. There are different approaches to the dichotomy between the law and the gospel. We have seen some indications of both development and diversity on this issue in the tradition. But such variations must not blind us to the fact that the entire tradition maintained *in some form* this dichotomy or contrast. There are different approaches to the definition of faith with regard especially to its relations to assurance. In this author's opinion there is an undeniable tendency in both Luther and Calvin to speak of assurance of salvation as essential to faith. There is just as clearly (also in my opinion) a clearly visible desire to distinguish faith and assurance of salvation in the Westminster complex of documents. Again, however, this must not disguise for us what is plainly visible throughout the entire tradition—that justifying faith is understood in passive terms. It justifies, in other words, because it rests in, receives, or applies Christ—not because of any obedience it produces and not even because it has the character of obedience. There is simply no major difference of opinion in Luther, Calvin, or the confessional tradition at this point.[1] With respect to the doctrine of justification by faith alone, there is substantial unity in the Reformation tradition.[2] The trenchant words of Pelikan bear repeating here:

---

[1] Perhaps there were also differences in the precision with which the doctrine of the imputation of an alien righteousness was understood and articulated in the Reformation tradition. Even if this is the case, it would be simply another illustration of variation within the substantial unity of the tradition's affirmation of justification *sola fide*.

[2] I lodge my protest again against the implication that substantial diversity existed in the Reformation tradition with regard to justification *sola fide*. Statements like those of Thomas R. Schreiner and Ardel B. Caneday, *The Race Set before Us: A Biblical Theology of Perseverance & Assurance* (Downers Grove, IL: InterVarsity Press, 2001), 88, are not helpful: "Few disagreements, however, are as divisive and generate as much heat as the conflict that concerns the nature of faith's relationship to obedience and good works. The familiar motto *sola fide* ('by faith alone') was central to the Protestant Reformation of the church. This was the source of the famous disputation between the reformer Martin Luther and Desiderius Erasmus, the Roman Catholic. Protestants have continued to debate the meaning of 'by faith alone.' Each generation debates this Protestant motto, usually with some acrimony, because few issues concerning the gospel of Jesus Christ are as crucial as the question concerning the relationship of faith and obedience." When Norman Shepherd, "Justification by Faith Alone," *Reformation and Revival Journal* 2, no. 2 (Spring 2002), 81, asserts, ". . . there is also a difference between the classic Lutheran and Reformed doctrines of justification," the notion conveyed is downright misleading.

Although Luther's discovery of justification by faith took place in the struggle of his own conscience as it sought an answer to the question, "How do I obtain a God who is gracious to me?" the doctrine of justification by faith was to become one that "all churches reformed, with a sweet consent, applaud, and confess," including those churches that opposed Luther on many other points. Thus the seventeenth-century Reformed followers of John Calvin knew that they disagreed with the followers of Luther on many questions, but they recognized that all of them agreed on this doctrine of the entire Reformation, in fact, the chief doctrine of Christianity and the chief point of difference separating Protestantism from Roman Catholicism. Repeatedly, the various efforts in the sixteenth and seventeenth centuries to unite Lutheran and Reformed teachings were able to affirm this doctrine as one that they shared, diverge though they did on other doctrines. It was a Swiss Reformed theologian, Heinrich Bullinger, who, in the title of a book published in 1554 and dedicated to the Lutheran king of Denmark, managed to include all the constituents of this common confession more trenchantly than any one title had: *The Grace of God that Justifies Us for the Sake of Christ through Faith Alone, without Good Works, while Faith Meanwhile Abounds in Good Works.*[3]

Justification *sola fide* is the proper lens, therefore, through which to see the unity of the tradition. There are differences of opinion both today and in the tradition that are consistent with the tradition and within the boundaries of justification *sola fide*. There are also, of course, differences that are not! Whether or not one agrees with every jot and tittle of his article, Mark Seifrid has a point, when he says:

> Surely the outcome of their debate is instructive for us. Although they maintained their differences, Luther and Melanchthon accepted one another's teaching on justification. That is not at all to say that there were no boundaries.[4]

It is hoped that this study has clarified to some extent where those boundaries are.

---

[3] Jaroslav Pelikan, *The Reformation of Church and Dogma*, vol. 4 of *The Christian Tradition: A History of the Development of Doctrine* (Chicago: The University of Chicago Press, 2000), 138-139.

[4] Mark Seifrid, "Luther, Melanchthon, and Paul on the Question of Imputation," in *Justification: What's at Stake in the Current Debate?* ed. Mark Husbands and Daniel J. Treier (Downers Grove, IL: InterVarsity, 2004), 150. See Seifrid's comments in the same article, page 149.

- **The Necessity of a Clear Distinction between the "Already" and "Not Yet" in the Study of Justification**

One of the significant gains of evangelical theology over the last century is an increasing awareness of the fact that the New Testament presents its teaching with regard to a number of its crucial concepts in terms of "the already" and "the not yet." There is a paradoxical tendency to speak of kingdom, salvation, eternal life, redemption, and adoption (to mention only the first illustrations that come to mind) in terms of "the already" and "the not yet" phases of each. This same tendency is clearly present with regard to justification. There is clearly a sense in which believers are *already* justified (Luke 18:14; Rom. 3:24; 4:5; 5:1, 9; 1 Cor. 6:11; Titus 3:7) and a sense in which believers are *not yet* justified (Matt. 12:37; Rom. 2:13; Gal. 5:5).

An increased awareness of this important, exegetical fact has, it is to be feared, resulted in not a little fuzzy thinking among evangelicals with regard to justification. The fact that justification is both *already* and *not yet* does not mean that these two phases of justification are identical or may be merged into one another. A biblical parallel may make the matter clear. Adoption, as noted previously, is also presented in terms of a tension between the *already* and the *not yet*. See Galatians 4:5-7 and Romans 8:15 (where the *already* dimension of adoption is emphasized) and Romans 8:23 and possibly Ephesians 1:5 (where the *not yet* dimension is emphasized). According to Romans 8:23, our yet future adoption involves the redemption of our bodies. Quite clearly, our *already* adoption does not and is, thus, in this respect quite different. Even so, however helpful and necessary it may be to see the connection between the *already* and *not yet* aspects of justification, this clearly does not give us the right to simply merge the two phases of justification into one or treat them as theologically equivalent.

If, however, we have read Fuller, Shepherd, and Garlington aright, this is exactly what they are doing. *If* the Reformation tradition tended to lay exclusive emphasis on the *already* dimension of justification, such writers tend not only to emphasize the *future* or *not yet* dimension, but also to merge the two into one. We have noted this tendency at several points in this study. What else can the idea that justification is conditioned on perseverance imply?[5]

---

[5]Norman Shepherd, *The Call of Grace: How the Covenant Illuminates Salvation and Evangelism* (Phillipsburg, NJ: P&R Publishing, 2000), 16, 50, and Daniel P. Fuller, *The Unity of the Bible* (Grand Rapids: Zondervan, 1992), 310, 315, argue that justification is

It seems to be a common tendency among evangelical theologians today to merge the two phases of justification into a justification that is characteristically future. It is not necessary to exclusively emphasize the *already* dimension of justification in order to maintain the Reformation view of justification *sola fide*. It is, however, necessary carefully to distinguish the *already* from the *not yet* dimension. Without such a careful distinction, confusion will abound—as this study shows. Justification by faith alone must in the face of such confusion either be denied or provided with a meaning that it does not possess in the Reformation tradition.

- **The Irrelevance for Justification *Sola Fide* of a Distinction between Works of Faith and Works of Merit**

This study shows that the most common way of providing *sola fide* with a meaning that will make sense within and fit into contemporary biblico-theological tendencies is to assert that justification *sola fide* is to be understood in terms of a distinction between two kinds of works. Shepherd[6] and Fuller[7] both in their own way distinguish between works of merit and works of faith. Garlington, following the typical path of "the new perspective on Paul," and especially James D.G. Dunn,[8] distinguishes "the obedience of faith" from the peculiarly Jewish works of the law.[9]

Some such distinction maintained by Shepherd and Fuller is found in the Bible. This distinction is even important in its own way. It is just that it is irrelevant when it comes to specifying the meaning of *sola fide*. As we have shown conclusively, *sola fide* was not just opposed to the works of the law, it was also distinguished from the works of faith. It was understood in the Reformation tradition that faith was a form of obedience. It was also understood that faith produced obedience. It was just that faith did not justify because it was obedient or virtuous, but because it rested in Christ. Resting in Christ and not working through love was the meaning of *sola fide*.

---

conditioned on perseverance. This view can only mean that the *already* and *not yet* phases of justification are merged into a view of justification that sees it as mainly future.

[6]Shepherd, *Call of Grace*, 60-61, and "Justification by Faith Alone," 88.

[7]Fuller, *The Unity of the Bible*, 311, 314, 323, 335.

[8]See Dunn's treatment of Galatians 2:16 in *Jesus, Paul, and the Law: Studies in Mark and Galatians* (Louisville: Westminster/John Knox Press, 1990).

[9]See Don B. Garlington, *Faith, Obedience, and Perseverance* (Tubingen: J. C. B. Mohr, 1994), 5, and idem, *The Obedience of Faith*, (Tubingen: J. C. b. Mohr, 1991), 247.

- ## The Indispensability of Calvin's Approach to James 2

The author confesses that he entered upon this study somewhat ambivalent with regard to the proper approach to James 2 and the proper way of reconciling it to Paul's teaching of justification *sola fide*. The foregoing observations clearly imply why he can no longer entertain such ambivalence. Both Shepherd and Fuller argue that James 2 is speaking of the works of faith and asserting that we are justified by the works of faith.[10] They reconcile James with Paul by arguing that being justified by faith alone means being justified by the works of faith alone and not by some other kind of works. Hence, they both assume that the meaning of justification in James 2 is the same as its meaning, for instance, in Romans 3 and 4. Calvin, on the other hand, insists:

> That we may not then fall into that false reasoning which has deceived the Sophists, we must take notice of the two-fold meaning of the word *justified*. Paul means by it the gratuitous imputation of righteousness before the tribunal of God; and James, the manifestation of righteousness by the conduct, and that before men.[11]

It should be clear now why an approach like that of Calvin which distinguishes "the two-fold meaning of the word *justified*" is necessary. Justification *sola fide* for Calvin and the whole Reformation tradition must be distinguished from justification by any works of ours whatever—not just works of the law or works of merit, but even works of faith. Thus, James cannot be using the term *justified* in the same sense as Paul. If he is, there would be direct contradiction.[12] Shepherd and Fuller manifest in their interpretation of James 2 the contemporary predilection to merge the *already* and *not yet* phases of justification into a justification that is characteristically future. On the other hand, Calvin's idea that there is a twofold meaning of justification is completely unobjectionable from an exegetical viewpoint. It is clear—as even Shepherd and Fuller admit—that both the words *faith* and *works* have different denotations in James 2. Why, then, is it hard to see that the word *justified* does as well?

---

[10]Norman Shepherd, "The Grace of Justification," (unpublished paper written in 1979), 2; Fuller, *The Unity of the Bible*, 311.

[11]*Comm*. Jas. 2:21. Footnote citations written as *Comm*. are from *Calvin's Commentaries*, 22 vols. (Grand Rapids: Baker Book House, 1981).

[12]To this extent, Luther is right. There is direct contradiction between Paul and James—*if* justification means the same in both.

Principal Observations

- **The Misleading Nature of the Claims of Garlington, Fuller, and Shepherd**

Here it is only necessary to remind the reader of the thesis of this study. The classic articulation of justification *sola fide* is found in the Reformation tradition. To affirm *sola fide* and not mean by this phrase what it meant for the whole Reformation tradition is simply misleading. The fact is, however, that this is exactly what Garlington, Fuller, and Shepherd actually do. They do not hold the definition of justifying faith held by the Reformation tradition. They do not hold the distinction between justifying faith and evangelical obedience held by the Reformation tradition. They do not hold the dichotomy between law and gospel held by the Reformation tradition. They do not hold *sola fide* in any of its fundamental characteristics in the tradition. They do not hold justification *sola fide* in any familiar or meaningful sense. Their affirmation of *sola fide*, then, only serves to cloud and confuse the true meaning and real purport of their theologies. It would be helpful and clarifying, then, if they would cease attempting to articulate their views in terms of a doctrine they really do not hold. It would also be helpful and clarifying if they would make clear that they are not Reformation evangelicals in any historic sense.

- **The Enormous Consequences of Departure from the *Sola Fide* of the Reformation**

The enormous consequences of what has just been said must be carefully weighed. The cardinal doctrine of the Reformation, its peculiar contribution to the advancement of biblical truth in the church, is the doctrine of justification by faith alone. In some sense this is the central meaning of the Reformation. Yet Garlington, Fuller, and Shepherd no longer hold this doctrine in any meaningful sense. Though not affirming that they have reverted to Tridentine Catholicism, their formulations are closer to those of Trent than historic Protestantism. Whatever they are, they are not Reformation evangelicals in an historical sense.

- **The Widespread Confusion over the Meaning of Justification by Faith Alone**

We began this study with the remark of John Piper that "a detailed defense still needs to be done on the historic Reformation view of the relationship between faith and obedience, so that the two are not conflated in the instrumentality of justification, as many in biblical-theological circles are doing these days."[13] This study has confirmed (in my thinking) that Piper is correct when he remarks that "many" are conflating faith and obedience in the instrumentality of justification.

Garlington, Fuller, and Shepherd were examined because, in this author's opinion, they are the clearest and most serious illustrations of this tendency within evangelical circles. It has, nevertheless, also become clear that each of these men represent a circle that to some extent supports their views. Many evangelicals are being influenced by "new perspective" views like those of Garlington. Many evangelicals have been significantly influenced by Fuller. His distinctive views are, however, in some respects quite different than those of the "new perspective." Shepherd represents many in Presbyterian circles, especially those in the orbit of the *Auburn Avenue Theology*, who share his perspectives. In light of this, it is a fair characterization to say there is a widespread penumbra of confusion among evangelicals regarding faith, obedience, and justification. It is feared that there is wide recession from the careful and crucial statements of our Reformation forefathers on justification *sola fide*. Vast ignorance of their careful formulations of this great truth has resulted in those formulations appearing increasingly alien to evangelicals today.

- **The Vital Importance of the Classical Articulation of Justification by Faith Alone for Exegesis and Doctrine**

There is a kind of morbid fear among evangelicals today that too much study of the great creeds and important theologians of the church will hinder them from reading the Bible *for themselves*. Also infecting evangelicalism and its scholars is a kind of *pride of modernity* that looks at the past with condescension inconsistent with the teachable spirit that ought to characterize our interaction with the great teachers Christ has

---

[13] John Piper, *Counted Righteous in Christ* (Wheaton, IL: Crossway Books, 2002), 42.

given His church. Not a little of the ignorance and confusion that characterizes evangelicalism today may be explained on the basis of such subtle self-sufficiency and pride.

In such a context, this study is a call and a testimony. It is a call to respectful study of the great developments of historical theology, and especially those developments associated with the cardinal doctrine of the Reformation–*sola fide*. It is this author's testimony that he has found in such a study not darkness and obscurity, but light that has guided his steps into the truth of Scripture and the blessedness of being justified by faith alone.

BIBLIOGRAPHY

General Evangelical Discussion of *Sola Fide*

1. Books

Anderson, H. George, and Murphy, T. Austin. *Justification by Faith.* Minneapolis: Auguburg, 1985.
Anderson, H. George, Murphy, T. Austin, and Burgess, Joseph A., eds. *Justification by Faith: Lutherans and Catholics in Dialogue VII.* Minneapolis: Augsburg Publishing House, 1985.
Belcher, Richard P. *A Layman's Guide to the Lordship Controversy.* Southbridge, MA: Crowne Publications, 1990.
Carson, D.A., ed. *Justification and Variegated Nomism.* Vol. 1, *The Complexities of Second Temple Judaism.* Grand Rapids: Baker, 2001.
Chantry, Walt J. *Today's Gospel: Authentic or Synthetic?* Edinburgh: Banner of Truth Trust, 1970.
Colson, Charles and Neuhaus, Richard John, eds. *Evangelicals and Catholics Together: Toward a Common Mission.* Dallas: Word Publishing, 1995.
Das, A. Andrew. *Paul, the Law, and the Covenant.* Peabody, MA: Hendrickson Publishers, 2001.
Dunn, James D.G. *The Theology of Paul the Apostle.* Grand Rapids: Eerdmans, 1998.
Eveson, Philip H. *Justification by Faith Alone in the Light of Recent Thought.* Bromley, England: Day One, 1996.
Forde, Gerhard O. *The Law-Gospel Debate: An Interpretation of Its Historical Development.* Minneapolis: Augsburg, 1968.
Hodges, Zane C. *Absolutely Free: A Biblical Reply to Lordship Salvation.* Dallas: Redención Viva, 1989.
_____. *The Gospel under Siege: Faith and Works in Tension.* Dallas: Redención Viva, 1992.
_____. *The Hungry Inherit: Winning the Wealth of the World to Come.* Dallas: Redención Viva, c1997.
Horton, Michael S. *Covenant and Eschatology.* Louisville: Westmminster John Knox, 2002.
Joint Declaration on the Doctrine of Justification. English Language ed. Grand Rapids: Eerdmans, 2000.

Karlberg, Mark W. *The Changing of the Guard—Westminster Theological Seminary in Philadelphia.* Unicoi, TN: The Trinity Foundation, 2001.

_____. *Covenant Theology in Reformed Perspective.* Eugene, OR: Wipf and Stock Publishers, 2000.

Kim, Seyoon. *Paul and the New Perspective: Second Thoughts on the Origins of Paul's Gospel.* Grand Rapids: Eerdmans, 2002.

MacArthur, John. *Faith Works: The Gospel According to the Apostles.* Dallas: Word, 1993.

_____. *Justification by Faith.* Chicago: Moody Press, 1985.

_____. *The Gospel According to Jesus: What Does Jesus Mean When He Says, "Follow Me"?* Grand Rapids: Zondervan, 1994.

McGoldrick, James Edward. *Baptist Successionism: A Crucial Question of Baptist History.* Metuchen, NJ: The Scarecrow Press, 1994.

Orr, James. *The Progress of Dogma.* Old Tappan, NJ: Fleming H. Revell, 1901.

Piper, John. *Counted Righteous in Christ.* Wheaton, IL: Crossway Books, 2002.

Robertson, O. Palmer. *The Current Justification Controversy.* Unicoi, TN: The Trinity Foundation, 2003.

Sanders, E.P. *Paul.* Oxford: Oxford University Press, 1991.

_____. *Paul and Palestinian Judaism: A Comparison of Patterns of Religion.* Philadelphia: Fortress, 1977.

_____. *Paul, the Law, and the Jewish People.* Philadelphia, Fortress, 1983.

Schreiner, Thomas R. and Ardel B. Caneday. *The Race Set Before Us: A Biblical Theology of Perseverance and Assurance.* Downers Grove, IL: InterVarsity Press, 2001.

Seifrid, Mark A. *Christ, Our Righteousness: Paul's Theology of Justification.* Downers Grove, IL: InterVarsity Press, 2000.

_____. *Justification by Faith: The Origin and Development of a Central Pauline Theme.* New York: E.J. Brill, 1992.

Strickland, Wayne G., ed. *Five Views of Law and Gospel.* Grand Rapids: Zondervan, 1993.

Stuhlmacher, Peter. *Revisiting Paul's Doctrine of Justification: A Challenge to the New Perspective.* Downers Grove, IL: InterVarsity Press, 2001.

Toon, Peter. *The Development of Doctrine in the Church.* Grand Rapids: Eerdmans, 1979.

Waldron, Samuel E. *Easy Christianity.* Grand Rapids: Truth for Eternity Ministries, 1984.

Westerholm, Stephen. *Israel's Law and the Church's Faith: Paul and His Recent Interpreters*. Grand Rapids: Eerdmans, 1988.

_____. *Perspectives Old and New on Paul: The "Lutheran" Paul and His Critics*. Grand Rapids: Eerdmans, 2004.

Wright, N.T. *Jesus and the Victory of God*. Minneapolis: Fortress Press, 1996.

_____. *The Climax of the Covenant: Christ and the Law in Pauline Theology*. Minneapolis: Fortress Press, 1991.

_____. *The New Testament People of God*. Minneapolis: Fortress Press, 1992.

_____. *The Resurrection of the Son of God*. Minneapolis: Fortress Press, 2003.

_____. *What Saint Paul Really Said*. Grand Rapids: Eerdmans, 1997.

2. Articles

Allen, Kenneth W. "Justification by Faith." *Bibliotheca Sacra* (April/June 1978), 109-116.

Barth, Karl L. "Cardinal Principles of Lutheranism and 'Evangelical Theology.'" *Concordia Journal* 7, no. 2 (March 1981), 50-57.

Bayer, Oswald. "Justification as the Basis and Boundary of Theology." *Lutheran Quarterly* 15, no. 3 (Autumn, 2001), 273-292.

Bloesch, Donald G. "Faith Alone: The Evangelical Doctrine of Justification." *Christianity Today* 40 (October 1996), 54-55.

Carson, D.A. "The Vindication of Imputation: On Fields of Discourse and Semantic Fields." In *Justification: What's at Stake in the Current Debates?* ed. Mark Husbands and Daniel J. Treier, 46-78. Downers Grove, IL: InterVarsity Press, 2004.

Dunn, James D.G. "The New Perspective on Paul and the Law." In *Romans 1-8*. Waco, TX: Word, 1988.

Forde, Gerhard O. "Justification by Faith Alone: The Article by Which the Church Stands of Falls?" *Dialog* 27 (Autumn 1988), 260-267.

Gaffin, Richard B., Jr. "Paul and the Theologian." *Westminster Theological Journal* 62 (Spring 2000), 121-141.

Garlington, Don. "A Study of Justification by Faith." *The Reformation and Revival Journal* 11, no. 2 (Spring 2002), 55-74.

Gathercole, Simon J. "After the New Perspective." *Tyndale Bulletin* 52, no. 2 (2001), 303-306.

_____. "The Gift of Salvation." *First Things* 79 (1998), 20-23.

_____. "The 'New Perspective' on Paul's Conversion and Justification." *Reformation Today*. 188 (July-August 2002), 7-16.

_____. *Where Is Boasting? Early Jewish Soteriology and Paul's Response in Romans 1-5*. Grand Rapids: Eerdmans, 2002.

Hinlicky, Paul R. "Faith Alone." *Lutheran Forum* 23, no. 2 (1989), 4-27.

Keeling, Alma Lauder. "Not By Faith Alone." *Journal of Religion and Psychical Research* 5, no. 1 (January 1982), 50-53.

Keifert, Patrick. "Faith Alone: Lutheran-Roman Catholic Convergence?" *Lutheran Forum* 23, no. 2 (1989), 19-20, 35.

Lightner, Robert P. "Faith Alone: The Evangelical Doctrine of Justification." *Bibliotheca Sacra* 153 (April-June 1996), 234.

Lusk, Rich. "N.T. Wright and Reformed Theology: Friends or Foes?" *The Reformation and Revival Journal* 11, no. 2 (Spring 2002), 35-54.

Moore, Russell D. "A Review of *the Race Set Before Us: A Biblical Theology of Perseverance and Assurance*." *The Southern Baptist Theological Journal* (Summer 2002), 80-81.

Peter, Carl J. "Justification by Faith Alone: The Article by Which the Church Stands or Falls? A Reply." *Dialog* 29 (Winter 1990), 55-58.

Peterson, Robert A. "Perseverance and Apostasy: A Bibliographic Essay." *Covenant Seminary Review—Presbyterion* 16, no. 2 (1990), 119-125.

Sandlin, P. Andrew. "Lutheranized Calvinism: Gospel or Law; or Gospel and Law." *The Reformation and Revival Journal* 11, no. 2 (Spring 2002), 123-136.

Shepherd, Norman. "Justification by Faith Alone." *The Reformation and Revival Journal* 11, no. 2 (Spring 2002), 75-92.

Sorum, Jonathan D. "Cheap Grace, Costly Grace, and Just Plain Grace: Bonhoeffer's Defense of Justification by Faith Alone." *Lutheran Forum* 27 (August 1993), 20-23.

Strickland, Wayne G. "Preunderstanding and Daniel Fuller's Law-Gospel Continuum." *Bibliotheca Sacra* (1987), 181-193.

Tamerius, Travis. "Sounding the Alarm: N.T. Wright and Evangelical Theology." *The Reformation and Revival Journal* 11, no. 2 (Spring 2002), 11-34.

_____. "The RRJ Interview with N.T. Wright, Part Two." *The Reformation and Revival Journal* 11, no. 2 (Spring 2002), 137-154.

VanDrunen, David. "When the Covenant Obscures Justification: Review of *The Call of Grace: How the Covenant Illuminates Salvation and Evangelism*." *Modern Reformation* 11, no. 2 (March/April 2002), 38-40.

Wilson, Douglas. "A Collection of Short Credos." *Credenda Agenda* 15, no. 5 (2003), 22-26.

_____. "A Pauline Take on the New Perspective." *Credenda Agenda* 15, no. 5 (2003), 5-20.

Withrow, Brandon. "Jonathan Edwards and Justification by Faith." *The Reformation and Revival Journal* 11, no. 2 (Spring 2002), 93-110.

3. Theses and Dissertations

Vickers, Brian. "The Imputation of Christ's Righteousness: A Study of Key Pauline Texts." Ph.D. diss., The Southern Baptist Theological Seminary, 2003.

4. Internet Links

The Justification Controversy. [on-line]. Accessed 1 September 2003. Available from www.pcanet.org/history/documents/shepherd/justification.html

Keathley, Ken. "Does Anyone Really Know If They are Saved? A Survey of the Current Views on Assurance with a Modest Proposal." *Journal of the Grace Evangelical Society* 15, no. 28 (Spring 2002) [on-line]. Accessed 19 April 2003. Available from www.faithalone.org/journal/index.html#SPRING%202002

Robbins, John. "Justification and Judgment." *Journal of the Grace Evangelical Society* 15, no. 28 (Spring 2002). Accessed April 19, 2003. Available from www.faithalone.org/journal/index.html#SPRING%202002

Wilkin, Robert N. "Striving for the Prize of Eternal Salvation: A Review of Schreiner and Caneday's *The Race Set Before Us*" [on-line]. Accessed ca. January 1, 2003. Available from http://www.faithalone.org/journal/2002i/wilkin/html

Luther and *Sola Fide*

1. Primary Sources

Luther, Martin. *A Commentary on Saint Paul's Epistle to the Galatians.* New York: Robert Carter, 1845.

_____. *A Commentary on St. Paul's Epistle to the Galatians, A revised and completed translation based on the 'Middleton' edition of the English version of 1575.* London: James Clarke & Co. Ltd., 1953.

_____. *American Edition of Luther's Works*. Translated by Tappert. Philadelphia and St. Louis, 1955-.

_____. *Kritische Gesamtausgabe der Werke, D. Martin Luther*. 67 vols. to date. Weimar: Hermann Bohlaus Nachfolger, 1883-.

_____.*Kritische Gesamtausgabe, D. Martin Luther's Werke: Tischreden*. Weimar: H. Böhlaus Nachfolger, 1912-1921.

_____. *Luther: Lectures on Romans*. Translated and edited by Wilhelm Pauck. London: S.C.M. Press, 1961.

_____. *Luther's Works: American Edition*. Edited by J. Pelikan. 55 vols. Saint Louis: Concordia Publishing House, 1955-1986.

_____. *Martin Luther's Basic Theological Writings*. Edited by Timothy F. Lull. Minneapolis: Fortress Press, 1989.

_____. *On the Bondage of the Will*. Grand Rapids: Associated Publishers and Authors, n.d.

_____. *Reformation Writings of Martin Luther*. Translated with introduction and notes from the definitive Weimar Edition by Bertam Lee Woolf. London: Lutterworth Press, 1952.

_____. *Three Treatises*. Philadelphia: Fortress Press, 1978.

_____. *Tischreden: D. Martin Luther Werke*. Weimar: Hermann Bohlaus Nachfolger, 1912-1921.

2. Books

Althaus, Paul. *The Ethics of Martin Luther*. Translated and with a foreword by Robert C. Schultz. Philadelphia: Fortress Press, 1972.

_____. *The Theology of Martin Luther*. Philadelphia: Fortress Press, 1966.

Atkinson, James. *The Great Light*. Grand Rapids: Eerdmans, 1968.

Bainton, Roland H. *Here I Stand: A Life of Martin Luther*. New York: The New American Library, 1950.

Bayer, Oswald. *Promissio: Geschichte der reformatorischen Wende in Luthers Theologie*. Göttingen: Vandenhoeck&Ruprecht, 1971.

Braaten, Carl E. and Jenson, Robert W., eds. *Union with Christ: The New Finnish Interpretation of Luther*. Grand Rapids: Eerdmans, 1998.

Brecht, Martin. *Martin Luther: His Road to Reformation, 1483-1521*. Translated by James L. Schaaf. Fortress Press: Philadelphia, 1985.

Chadwick, Henry. *The Reformation*. Harmondsworth, England: Penguin Books, 1978.

Cunningham, William. *The Reformers and the Theology of the Reformation*. Edinburgh: Banner of Truth Trust, 1979.

D'Aubigne, J.H. Merle. *History of the Reformation of the Sixteenth Century*. Grand Rapids: Baker Book House, 1976.

Douglass, E. Jane Dempsey. *Justification in Late Medieval Preaching: A Study of John Geiler of Keisersberg*. Leiden: E.J. Brill, 1966.

Ebeling, Gerhard. *Luther: An Introduction to His Thought*. Translated by R. A. Wilson. Philadelphia: Fortress Press, 1970.

Feuerbach, Ludwig. *The Essence of Faith According to Luther*. Translated by Melvin Cherno. New York: Harper & Row, 1967.

Herman, Rudolf. "Beobachtungen zu Luthers Rechtfertigungslehre." In *Gesammelte Studien zur Theologie Luthers under der Reformation*. Gottingen: Vandenhoeck & Ruprecht, 1960.

Holl, Karl. *Gesammelte Aufsatze zur Kirchengeschichte*, 3 vols. Tubingen, 1928.

_____. *What Did Luther Understand by Religion?*. Edited by James Luther Adams and Walter F. Bense. Translated by Fred W. Meuser and Walter R. Wietzke. Philadelphia: Fortress Press, 1977.

Kerr, Hugh Thomson. *A Compend of Luther's Theology*. Philadelphia: The Westminster Press, 1943.

Kittelson, James M. *Luther the Reformer: The Story of the Man and His Career*. Minneapolis: Augsburg Publishing House, 1986.

Knox, David Broughton. *The Doctrine of Faith in the Reign of Henry VIII*. London: James Clarke & Co., 1961.

Kooiman, W.J. *By Faith Alone: The Life of Martin Luther*. Translated by Bertram Lee Woolf. London:Lutterworth Press, 1954.

Lenker, John Nicholas. *Luther's Catechetical Writings*. Minneapolis: The Luther Press, 1907.

Lindsay, Thomas M. *A History of the Reformation*. 2 vols. New York: Charles Scribner's sons, 1936.

Lohse, Bernhard. *Martin Luther: An Introduction to His Life and Work*. Translated by Robert C. Schultz. Philadelphia: Fortress Press, 1986.

Luther's Lives: Two Contemporary Accounts of Martin Luther. Translated and annotated by Elizabeth Vandiver, Ralph Keen, and Thomas D. Frazel. New York: Manchester University Press, 2002.

Mannermaa, Tuomo. *Christ Present in Faith: Luther's View of Justification*. Edited and introduced by Kirsi Stjerna. Minneapolis: Fortress Press, 2005.

_____. *Luther's English Connection*. Milwaukee: Northwestern Publishing House, 1979.

McGrath, Alister. *Iustitia Dei: A History of the Christian Doctrine of Justification*. Second Edition. Cambridge, UK: Cambridge University Press, 1998.

_____. *Justification by Faith*. Grand Rapids: Zondervan, 1988.
_____. *Luther's Theology of the Cross*. Cambridge, MA: Blackwell, 1998.
Melanchthon, Philip. *Melanchthon on Christian Doctrine: Loci Communes 1555*. Translated and edited by Clyde L. Manschreck. Grand Rapids: Baker Book House, 1965.
Oberman, Heiko. *The Dawn of the Reformation*. Edinburgh: T & T Clark, 1986.
_____. *The Forerunners of the Reformation: The Shape of Late Medieval Thought*. Translated by Paul L. Nyhus. New York: Holt, Rinehart, and Winston, 1966.
_____. *The Harvest of Medieval Theology*. Grand Rapids: Baker Book House, 1983.
Pelikan, Jaroslav. *The Christian Tradition: A History of the Development of Doctrine*. Vol. 4, *The Reformation of Church and Dogma*. Chicago: The University of Chicago Press, 2000.
Rupp, Gordon E. *The Righteousness of God*. London: Hodder and Stoughton, 1953.
Sears, B. *Select Treatises of Martin Luther*. Andover, MD: Allen, Morrill, and Wardwell, 1846.
Seeberg, Reinhold. *History of Doctrines*. Translated by Charles E. Hay. Grand Rapids: Baker Book House, 1978.
Stump, Joseph. *Life of Philip Melanchthon*. 2d. Edition. New York: Pilger Publishing House, 1897.
Warfield, B.B. *The Works of Benjamin B. Warfield*, Vol. 4, *Tertullian and Augustine*. Grand Rapids: Baker Book House, 1981.
Wengert, Timothy J. *Law and Gospel: Philip Melanchthon's debate with John Agricola of Eisleben over Poenitentia*. Grand Rapids: Baker Book House, 1997.

3. Articles

Anderson, Marvin W. "Luther's *Sola Fide* in Italy: 1542-1551." *Church History* 38 (March 1969), 25-42.
Arand, Charles P. "Melanchthon's Rhetorical Argument for *Sola Fide* in the Apology." *Lutheran Quarterly* 14, no. 3 (Autumn 2000), 280-308.
Baker, Wayne J. "*Sola Fide, Sola Gratia*: The Battle for Luther in 17th Century England." *Sixteenth Century Journal* 16 (1985), 115-133.
Bayer, Oswald. "Rupture of Times: Luther's Relevance for Today." *Lutheran Quarterly* 13 (1999), 35-50.

_____. "The Being of Christ in Faith." *The Lutheran Quarterly* 10 (1996), 135-150.

Braaten, Carl. "The Gospel of Justification *Sola Fide*." *Dialog* 15 (Summer 1976), 207-213.

Cameron, James K. "Aspects of the Lutheran Contribution to the Scottish Reformation 1528-1552." *Lutheran Theological Journal* 19 (May 1985), 12-20.

_____. "The Communion of Saints." *First Things* 131 (2003), 26-33.

Dorman, Ted. "The Catholic Luther." *First Things* 98 (December 1999), 49-52.

Heckel, Matthew C. "Is R.C. Sproul Wrong about Martin Luther? An Analysis of R.C. Sproul's *Faith Alone: The Evangelical Doctrine of Justification* with respect to Augustine, Luther, Calvin, and Catholic Luther Scholarship." *Journal of the Evangelical Theological Society* 47, no.1 (2004), 89-120.

Jenson, Robert W. "Response to Mark Seifrid, Paul Metzger, and Carl Trueman on Finnish Luther Research." *Westminster Theological Journal* 65, no. 2 (Fall 2003), 245-250.

Kittelson, James M. "To the Finland Station: A Review Essay," *Dialog* 38, no. 3 (Summer 1999), 235-237.

Kolb, Robert. "Luther on the Two Kinds of Righteousness; Reflections on His Two-dimensional Definition of Humanity at the Heart of His Theology." *Lutheran Quarterly* 13 (1999), 449-466.

Laird, Martin. ""By Faith Alone": A Technical Term in Gregory of Nyssa." *Vigiilae Christianae* 54, no. 1 (2000), 61-79.

Lowrie, Walter. "About "Justification by Faith Alone"." *The Journal of Religion* 32 (October 1952), 231-241.

Metzger, Paul Louis. "Mystical Union with Christ;" *Westminster Theological Journal* 65, no. 2 (Fall 2003), 201-215.

Seifrid, Mark A. "Luther, Melanchthon, and Paul: Recommendations on a Current Debate." In *Justification: What's at Stake in the Current Debates?* eds. Mark Husbands and Daniel J. Treier, 137-152. Downers Grove, IL: InterVarsity Press, 2004.

Steinmetz, David C. "A Review of *Faith Alone: The Evangelical Doctrine of Justification.*" *Review and Expositor* 92 (1995), 437.

_____. "Luther against Luther." In *Luther in Context*, 1-11. Bloomington, Indiana: University Press, 1986.

_____. "Paul, Luther, and Justification." *Westminster Theological Journal* 65, no. 2 (Fall 2003), 215-230.

Trueman, Carl R. "Is the Finnish Line a New Beginning? A Critical Assessment of the Reading of Luther Offered by the Helsinki

Circle." *Westminster Theological Journal* 65, no. 2 (Fall 2003), 231-244.

Wengert, Timothy J. "Review of "*Union with Christ: The New Finnish Interpretation of Luther.*" *Theology Today* 56, no. 3 (October 1999), 432-434.

Calvin and *Sola Fide*

1. Primary Sources

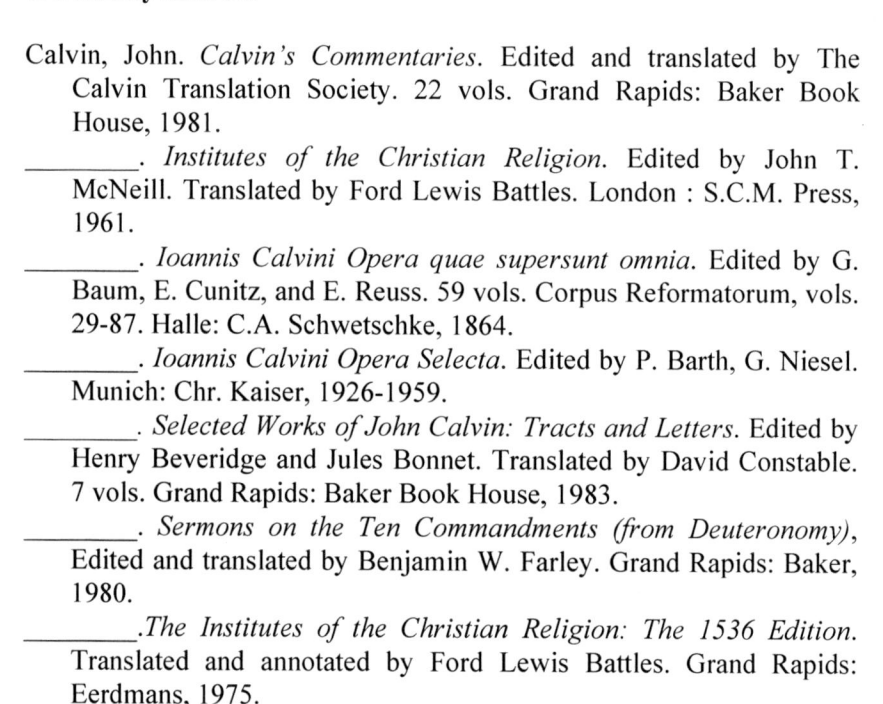

Calvin, John. *Calvin's Commentaries*. Edited and translated by The Calvin Translation Society. 22 vols. Grand Rapids: Baker Book House, 1981.

_____. *Institutes of the Christian Religion*. Edited by John T. McNeill. Translated by Ford Lewis Battles. London : S.C.M. Press, 1961.

_____. *Ioannis Calvini Opera quae supersunt omnia*. Edited by G. Baum, E. Cunitz, and E. Reuss. 59 vols. Corpus Reformatorum, vols. 29-87. Halle: C.A. Schwetschke, 1864.

_____. *Ioannis Calvini Opera Selecta*. Edited by P. Barth, G. Niesel. Munich: Chr. Kaiser, 1926-1959.

_____. *Selected Works of John Calvin: Tracts and Letters*. Edited by Henry Beveridge and Jules Bonnet. Translated by David Constable. 7 vols. Grand Rapids: Baker Book House, 1983.

_____. *Sermons on the Ten Commandments (from Deuteronomy)*, Edited and translated by Benjamin W. Farley. Grand Rapids: Baker, 1980.

_____.*The Institutes of the Christian Religion: The 1536 Edition*. Translated and annotated by Ford Lewis Battles. Grand Rapids: Eerdmans, 1975.

2. Books

Beeke, Joel R. *Assurance of Faith: Calvin, English Puritanism, and the Dutch Second Reformation*. New York: P. Lang, 1991.

Cranfield, C.E.B. *The International Critical Commentary: The Epistle to the Romans*. Edinburgh: T. and T. Clark Limited, 1975-1979.

Cunningham, William. *Reformers and the Theology of the Reformation*. Edinburgh: T. and T. Clark, 1862.

Dowey, Edward A. *The Knowledge of God in Calvin's Theology*. Grand Rapids: Eerdmans, 1994.

George, Timothy. *Theology of the Reformers*. Nashville: Broadman Press, 1988.
Hesselink, I. John. *Calvin's Concept of the Law*. Allison Park, PA: Pickwick Publications, 1992.
Kendall, R.T. *Calvin and English Calvinism to 1649*. New York: Oxford University Press, 1979.
Muller, Richard A. *The Unaccomodated Calvin: Studies in the Foundation of a Theological Tradition*. New York: Oxford University Press, 2000.
Parker, T.H.L. *John Calvin*. Tring, Herts, England: Lion Publishing, 1988.
_____. *The Oracles of God: An Introduction to the Preaching of John Calvin*. London; Redhill: Lutterworth Press, 1947.
Pitkin, Barbara. *What Pure Eyes Could See: Calvin's Doctrine of Faith in Its Exegetical Context*. New York: Oxford University Press, 1999.
Shepherd, Victor H. *The Nature and Function of Faith in the Theology of John Calvin*. Mercer University Press, 1983.
Stuermann, Walter E. *A Critical Study of Calvin's Concept of Faith*. Ann Arbor, MI: Edwards Brothers, 1952.
Wallace, Ronald S. *Calvin, Geneva, and the Reformation*. Grand Rapids: Baker Book House, 1988.
Wendel, Francois. *Calvin: Origins and Development of His Religious Thought*. Translated by Philip Mairet. Grand Rapids: Baker, 2002.

3. Articles

Bandstra, Andrew J. "Law and Gospel in Calvin and in Paul." In *Exploring the Heritage of John Calvin: Essays in Honor of John Bratt*. ed. David E. Holwerda. 11-39. Grand Rapids: Baker Book House, 1976.
Beeke, Joel R. "Does Assurance Belong to the Essence of Faith? Calvin and the Calvinists." *Master's Seminary Journal* 5, no. 1 (1994), 43-71.
Belting, Natalia M. "Calvin and Justification by Faith." *Christian Scholar* 45 (1962), 198-205.
Bulman, James M. "The Place of Knowledge in Calvin's View of Faith." *Review and Expositor* 50 (July 1953), 323-329.
Dowey, Edward A., Jr. "Law in Luther and Calvin," *Theology Today* 41 (July 1984), 146-153.
Gerrish, Brian A. "The Doctrine of Faith." *Princeton Seminary Bulletin* 16, no.2 (1995), 202-215.

Gordh, George. "Calvin's Conception of Faith." *Review & Expositor* 50 (1953), 207-215.
Harper, George W. "Calvin and English Calvinism to 1649: A Review Article," *Calvin Theological Journal* 20 (1985), 255-262.
Reid, W. Stanford. "Justification by Faith according to John Calvin." *Westminster Theological Journal* 42, no. 2 (1980), 290-307.
Smith, John Clark. "Calvin: Unbelief in the Elect." *Evangelical Quarterly* 54 (1982), 14-24.
Steinmetz, David C. "Calvin and Abraham: The Interpretation of Romans 4 in the Sixteenth Century." *Church History* 57 (December 1988), 443-455.
Thorson, Stephen. "Tensions in Calvin's View of Faith: Unexamined Assumptions in R.T. Kendall's *Calvin and English Calvinism to 1649.*" *Journal of the Evangelical Theological Society* 37 (1994), 413-426.

The Protestant Confessions and *Sola Fide*

1. Primary Sources

Creeds and Confessions of Faith in the Christian Tradition. Edited by J. Pelikan, V. Hotchkiss. 4 vols. New Haven: Yale University Press, 2003.
The Constitution of the Presbyterian Church (U.S.A.), Part I, Book of Confessions. Louisville: Geneva Press, 1996.
The Creeds and Platforms of Congregationalism. Edited by Williston Walker. New York: Pilgrim Press, 1991.
The Creeds of Christendom with a History and Critical Notes. Edited by Philip Schaff. Revised by David S. Schaff. 3 vols. Grand Rapids: Baker Book House, 1983.
The Savoy Declaration of Faith and Order 1658. Darlington, England: Evangelical Press, 1971.
The Westminster Confession of Faith. n.p.: Publications Committee of the Free Church of Scotland, 1970.

2. Books

A Confession of Faith. Put Forth by the Elders and Brethren of Many Congregations of Christians (Baptized upon Profession of Their Faith) in London and the Country Printed in the Year, 1677. AKA:

Bibliography

the *"1689"& The Second London Baptist Confession*. Facsimile ed. Auburn, MA: B & R. Press, 2000.

Arminius, James. *The Writings of James Arminius*. Translated by James Nichols. 3 vols. Grand Rapids: Baker Book House, 1956.

Armstrong, William Park, ed. *Calvin and the Reformation*. Grand Rapids: Baker Book House, 1980.

Berkouwer. G.C. *Studies in Dogmatics: Faith and Justification*. Translated by Lewis B. Smedes. Grand Rapids: Eerdmans, 1954.

Buchanan, James. *The Doctrine of Justification: An Outline of Its History in the Church and of Its Exposition from Scripture*. Grand Rapids: Baker Book House, 1977.

Cunningham, William. *Historical Theology*. 2 Vols. Edinburgh: The Banner of Truth Trust, 1969.

_____. *The Reformers and the Theology of the Reformation*. Edinburgh: The Banner of Truth Trust, 1979.

Dejong Peter Y., ed. *Crisis in the Reformed Churches*. Grand Rapids: Reformed Fellowship Inc., 1968.

Dunn, Alan. *The London Baptist Confession of Faith with a Key to Its Sources*. Flemington, NJ: Unpublished Manuscript, 1983.

Eaton, Michael. *No Condemnation: A New Theology of Assurance*. Downers Grove, IL: InterVarsity Press, 1997.

Edwards, Jonathan. *Justification by Faith Alone*. Edited by Don Kistler. Morgan, PA: Soli Deo Gloria Publications, 2000.

Flavel, John. *The Works of John Flavel*. 6 vols. Edinburgh: Banner of Truth Trust, 1968.

Helm, Paul. *Calvin and the Calvinists*. Edinburgh: The Banner of Truth Trust, 1982.

Heppe, Heinrich. *Reformed Dogmatics (Set Out and Illustrated from the Sources)*. Revised and edited by Ernst Bizer. Translated by G.T. Thomson. Grand Rapids: Baker Book House, 1950.

Hetherington, William M. *History of the Westminster Assembly of Divines*. 3d. ed. Edmonton, AB: Still Waters Revival Books, 1991.

Hodge, A. A. *The Confession of Faith*. Edinburgh: Banner of Truth Trust, 1983.

Hoeksema, Herman. *The Triple Knowledge (An Exposition of the Heidelberg Catechism*. 3 vols. Grand Rapids: Reformed Free Publishing Association, 1970.

Lumpkin, William L. *Baptist Confessions of Faith*. Revised ed. Valley Forge, PA: Judson Press, 1969.

Manton, Thomas. *Manton's Complete Works*. 22 vols. Worthington, PA: Maranatha Publications, n.d.

Muller, Richard A. *Dictionary of Latin and Greek Theological Terms: Drawn Principally from Protestant Scholastic Theology.* Grand Rapids: Baker, 1985.

_____. *Post-Reformation Dogmatics (The Rise and Development of Reformed Orthodoxy, ca. 1520 to ca. 1725).* 4 vols. 2d ed. Grand Rapids: Baker, 2003.

Owen, John. *The Works of John Owen.* Vol. 5. Edited William H. Goold. Edinburgh: The Banner of Truth Trust, 1976.

Puritan Sermons: 1659-1689. Vol. 5. Wheaton, IL: Richard Owen Roberts, Publishers, 1981.

Reid, W. Stanford, ed. *John Calvin: His Influence in the Western World.* Grand Rapids: Zondervan, 1982.

Seeberg, Reinhold. *History of Doctrines.* Translated by Charles E. Hay. Grand Rapids: Baker Book House, 1978.

The Confession of Faith, The Larger and Shorter Catechisms with the Scripture Proofs at Large, Together with the Sum of Saving Knowledge. Applecross, Ross-shire, Scotland: The Publications Committee of the Free Presbyterian Church of Scotland, 1970.

Traill, Robert. *The Works of Robert Traill.* Vols. 1-2. Edinburgh: Banner of Truth Trust, 1975.

Van Baalen, Jan Karel. *The Heritage of the Fathers.* Grand Rapids: Eerdmans, 1948.

Waldron, Samuel E. *A Modern Exposition of the 1689 Baptist Confession of Faith.* Darlington, England: Evangelical Press, 1999.

Warfield, Benjamin B. *The Works of Benjamin B. Warfield.* Vol. 6. *The Westminster Assembly and Its Work.* Grand Rapids: Baker Book House, 1981.

Watson, Thomas. *A Body of Divinity.* Rev. ed. Edinburgh: Banner of Truth Trust, 1965.

Williamson, G.I. *The Westminster Confession for Study Classes.* Philadelphia: Presbyterian and Reformed, 1964.

Walker, Williston. *The Creeds and Platforms of Congregationalism.* Pasadena, TX: Pilgrim Press, 1969.

3. Articles

Baker, J. Wayne. "*Sola Fide, Sola Gratia*: The Battle for Luther in Seventeenth-Century England." *The Sixteenth Century Journal* 16, no.1 (1985), 115-133.

Joyce, G.C. "Grotius." In *Encyclopedia of Religion and Ethics*. Edited by James Hastings. 6:440-443. New York: Charles Scribner's Sons, 1922.

Packer, James I. "*Sola Fide*: The Reformed Doctrine of Justification." In *Soli Deo Gloria: Essays in Reformed Theology: Festschrift for John H. Gerstner*. 11-25. Presbyterian Reformed Publishing Co.: 1976.

Platt, Frederic. "Arminianism." In *Encyclopedia of Religion and Ethics*. Edited by James Hastings. 1:807-816. New York: Charles Scribner's Sons, 1922.

4. Internet Links

The Heidelberg Catechism. Accessed 1 November 2004. Available from www.reformed.org/documents/heidelberg.html

The Scottish Confession of Faith. Dallas: Accessed 12 November 2004. Available from www.swrb.com/newslett/actualNLs/ScotConf.html

5. Unpublished Materials

Renihan, James M. *A Theological Family Tree: The 2nd London Baptist Confession and Its Source Documents*. Escondido, CA: Unpublished Manuscript, 2000.

Daniel Fuller and *Sola Fide*

1. Primary Sources

Fuller, Daniel P. "A Response on the Subjects of Works and Grace." *Presbyterion* 9, no. 1-2 (1983), 72-79.

_____. "Another Reply to *Counted Righteous in Christ*." Reformation and Revival Journal 2, no. 2 (2002), 115-120.

_____. "Biblical Theology and the Analogy of Faith." In *Unity and Diversity in New Testament Theology: Essays in Honor of George E. Ladd*, ed. Robert A. Guelich, 195-213. Grand Rapids: William B. Eerdmans, 1978.

_____. "Daniel P. Fuller's Reply to Paul Feinberg's Critique of *Gospel & Law: Contrast or Continuum*." Paper presented at the annual meeting of the Evangelical Theological Society, Toronto, ON, 28 December 1981.

_____. *Give the Winds a Mighty Voice*. n.p.: Word, 1972.

_____. *Gospel & Law: Contrast or Continuum*. Grand Rapids: Eerdmans, 1980.
_____. "Paul and 'The Works of the Law'." *Westminster Theological Journal* 38 (1975-76), 28-42.
_____. "The Hermeneutics of Dispensationalism." Th.D. diss., Northern Baptist Theological Seminary, 1957.
_____. "The Holy Spirit's Role in Biblical Interpretation." In *Scripture, Tradition, and Interpretation*, ed. W. Ward Gasque and William Sanford LaSor, 189-198. Grand Rapids: Eerdmans, 1978.
_____. *The Unity of the Bible*. Grand Rapids: Zondervan, 1992.

2. Books

Hafemann, Scott J. *The God of Promise and the Life of Faith*. Wheaton, IL: Crossway Books, 2001.
Murray, John. *The Epistle to the Romans*. Grand Rapids: Eerdmans, 1965.
Piper, John. *Future Grace*. Sisters, OR: Multnomah Publishers, 1995.

3. Articles

Barth, Karl. "Gospel and Law." In *God, Grace, and Gospel*. Translated by J.S. McNab, 1-28. Scottish Journal of Theology Occasional Papers, no. 8.
Godfrey, W. Robert. "Back to Basics: A Response to the Robertson-Fuller Dialogue." *Presbyterion* 9, no. 1-2 (1983), 80-92.
Hoekema, Anthony A. "*Gospel & Law*: A Review." *Calvin Theological Journal* 17 (April 1982), 11-12.
Huckaby, Charles P. "A Modern Evangelical Dialogue with Martin Luther: Interaction with the German Reformer in Daniel P. Fuller's *The Unity of the Bible*." *Reformation & Revival* 8 (1999), 217-236.
Karlberg, Mark W. "Legitimate Discontinuities between the Testaments." *Journal of the Evangelical Theological Society* 28, no. 1 (1985), 9-20.
Moo, Douglas. "Review of *Gospel & Law: Contrast or Continuum? The Hermeneutics of Dispensationalism and Covenant Theolog.*" *Trinity Journal* 3, no. 1 (1982), 99-103.
Murray, John. "The Adamic Administration." In *Collected Writings*. Vol. 2, *Systematic Theology*, 47-59. Edinburgh: Banner of Truth Trust, 1977.

Robertson, O. Palmer. "Daniel P. Fuller's *Gospel & Law: Contrast or Continuum*: a Review Article." *Presbyterion* 8, no. 1 (1982), 84-91.

Wallis, Wilber. "Review of *Gospel & Law: Contrast or Continuum? The Hermeneutics of Dispensationalism and Covenant Theology.*" *Presbyterion* 8, no. 1 (1982), 72-82.

Norman Shepherd and *Sola Fide*

1. Primary Sources

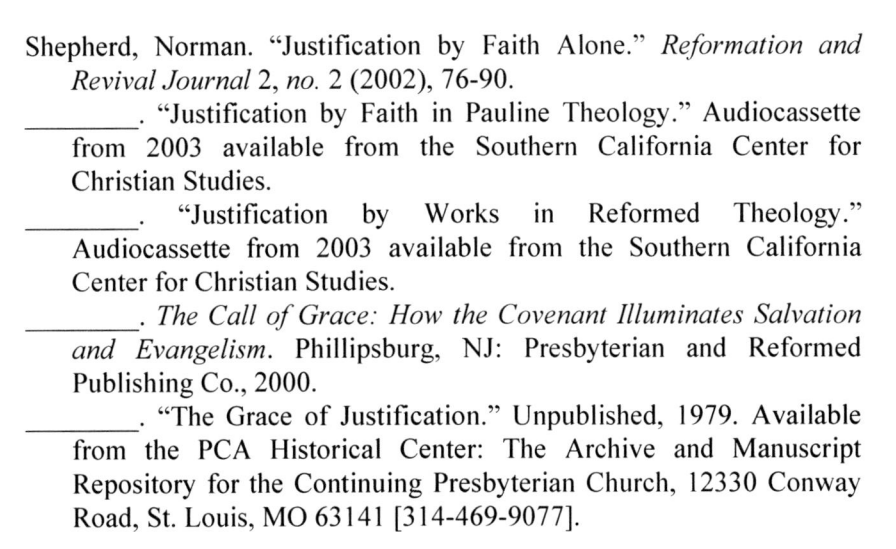

Shepherd, Norman. "Justification by Faith Alone." *Reformation and Revival Journal* 2, no. 2 (2002), 76-90.

———. "Justification by Faith in Pauline Theology." Audiocassette from 2003 available from the Southern California Center for Christian Studies.

———. "Justification by Works in Reformed Theology." Audiocassette from 2003 available from the Southern California Center for Christian Studies.

———. *The Call of Grace: How the Covenant Illuminates Salvation and Evangelism.* Phillipsburg, NJ: Presbyterian and Reformed Publishing Co., 2000.

———. "The Grace of Justification." Unpublished, 1979. Available from the PCA Historical Center: The Archive and Manuscript Repository for the Continuing Presbyterian Church, 12330 Conway Road, St. Louis, MO 63141 [314-469-9077].

2. Books

Beisner, E. Calvin, ed. *The Auburn Avenue Theology Pros & Cons: Debating the Federal Vision (The Knox Theological Seminary Colloquium on the Federal Vision.* Fort Lauderdale, FL: Knox Theological Seminary, 2004.

Robertson, O. Palmer. *The Current Justification Controversy.* Unicoi, TN: The Trinity Foundation, 2003.

3. Articles

Van Drunen, David. "When the Covenant Obscures Justification." *Modern Reformation* (March/April 2002), 38-43.

Venema, Cornelis P. "*The Call of Grace: How the Covenant Illuminates Salvation and Evangelism*: A Review Article." *Mid-America Journal of Theology* 13 (2002), 232-248.

"Westminster Seminary Fires Theologian." *Christianity Today* 26 (January 1 1982), 49.

4. Internet Links

Report of the Special Committee to Study Justification in Light of the Current Justification Controversy. Presented to the 258th Synod of The Reformed Church Of The United States. Accessed 5 January 2005. Available from www.trinityrcus.com/Articles/reportshepherd1.htm

Van Drunen, David. "Justification by Faith in the Theology of Norman Shepherd." [on-line] Accessed 7 January 2005. Available from www.banneroftruth.org/pages/articles/article_detail.php?186

Don Garlington and *Sola Fide*

1. Primary Sources

Garlington, Don B. "A Study of Justification by Faith." *Reformation and Revival Journal* 2, no. 2 (2002), 54-91.

_____. *Faith, Obedience, and Perseverance*. Tubingen: J.C.B. Mohr, 1994.

_____. "Imputation or Union with Christ." *Reformation and Revival Journal* 2, no. 4 (2003), 45-113.

_____. *The Obedience of Faith*. Tubingen: J.C.B. Mohr, 1991.

2. Books

Dunn. James D.G. *Jesus, Paul, and the Law: Studies in Mark and Galatians*. Louisville: Westminster/John Knox Press, 1990.

3. Articles

Byrne, Brendan. "*Faith, Obedience, and Perseverance: Aspects of Paul's Letter to the Romans*: A Review Article." *Catholic Biblical Quarterly* 58 (1996), 787.

deSilva, David A. "*Faith, Obedience, and Perseverance: Aspects of Paul's Letter to the Romans*: A Review Article." *Critical Review of Books in Religion* 9 (1996), 208.

Gundry-Volf, Judith M. "*Faith, Obedience, and Perseverance: Aspects of Paul's Letter to the Romans*: A Review Article." *The Evangelical Quarterly* 69, no. 1 (1997), 84.

Schreiner, Thomas R. "*Faith, Obedience, and Perseverance: Aspects of Paul's Letter to the Romans*: A Review Article." *Journal of the Evangelical Theological Society* 41, no. 4 (December 1998), 654-655.

Vos, Geerhardus. "The Doctrine of the Covenant in Reformed Theology." In *Redemptive History and Biblical Interpretation*, 234-267. Phillipsburg, NJ: Presbyterian and Reformed Publishing Co., 1980.

_____. "The Idea of Biblical Theology." In *Redemptive History and Biblical Interpretation*. 3-24. Phillipsburg, NJ: Presbyterian and Reformed Publishing Co., 1980.

Scripture Index

Genesis
2:17, *138, 145*
2:24, *39*
15:6, *64n, 133n, 141n, 184*
22:18, *147*

Exodus
19:1, *68n*
19:8, *135*

Leviticus
18:5, *134, 137(2)*

Deuteronomy
27:15-26, *137*
30:11, *68n*

Psalms
19:7, *68n*
32:2, *97*
130:4, *62, 62n, 173n*

Matthew
12:37, *228*
16:18, *9*
28:18-20, *9*

Mark
4:26-29, *9*

Luke
13:13-20, *9*
18:14, *228*
24:46, *62n*

John
1:13, *60*
6:29, *56*

Acts
11:18, *62n*
16:31, *177n*
17:25, *138*
17:31, *62n*
20:21, *61, 61n, 173n*

Romans
1:5, *48(2), 49n, 137, 185, 187, 188, 194, 208*
1:16-17, *47n*
1:17, *29(2), 30*
1:20, *26*
2:13, *188, 191, 200, 228*
2:22, *188(2)*
3-4, *18, 41n, 77, 79, 148, 201, 230*
3:20, *67*
3:21-26, *214*
3:22, 24, *64n, 121n, 141n, 174n*
3:23, *212, 212n*
3:24, *121n, 228*
3:24-25, *115*
3:27, *56*
3:27-28, *47n, 147*
3:28, *166, 201*
4:3-5, *147*
4:5, *113n, 228*
4:6, *147*
4:7-8, *26, 32*
4:11, *185*
4:15, *68n*
4:25, *94*
5, *217*
5:1, 9, *228*
5:1-11, *213*
5:12, *211, 212*
5:12-19, *188, 208, 209, 211, 213*
5:16, *209, 213, 220n*
5:20, *67, 68n*
6, *217*
6:1-11, *215*
6:7, *217(2)*
6:15-23, *210*
7:14-25, *188(2), 215n*
8:2, *210*
8:3, *93*
8:15, *68n, 69, 69n, 228*
8:23, *228(2)*
9:31-32a, *134*
9:32, *147, 185*
9:32b-33, *134*
10:4, *93*

10:5, *68n, 137*
10:5-8, *136, 137(4), 143n*
10:6, *137*
10:10, *194, 219*
11:6, *92*
12:3-8, *9*
16:26, *48, 137, 185, 188n*

1 Corinthians
6:11, *228*
12:27-31, *9*

2 Corinthians
3:6, *68n, 93*
5:19ff., *94*
5:21, *214*

Galatians
2-3, *201*
2:16, *44n, 46n, 47n*
2:18, *45n*
2:19, *68n*
3:3, *161*
3:10, *137*
3:10-12, *136, 137(5), 143n*
3:13, *45n, 93*
3:19-20, *68n*
4:5-7, *228*
5:5, *228*
5:6, *47n, 49(3), 50n, 56(3), 70, 91, 146, 147, 148, 151, 167, 175, 178*

Ephesians
1:5, *228*
1:19, *141*
2:1-3, *210*
2:9, *147*
2:14, *204*
4:11-13, *9*
4:11-15, *9*
5:29-32, *39*

Philippians
3:9, *214*

1 Thessalonians
1:3, *147*

2 Thessalonians
1:11, *147*
2:3, *208*

1 Timothy
1:5, *90*

2 Timothy
3:5-17, *9*

Titus
3:4-5, *147*
3:7, *228*

Hebrews
4:16, *30n*
13:4, *67*

James
1:15, *210n*
2, *148, 175(5), 175n, 179(3), 230(5)*
2:14ff., *91*
2:17, 26, *167*
2:21, *175, 179n, 230n*
2:24, *175*
2:24-25, *179n*

1 Peter
2:22, *197n, 208(2), 209*
4:10-11, *9*

2 Peter
2:19, *62n*

1 John
2:25, *177n*
5:16, *210n*

Name and Subject Index

Adam, *26, 39, 104(2), 122, 123(2), 125(2), 128, 134, 137, 138(2), 145(3), 183, 185, 205, 208(3), 209(10), 210, 211, 212(6), 214(2)*
Antinomian, *116*
Arminian, *75, 112, 113, 114(2), 115, 116(2)*
Arminianism, *113(5), 113n, 114(3), 114n, 115, 116*
Arminius, *112, 113, 113n*
assurance, *4n, 7n, 25, 27(2), 39, 53, 53n, 54(7), 55n, 57, 77, 78(2), 79(2), 85, 95, 98, 105(2), 109(2), 119(2), 119n, 120n, 125(2), 142, 150, 153(7), 153n, 154, 171, 192, 209, 226(3), 226n*
Auburn Avenue Theology, *157n*
Augustine, *10, 11(4), 30, 31(3), 33(3), 34(3), 35(4), 41, 44(2), 83, 113(5), 218*
Augustinian, *11, 21, 24(2), 26, 31(5), 31n, 32n, 33, 33n, 34, 36(2), 44, 55n, 83(3), 112, 113, 115*
Augustinianism, *31, 31n, 34, 35*

Barth, Karl, *127(8), 128*
Beza, *88*
Biel, Gabriel, *24(2), 25(2), 25n*
Bullinger, *5n, 16, 18, 88, 89(2), 91(3), 92, 94, 103n, 227*

calling, effectual, *170(2), 171*
Calvin, John, *5n, 6n, 7n, 10n, 16n, 19n, 20n, 31n, 34n, 47n, 48n, 50n, 52n, 53n, 55n, 56n, 58n, 60n, 65n, 66n, 67n, 68n, 69n, 70n, 103n, 121n, 130n, 132n, 140n, 152n, 153n, 171(3), 173(4), 174, 174n, 178n, 179(4), 179n, 189, 189n, 192(2), 198, 200n, 205(2), 212, 226(2), 227, 230(5), 230n*

Calvinism, *7n, 53n, 55n, 66, 66n, 82, 92n, 108, 116, 134*
Calvinist, *50n, 53n, 125*
Carson, D.A., *7n, 12n*
Catholic, *9, 10n, 12n, 14n, 33n, 34n, 97, 188n*
  Roman, *4n, 11, 11n, 25, 47(3), 176, 178, 180, 181, 205, 226n*
Catholicism,
  Medieval, *19, 35, 218*
  Roman, *3n, 18, 80, 163, 227*
  Tridentine, *201(2), 211, 231*
Catechism(s), *1n, 5, 74(2), 74n, 75(2), 76, 99, 100, 115, 118, 125, 165*
  Anglican, *75*
  Heidelberg, *88, 97(3), 98, 98n, 100n, 117*
  Luther's,
    Large, *75n*
    Small, *75, 84*
  Westminster,
    Larger, *75, 102n, 117, 119n, 120, 120n, 142*
    Shorter, *75, 116, 117(2), 119n, 120n, 124n*
cause,
  efficient, *121n, 141*
  meritorious, *64, 141*
Christ,
  obedience of, *93, 102, 125, 185, 188, 208(2)*
  union with, *58, 58n, 59(3), 61(2), 62, 63(3), 101, 173(2), 189, 211(2), 212, 221, 222(3), 240, 243, 244, 252*
condition, *32, 64(2), 67, 69, 111, 113(5), 114, 122, 135(11), 136, 137(3), 138(4), 140(6), 141(3), 145(6), 147, 148(4), 149(6), 153, 173(2), 174, 176(3), 185n, 193*
Confession,
  Augsburg, *5, 5n, 17(7), 17n, 18n, 20n, 41, 41n, 76(2), 77(5), 77n,*

78, 78n(7), 79n(4), 80, 81, 81n(2), 84, 85, 87, 189, 189n
Belgic, 5, 101(4), 101n, 102, 102n(3), 103n(3), 104, 104n, 168, 168n
First Scottish, 5, 104(2)
Gallican, 5, 94(3), 95, 95n(3), 96, 96n(4), 97(2), 97n(2)
Second Helvetic, 5, 5n, 88(4), 88n(3), 92, 93n, 94(2), 103n, 114, 114n
the 1689 Baptist, 50n, 75, 76n, 117, 117n, 119n, 122n(2), 123n(3), 125n(2), 248
Westminster, 6, 6n, 50n, 53n(2), 75(5), 101, 102n, 108(2), 111, 115(2), 116, 117(5), 118, 118n(5), 119, 119n(3), 120, 120n, 121n, 122, 122n(3), 123(3), 123n, 124(2), 124n(3), 125, 144n, 146n, 151n, 152, 152n, 153n, 166, 167, 168, 169, 171, 171n, 174, 180, 186(2), 192n(3), 195n, 205, 246, 248
Covenant,
Abrahamic, 183(5), 184(2)
Davidic, 135(2), 141
Mosaic, 123, 125, 136, 139(6), 141, 143n, 183, 185
New, 114, 129, 134, 135(3), 136(4), 138(2), 161, 162, 173, 183(2)
of grace, 69, 114, 119, 121, 122(7), 123(4), 123n(2), 124(2), 124n, 125(2), 134, 135, 137, 138(2), 139(3), 142, 152n, 186
of works, 104, 121, 122(2), 123(6), 123n(3), 125(2), 134, 135, 137, 138(6), 139(3), 142n, 143n(4), 144, 145, 183(2), 185(2), 185n(5), 186,190, 205(2)
Old, 123, 134, 135, 139, 143n, 205

dichotomy, vi, 6(4), 7, 45, 46, 68n, 73(2), 76, 80(2), 81, 87, 92(3), 93(2), 97(3), 99(2), 103, 103n(2), 106, 107, 111(2), 115, 121(2), 123(3), 123n, 125, 133, 134, 140n, 166, 182(2), 185, 186, 192, 195, 205(4), 223(3), 225, 226, 231
Dort, Canons of, 83, 114, 115, 115n, 116
Dowey, Edward A., 66, 66n(3), 69n
Dunn, James D.G., 132, 133n(2), 187, 188(3), 190, 201(2), 202(2), 202n, 203, 206, 229, 229n, 235, 237, 247, 252

Eastern Orthodoxy, 14
easy-believism, 2, 2n, 3n, 4n, 133n, 160(2), 161, 161n, 198
Edwards, Jonathan, 127(2), 143n, 145(3), 145n, 146(3), 146n
Erasmus, 4n, 33, 226n
evangelical(s), 2(3), 2n, 3, 3n, 4(2), 4n, 5n, 6, 8(2), 8n, 9, 10, 10n, 12, 34n, 48, 70, 71, 73(3), 111, 115, 126, 127(3), 129n, 130, 131(3), 133n, 134, 142n, 157(2), 159, 163(2), 163n, 166, 180, 187(3), 198, 210n, 222, 225(3), 228(2), 229, 231(2), 232(6),
evangelicalism, 2, 3n, 8n, 127, 129(2), 157, 161n, 162, 232, 233

faith,
justifying, 2n, 6(5), 6n, 7, 7n, 18(2), 42, 42n, 43(2), 44, 46(2), 47(4), 48(4), 51(3), 53n, 56, 57, 64, 65, 70, 73(5), 76(2), 77, 79, 80(2), 83, 84(6), 86(3), 87, 88, 89, 90(3), 91(2), 92(2), 95(3), 96(2), 97(2), 98(2), 99(3), 101(3), 102(2), 105(3), 107(2), 109(5), 110, 115(2), 118(2), 119(4), 120(2), 120n, 121, 122, 123(2), 125(3), 129, 144, 145(5), 150(3), 151, 152, 153(2), 154(5), 155(4), 166(2),

Name and Subject Index 259

167(3), 168(2), 169(3), 170, 172, 173(2), 177(3), 177n, 178, 182(3), 192(6), 193, 195(2), 198, 199, 200, 205(2), 225(2), 226, 231(2)

obedience of, 48, 49, 49n, 114, 115(3), 128(2), 128n, 131, 131n, 134, 135, 137(2), 138, 139, 140, 141, 144, 152(2), 153n, 182, 184(4), 185(2), 186, 187(2), 187n, 188(3), 188n, 189n, 190(3), 191(2), 193n, 195(2), 196, 196n, 197(2), 197n, 199, 199n, 200(3), 202, 202n, 203(3), 203n, 204(2), 206n, 207n, 208, 210n, 211, 214, 216n, 219(2), 220, 229, 229n

persevering, 145(3), 146, 148(4), 153(2)

saving, 6n, 43, 49, 50(3), 51, 52, 55n, 57(2), 104, 119(5), 120n, 122(2), 123, 124, 125, 141, 152n, 154, 167, 170(9), 171(2), 192

works of, 147, 176(5), 180, 181(2), 182(2), 183, 184, 229(3), 230(4)

faithfulness, 70, 162(2), 174(2), 177(2), 181(2), 183(2), 185, 189, 193(2), 193n, 194(2), 196, 196n, 208(2), 209(2), 214, 217, 219(2), 220(3)

forensic, 6(2), 7n, 15(2), 17, 18(3), 19n, 37(3), 41, 59, 82, 143, 170, 175, 179, 180, 189, 207, 211, 215, 216, 217(3), 218(2), 220(2), 220n, 221(2), 222(2)

forgiveness, 7n, 17, 18(3), 19n, 41, 41n, 44, 58(2), 59(4), 60(2), 62(2), 77, 79(3), 81, 97, 100, 109, 143, 143n, 144(2), 145, 149(2), 173(5), 179(4), 180, 180n, 181(2), 218n

Formula of Concord, 5n, 17(6), 82(4), 83(2), 84(2), 84n, 85, 85n, 86, 86n, 87(2), 87n, 102n, 103

Fuller, Daniel P., 2, 2n, 3n, 4n, 8(2), 8n, 127(12), 127n, 128(7), 128n, 129(10), 129n, 130(4), 130n, 131(10), 131n, 132(11), 132n, 133(7), 133n, 134(4), 135, 135n, 136, 136n, 137(2), 138(7), 138n, 139(9), 139n, 140(3), 140n, 141, 141n, 142n, 143(5), 143n, 144(5), 144n, 145(8), 145n, 146(3), 146n, 147, 147n, 148(2), 148n, 149(3), 149n, 150(8), 151(5), 151n, 152(4), 152n, 153(4), 153n, 154(6), 154n, 155(2), 203n, 206n, 228, 228n, 229(2), 229n, 230(3), 230n, 231(3), 232(2), 238

Garlington, Don, 4n, 8(2), 8n, 49n, 187(9), 187n, 188(3), 188n, 189(8), 189n, 190n, 191(2), 191n, 192(3), 193(4), 193n, 194n, 195(6), 195n, 196, 196n, 197(4), 197n, 198(3), 198n, 199, 199n, 200(6), 200n, 201(6), 202(3), 202n, 203(2), 203n, 204(3), 205(6), 206(5), 206n, 207(5), 207n, 208(2), 208n, 209(3), 210(6), 210n, 211(6), 211n, 212(5), 212n, 213(5), 213n, 214(4), 215(6), 215n, 216(2), 216n, 217(4), 217n, 218(7), 219(4), 219n, 220(3), 220n, 221(4), 221n, 222(7), 223(3), 228, 229, 231(3), 232(2)

George, Timothy, 23, 23n, 26n, 27, 27n

Godfrey, Robert W., 129n, 131n, 144n, 150(2), 150n

gospel, 2, 2n, 3n, 4n, 6(2), 7, 7n, 11, 15n, 19n, 21n, 28, 29, 32, 43, 45, 46, 47, 47n, 49(5), 50, 51n, 52, 55, 56, 59, 60(2), 64(5), 65(4), 65n, 66(3), 66n, 67(6), 68(7), 68n, 69(7), 69n, 70, 71,

73(2), 76, 77, 78, 79, 80(5), 81(3), 83(2), 84(3), 85(3), 86, 87(6), 90(3), 92n, 93(4), 96, 97(4), 98, 99(2), 103(2), 103n, 106(2), 107, 109(2), 111(2), 112(3), 115, 121(2), 123(3), 123n, 124n, 125, 127(3), 127n, 128, 128n, 129(3), 129n, 130(2), 130n, 131, 131n, 132(2), 132n, 133(5), 133n, 134(8), 135(2), 135n, 136(4), 136n, 137(6), 138(2), 138n, 139(4), 139n, 140(6), 140n, 141, 143, 144(8), 145, 145n, 147n, 149n, 152n, 155, 161, 165, 166, 167(2), 177n, 180, 181, 182(4), 185(5), 186(3), 192, 199, 205(7), 210n, 222(2), 223(5), 225, 226, 226n, 231
grace, *3n, 17, 19, 21n, 24(5), 24n, 25(2), 26(2), 27, 31(3), 32(2), 32n, 33(4), 34, 38, 39, 41n, 44, 50, 51, 52(2), 54, 56(2), 60, 61, 63(5), 64(4), 65, 65n, 67(3), 68n, 69(2), 70(2), 77(3), 78, 79(3), 80(2), 81, 82(2), 83(6), 84(2), 85, 87(2), 89(3), 90(5), 92(6), 94, 95, 96(2), 97, 98, 99, 103(2), 105, 112, 113(4), 114(4), 115(4), 118, 119, 119n, 120(3), 120n, 121(2), 122(6), 123(3), 124(3), 124n, 125(2), 129, 131, 132, 132n, 134, 137, 138(5), 139(4), 142(2), 145, 146, 147, 158, 159, 161(5), 162(3), 163(2), 163n, 164(5), 165(4), 171, 175, 176(3), 177, 178(4), 179(3), 180(5), 183(3), 185, 191, 192(3), 194, 198, 205(6), 206, 208*

Hafemann, Scott, *2n, 7n, 131, 131n*
Hesselink, I. John, *65, 66n, 69, 69n*

imputation, *1, 3n, 7n, 12n, 15, 33, 34(2), 40, 45, 46, 59, 60, 126, 132, 143(4), 144(4), 144n, 179n, 180, 189(2), 189n, 191n, 195n, 207, 207n, 210(3), 210n, 211(6), 211n, 212(2), 212n, 213n, 215, 215n, 217n, 218(2), 219n, 220n, 221, 221n, 222(15), 226n, 227n, 230*
imputed, *1, 6(2), 7n, 19n, 20n, 30n, 37(2), 38(2), 39(2), 40, 40n, 41, 44, 82, 86(3), 93(4), 95, 96, 97, 100n, 103, 112, 114n, 120, 121, 124(3), 126, 144(2), 164, 165, 167, 168, 178(2), 184, 185, 205, 207, 210, 211, 213(2), 215, 218(3), 219(2), 220, 222(2), 223(3)*
Institutes, *15, 16n, 19, 49(2), 51, 52, 55, 56, 57, 59, 64, 65, 68(3), 80, 98, 139, 140(2), 173*
Irish Articles, *108(4), 109(2), 109n, 110n, 111(2), 111n, 112(2), 112n*
iustitia Dei, 25(2), 26, 29

Judaism, *133, 133n, 187(4), 188(2), 189n, 190, 194, 196, 197, 199, 202, 203, 205(3), 206(4)*
justification,
condition of, *113, 145(5), 148(3), 149, 153, 173(2), 176*
extrinsic, *35, 37*

Kendall, R.T., *7n, 52n, 53n, 55(2), 55n*

law,
and gospel, *2, 7n, 19n, 46, 65(3), 66(2), 66n, 67(2), 68(5), 68n, 69(3), 69n, 71, 73, 76, 80(3), 81, 87(2), 92(3), 93(2), 97(3), 99(2), 103(2), 106(2), 107, 111(2), 112, 115, 121(2), 123(3), 123n, 125, 127, 128, 129(2), 129n, 130n, 133(3), 134(2), 137(2), 139(3), 140(4), 140n, 143, 144, 145, 155, 166, 182(4), 185, 186(2), 192, 205(6), 223, 225, 231*

Name and Subject Index

of God, *35, 54, 62, 70, 93, 106, 192, 201, 202*
legalism, *66, 161, 162, 163, 206(2)*
Luther, Martin, *4n, 5(2), 5n, 6(5), 7, 7n, 8, 10(3), 10n, 11(4), 11n, 12, 13(18), 14(5), 14n, 15(10), 15n, 16(10), 17(10), 17n, 18(6), 19(7), 19n, 20(10), 20n, 21(10), 21n, 22(8), 22n, 23(5), 23n, 24(2), 24n, 25(8), 26(8), 26n, 27(9), 28(7), 28n, 29(4), 29n, 30(7), 30n, 31(2), 31n, 32(4), 32n, 33(5), 33n, 34(8), 34n, 35(3), 35n, 36(5), 36n, 37(6), 37n, 38(4), 38n, 39(3), 40(8), 40n, 41(6), 41n, 42(3), 42n, 43(9), 44(5), 44n, 45, 46(3), 47n, 53n, 55n, 65(5), 66(8), 66n, 67(2), 68, 69(2), 69n, 70(2), 73(7), 75(2), 75n, 76(4), 78, 79, 81, 82(2), 83(3), 84(2), 87, 113(3), 119, 123, 125(4), 129, 129n, 130n, 133(2), 142n, 144, 146(2), 148, 153(2), 155, 164, 166, 167n, 189, 189n, 198, 205(2), 214, 215(5), 215n, 218(2), 218n, 226(2), 226n, 227(4), 227n, 230n*
Lutheran(s), *1n, 3n, 5n, 14n, 15n, 17, 18(2), 19n, 36(3), 65, 66, 67(2), 68, 74, 74n, 76, 77(2), 80, 82, 84(2), 87(3), 92(3), 94(2), 103n, 125(2), 134, 165, 167(6), 168, 170(2), 187, 189n, 206, 226n, 227(2)*
Lutheranism, *66, 67n, 84, 134, 167(2), 167n, 168*

McGrath, Alister, *10n, 25, 26n, 29n, 30, 32n, 35, 35n, 36n, 40, 41(2), 41n, 42, 42n*
Melanchthon, *5n, 7n, 13, 14n, 15, 15n, 17(2), 17n, 18, 20(5), 20n, 21, 21n, 41, 42n, 76(5), 77n, 82, 83, 167n, 227, 227n*
merit(s), *17, 24(2), 24n, 41n, 45, 56, 66, 77, 79(2), 85, 87, 89, 90(6), 91, 94, 95, 96(3), 97, 98, 99, 101, 102(3), 103, 106, 107, 109(3), 110(2), 111(3), 115(2), 146, 163(5), 165, 174, 175, 176(5), 177, 180(2), 181(5), 182(4), 183(3), 183n, 185, 206n, 229(2), 230*
meritorious, *64, 111, 121n, 138, 141(2), 142n, 165n, 174, 177, 180(2), 181(3), 182(2), 183(2), 186, 194, 203n, 206, 207*
Muller, Richard, *52n, 55, 55n*
Murray, John, *137, 143n, 157, 159n, 172, 178n, 189, 189n*

New Perspective, *2, 2n, 3n, 8n, 12, 66, 66n, 67(2), 67n, 92n, 132(2), 133(2), 133n, 157(2), 157n, 187(2), 201, 202, 203, 206(2), 229, 232(2)*

obedience,
  evangelical, *2n, 44, 46, 47(2), 47n, 48(16), 57(2), 63, 73(2), 76, 84, 96(2), 97, 99(2), 102, 105, 107, 109, 114, 115, 118, 120(4), 123, 134, 148, 150, 169, 172, 177n, 195, 198, 223, 225, 231*
  of Christ, *93, 102, 125, 185, 188, 208(2)*
Oberman, Heiko, *11n, 24n, 25n, 31n*
ordo salutis, *57, 58, 191*

Pelagian, *10, 11, 24, 24n, 25, 31, 31n, 32, 116*
Pelikan, Jaroslav, *15n, 18, 19n, 21, 22n, 25n, 31n, 32n, 41n, 74n, 226, 227n*
Piper, John, *1(5), 1n, 2n, 3n, 130, 131(4), 132(7), 132n, 144(3), 144n, 189(3), 194, 212, 219, 220n, 221(3), 222, 232(2), 232n*

regeneration, *49, 50(2), 59(2), 60(3), 61(7), 62(2), 63, 85, 96, 100, 169, 170(7), 171(9)*

Reid, W. Stanford, *47n, 70, 70n*
repentance, *2n, 21, 42n, 49, 51, 57(3), 59(12), 60(7), 60n, 61(9), 62(10), 63(3), 71, 78, 80, 81, 85, 87(2), 109, 110(2), 121(4), 121n, 149, 161(2), 165(2), 169, 170(3), 171(2), 172(14), 173(16), 174(9), 174n, 176, 177(3), 179(4), 180, 181(2), 207, 210n*
righteousness,
  alien, *7n, 37, 38(9), 39(10), 40(3), 40n, 185, 215, 215n, 218(5), 219, 226n*
  extrinsic, *35, 40n, 215*
  gift of, *211, 214(2)*
  imputed, *1, 6(2), 7n, 19n, 30n, 37(2), 38, 39(2), 40, 41, 86(2), 93(2), 100n, 103, 112, 114n, 121, 124(2), 136, 144(2), 165, 205, 207, 210, 211, 213, 215, 218(3), 219(2), 220, 222(2), 223(3)*
  of God, *24, 30n, 32, 33, 35, 43, 134(2), 185, 212(2), 221(2)*
Robertson, O. Palmer, *130, 130n, 131n, 149, 154, 157n, 158n, 159n*
Romanism, *82*
Rome, *20, 51, 163(2), 163n, 176*

sanctification, *14(2), 14n, 42n, 49(4), 58n, 59, 62, 63, 82, 102, 105(2), 119, 122, 129(2), 132n, 133, 143, 150(2), 151(12), 151n, 152(12), 152n, 153n, 163, 164(5), 170(13), 171(10), 172(2), 173, 192, 215n, 216(5), 217(3)*
Sanders, E.P., *132, 133n, 187(3), 188(4), 190, 201, 202, 206*
Schaff, Philip, *17n, 41n, 74, 74n*
Scholastic, *21, 23, 25(4), 26, 27(2), 32*
Seifrid, Mark A., *7n, 14, 14n, 15, 15n, 20, 21n, 37n, 42n, 227, 227n*

Semi-Pelagian(ism), *211n*
Shepherd, Norman, *2n, 4n, 8(2), 8n, 58n, 61n, 62n, 65n, 92n, 131n, 157(7), 157n, 158(4), 158n, 159(4), 159n, 160(7), 160n, 161(4), 161n, 162(2), 162n, 163(6), 163n, 164(3), 164n, 165(2), 165n, 166(4), 166n, 167(3), 167n, 168(5), 168n, 169(9), 169n, 170(2), 170n, 171(4), 172(4), 172n, 173(2), 173n, 174(3), 175(5), 175n, 176(3), 176n, 177(3), 177n, 178(7), 179(5), 179n, 180(6), 180n, 181(6), 181n, 182(6), 183(4), 183n, 184(6), 184n, 185(5), 185n, 186(2), 226n, 228, 228n, 229(2), 229n, 230(3), 230n, 231(3), 232(2)*
sola fide, *1(2), 2n, 3, 4(3), 4n, 5(3), 5n, 6(6), 7(2), 7n, 8(2), 10(2), 10n, 11(5), 12n, 13(9), 15(2), 17, 18, 19(2), 19n, 20(2), 21(6), 22, 28(2), 30(2), 31(2), 33, 34(2), 34n, 35, 41, 42n, 43(3), 44, 46, 47(3), 47n, 48, 51(3), 65(3), 66(2), 70(2), 71, 73(10), 74, 75, 76, 77, 80, 81, 83(3), 84, 87(3), 89(3), 94, 95, 98, 102, 104(3), 107, 112, 115, 123(2), 125, 126(3), 127(2), 131, 133(3), 133n, 134, 144(3), 145(2), 146, 149(2), 150(2), 151(5), 152(3), 154, 155(2), 157(2), 158, 164(3), 166, 167(2), 168, 169(3), 172, 173(2), 178, 179(2), 180, 182(2), 184n, 186(2), 187(2), 190, 191(4), 192(3), 198(2), 200, 201(2), 201n, 205(3), 206(3), 207(3), 222(2), 223(4), 225(3), 226n, 227(2), 229(7), 230(2), 231(5), 232, 233*
sola gratia, *11(3), 24, 31(2)*
sola Scriptura, *9(3), 11(2), 27, 164*
Sproul, R.C., *10n, 11n, 34n*
Staupitz, *23(5), 23n, 27*

Name and Subject Index

Synod of Dort, *75, 101, 112(4), 116(2)*

Thirty-nine Articles, *75, 107(2), 107n, 108*

voluntarist, *52, 55(4), 55n, 57*

Westminster Seminary, *118n, 159, 159n, 160n*
Wilson, Douglas, *2n, 66, 67(5), 67n, 68(2), 92n*
work(s),
  good, *2n, 4n, 24, 38(2), 42(4), 43(2), 44, 49(3), 50(2), 79, 80(9), 83(3), 84, 86(4), 90, 91(3), 92, 96, 100, 103(6), 104, 105(2), 106, 108, 110(4), 113, 120, 132n, 149, 150(2), 151, 152n, 153n, 154(5), 165, 165n, 167(2), 168(7), 169(2), 170(2), 171, 173, 175, 180(3), 181(5), 202, 226n*
  of faith, *147, 176(5), 180, 181(2), 182(2), 183, 184, 229(2), 230(4)*
Wright, N.T., *2n, 7n, 66n, 132, 133n*

Zwingli, Ulrich, *5n, 11, 16(3), 19n, 31n, 75, 88, 94*